ENGLISH RECUSANT LITERATURE
1558—1640

Selected and Edited by
D. M. ROGERS

Volume 123

JOHN COLVILLE
The Paraenese
1602

ROBERT SOUTHWELL
An Humble Supplication
1595

JOHN COLVILLE

The Paraenese or
Admonition . . . unto his
Cuntrey Men
1602

The Scolar Press
1973

ISBN 0 85417 901 1

*Published and Printed in Great Britain by
The Scolar Press Limited, 20 Main Street,
Menston, Yorkshire, England*

NOTE

The following works are reproduced (original size), with permission, as follows:

(1) John Colville, *The paraenese*, 1602, from a copy in the Bodleian library, by permission of the Curators.
References: Allison and Rogers 249; STC. 5589.

(2) Robert Southwell, *An humble supplication to her maiestie*, 1595, from a copy in the library of Stonyhurst College, by permission of the Rector.
References: Allison and Rogers 784; STC. 7586.

THE PARÆNESE

or admonition of Io. Coluille (laitly returnit to the Catholique Romane Religion in vhilk he vas baptesit and brocht vp till he had full 14. years of age) vnto his cuntrey men.

The contentes of this treatise is to be found after the Epistles.

AT PARIS,

In the Typographie of Stephanus Preuosteau in S. Io. de Lateran. besyid the College of Cambrey.

1 6 0 2.

Hieremie 6.

This sayit the lord sland vpon the hie vayis and ask in the ancient streates vhilk is the good vay, and valk thairin and you salt fynd refreching vnto your soules.

Prouerb. 22.

Transgres not the auld termes vhilk thy fathers haue sett.

2.Thessal. 2.

Stand and hold the traditions vhilk you haue lernit ether by my sermon or my epistle.

1. Corint. 11.

I loue you that in all thingis you remēber on me holding my precepts as I haue by tradition geuin tham vnto you.

Rom. 16.

I besech you(my brethring)to mark thā yat bring in dissensiones and sklandres differing from the doctrin yat you haue lernit, and to declin from tham.

1. Corinth. 14.

Hes the vord of god procedit from you, or hes tt cum amang you only.

TO MY DEARLY-

*belouit brethring the Mini-
ſtres of Scotland.*

LBEIT (my dearly
belouit) the repre-
henſions or admo-
nitiõs of our freinds
be à thouſand fold
more frutfull and neidfull nor the
flattry of foes (according to yat of
Cicero vhar he ſayis *yat the Medi-* Prouerb. 27.
cin doth profit moſt vhilk cauſit greteſt
ſmart, and of yat of Solomon vhar it
is ſaid yat the vouƞds of à freind be bet-
ter nor the kiſſes of ane enemmie) yit
daylie experience doth tech vs no

á ij

thing to be more fafcheux and vn-
acceptabill fpecially vhen ve ad-
monifs our freinds to renúce fuch
vyces as be turnit in habituds and
to degrad thair felf of fuch dignitie as in thair opinion thai can not
veill depone vithout oppin difcre
dit. Vharof thair be fo many popular exemples boyth in hiftorcis
holy and prophane as I nead not
repeat any of tham namly vnto
you vhom I knou fo veill verfit in
fuch lecture. For this caufe did the
Comique Poet fay. *Obfequium ami-*
cos, veritas odium parit: For this cau-
fe both Elia and Michea fpeking the
piking veritie var vnuclcum and the
400. fals Prophets pronuncing plefant
lyes var acceptabill vnto Achab, and
for this fame caufe did the obftinat If-
Efay.30. *raëlites in the dayis of Efayas fay to*
the fears fee not and to thair vachmen

hear not viffing thair Prophets rather to ſpek plauſibill errors nor vnpleſant veriteis. Bot as in the corporall in-firmitie of my freind nether ſuld his ſeiknes ſtay me ſtill to hold him my freind, nor hinder me to help him to my pouer houſoeuer by force of his fiuer he be tranſ-ported and ſcheu him ſelf vnuil-ling to vſe my aſſiſtance: euin ſo (my veilbelouit) ſeing boyth you and tham yat you lead ſo dangeru-ruſly diſeaſit and almoſt ouergo-ne vith à mortall malady of the mynd I can not abſtene to haue compaſſion of your miſery the re-ther for yat I perſaue your diſeaſe accompaneit vith the verie Sintős of diſeaſes yat be incurabill‘in yat the ſame being inſenſibill you hold opiniõ yat you haue no nead of Medicin or admonition, *lyik vnto yat prouoking citie mentionat in Sophonia yat vold reſaue no inſtruc̄tiŏ, and lyik vnto the man mentionat in the 28. of the Prouerbs ⁊ho chuſit vnto him ſelf à vay ⁊hilk ſeamit rycht yit the end tharof ledit to damnatıon.* For this cauſe houſoeuer you lyiк or miſlyiк of my louing affection I vill not ſpair to preſent and perform all lefull offices of kynd-nes lying in my pouer vharun-to being obliſt boyth by the lau of God and nature if I ſuld faill thairin I ſuld proue rether ane ſtif-hartit ſtoik nor à téderhartit Chrĩ-ſtiá, ſeing ſum of you be my kinſ-men, ſum my alliance and ould ac-quentáce, all my cuntreymen and ve all born ſubiects to one ſouue-rane lord the ornaméts of our age ãd as *ſayit Malachy. Ve haue bot one God to our father ⁊ho hes created ⁊s* all , vharfor then fuld eury one of vs dispyife his brother.be ve not commandit eury one of vs to bear ane vthers burthing doing no thing (as fayis the fame Apoftle in ane vther place) by contenfion or for vane gloir bot in all humilite eury one efteming his felloubroiher better nor him felf. O vhat notable aduyfes vpon this fubiect of mutuall loue and charitie hes this holy Apoftle left vnto vs in many places of his diuyne Epiftles namlie in the 1.Cor.13. faying yat vithout this charitie, fayth and hoip and all vther Chriftian vertus be no thing at all and yat by this Chriftian dilection the houll lau is fulfillit vhilk lau cōfiftit allanerly in Loning our gratius God aboue all and our nychtbore as our fef: in place varof fayis the fayd Apoftle in ane vther place if ve fall mutually byit brab bill, and vrangill one vith ane vther ve fall att leuth bot confum one ane vther. O vhat fueit harmony is amang the Prophets, Euangelliftes and Apoftles fpeking vpon this purpos the Royall Prophet faying. *O hou Good and plefand is it to fe brethring duell togidde in vnitie.* Sanct Peter and Sanct Io. *faying yat vithout loue and charitie ye can not be eftemit the childring of God* and not only thai bot Cryft hym felf faying in one place *yat he geuit vs command not only to loue* one ane vther *bot euin to loue our enemis, for God is not the God of diffenfion bot of peace, and as Solomõ fayis in the 12. of his Prouerbs it is bot the lippes of the folish yat mellit vith ftryif and vhofe mouth prouoquit vnto chyding.* Yea this Chriftian charitie hes bene of fuch pryce amang the faid Apoftles yat albeit Sanct Paul to. tit. 3. *commandit to flee from ane Heretique*

Heretique after one or tuo admonitiõs yit the same Apostle interpreting him self in the 2.Thessall. 3.visit vs not to hold tham for our enemis yat vill not obey his Epistle bot to reprehend tham as our brethring . Yea in one vther place he is so transported vith affection vnto his brethring after the flesch tho thai ver bot infidells yat *for thair saluation he affirmit he* Rom.9. *culd viß him self ane anathem or cursing fro.n Cryst.*

To this purpos ane holy man interpreting this passage of Sanct Paul. Let him yat standit tak head he fall not. doth exhort vs so cheritably and fauorably to interprit the actions of our brethring yat fynding tham fall ve suld extend our ingyne to the vttermost to fynd out arguments hou to excuse thair errors, alleging yat sum gret

c̃

tentation had furprifit tham and yat if ve had bene in thair place ve had fallin more fearfully:for vhilk caufe ve fuld rether ferch out matter to thank God yat ve haue not bene fo tempted nor to difpyis him yat hes fallin into tentation: For treu charitie hes no indignation, bot much commiferation: and tharfor in the 6.to the Galats is faid. *My brethring if à man be furprifit vith à falt you yat be ſpirituall reſtor him by the ſpreit of manſuetud and tak head yat you your ſelf be not tempted.*

Then it is not the part of à peceabill hartit Chriſtian bot of one yat is to partiall and paſſionat incōtinent to obiect agans vthers yat be not of thair opiniō in matters of religion theifs paſſages of holy fcriptur quoted agans the

hair. *Tho it var thy brother child or* Deuter.13.
2 Epift.S.Io,
Math.18.
Math.15.
Marc.7.
vyf let not thy Ee spair tham : Salute
tham not for in saluting tham you art
maid participant af thair euill doing:
let tham be vnto the as Etniques and
publicans,and cast not the bread of chil-
dring vnto dogs. For à particular person or à particular numbre separating thair self from the hoill body and presuming to apply theis
passages agans the said vniuersall
body (as I my self once did agans
the Catholiques Romane) is to be
estemit so doing as iniurius and
impertinent as vas Achab imputing vnto Elias the trubling of If-
raell,or the debauschit vyfe of Pu-
tifer ád fals eldars accusing Ioseph
ád Susanna of adultery,or Sedecia
the sone of Canaana pusching
vyth his phantastique hornes of
Irin agans the the inuincibill veri-

ẽ ij

tie pronūcit by the mouth of Micheas.

Becaus Moyſes ſpekit expreſlie
in the place foiſaid agans thã yat
vold lead vs to ſerue ſtrãge Godds,
Sauĉt Iohne expreſlie agans tham
yat tech ane doĉtrin cõtrar to his
and Sanĉt Matheu expreſlie agans
thã yat vill not obey the church:

Bot Catholiques Romane *lead
you not to ſerue or follou any vther
God bot the God of Moyſes qui in
principio creauit cælum & terram: thai
thech you no vther doĉtrin bot yat of
Sanĉt Iohn , to vit : In principio erat
ϒerbum & verbum erat apud Deum,
& Deus erat ϒerbum : that ϒiß you
not to diſobey the church bot day and
nicht thai exhort you to obey hir ϒoyce.*
So the ſaid paſſages be moſt foo-
liſhly vſit agans Catholiques Romane vhilk agknouleg no vther

God bot the God of Moyſes, nor no
vther doctrin bot yat of S. Iohn,
nor can not abyid yat any ſuld
diſobey the church as the ſaid Moy
ſes, Sanct Iohn and holy Euangell
hes commandit in the places forſaid.

It is treu in dead yat the church
hauing the pouer to bynd and
looſs, to collect and cutt of, ſche
may iuſtly vhenas any of hir mébres becum incorrigibill ſned thá
of as inutill: Bot you or I to vſurp
yat pouer aboue hir it var bot the
part of à Mrriam agans Moyſes
and of à Cham going about to
vncouer the ſchame of his father:
It becummit vs rether to pyik out
all paſſages yat may perſuad vs úto
Chriſtian compaſſió and mutuall
charitie, knouing yat euin verey
dogs be permitted to gather of
é iij

the crommes yat fall from thair
masters tabill and yat Cryst Iesus
him self disdanit not the cumpany of Phariseis, Publicans and Infidells that he sittit in the heuins
and ranit vpon the vniust as veill
as on the iust, and yat he did once
descend from heauin to cuir the
seik and to saue the vniust commanding vs not only to loue our
freinds bot euin our foes after
his auin exemple vho did pray,
pardon and suffer for his enemis
according to yat of Sanct Matheu. *Ego autem dico vobis, diligi-*
te inimicos vestros, benefacite his qui
oderunt vos & orate pro persequenti-
bus vos, vt sitis filij patris vestri qui in
cælis est, qui Solem suu oriri facit super
iustos & iniustos.

By verteu of theiss cósideratiós
(veillbelouit) I am still resoluit to

loue you houſoeuer you miſlyik
of me,yea ſuppoſe you ſuld diſcry
me to the hoill vorld and viſs all
men dishant my cumpany as the
Ieuis did vnto the Samaritáns: yit
I ſall not ceaſſe to my pouer lyik
the Euágelique Samaritan to poor
ſuch oyill and vyne as I haue in to
your vounds ſeiking aluay your
conuerſion houſoeuer you be deliberat to vork my confuſion,and
in one vord except you cut out
my toung and hak of my handes
I ſall neuer ſpair to ſpek , vrit and
vork by all meanis in ſeaſon and
out of ſeaſon to reduce you vnto
the rycht vay from vhilk you hane
ſo dangeruſly ſtrayit cauſing the
ignorants ſo vith you to ſtray and
grou opiniaſtre in thair ignoráce
yat vithout tymlie repentáce you
be in danger one day(vhilk I pray

God fall not out) to hear that
fearfull threatinng of the Euangell: *Vo be vnto you yat fchoot vp the
kingdom of heauins ād nether vill your
felf entre nor fuffer tham to entre yat
vold.*

Eot to th' end yat on th' one part
I prefum not to fpek any rhing in
this matter(vhilk tuichis the high-
eft point of all to vit our faluatiō)
vithout Good ground, and on the
vther part yat my incredibill cōpaffion vpon my dearly belouit cā-
treymē(my flefch and blood, more pretieux vnto me as the lord
knouit nor becūmit me to fpek)
may appeir more by my vork nor
vords, I haue prefented vnto tham
à litill exhortation vharby thai
may clearlie fee hou to direct thair
cours in this vildirnes or varietie
of manifold religions vhilk vithin this

thin this 80. years as ane turbulent
inundatiõ and ſpeat vatter hes pitifully ouerrun the vynèyard of
the church : aduyſing thame in
theirs ſpirituall incurſions and de-
predations of thair ſaulles inui-
ronit vith ſo many contrarius and
crafty ſeduĉturs to vſe the ſelf ſame remeid vhilk ordinarly all mē
do for auoyding temporall irru-
ptions of thair temporall enemis.
For vhat ſogeor var he neuer ſo
hardy and aſſurit nedit not Principally and ſpecially by ſum ſpeciall ſignes to knou the colors of
his cumpany and place of the ca-
ſtell or fort vharunto he ſuld flee
finding him ſelf reducit vnto any
neceſſitie, vharof if he cháſe to be
ignorát he may as veill ſall vpõ the
troupes ád intráchméts of his foes
as of his freinds, euĩ ſo vndoutedly

ĩ

to discern the displyit enseignie, the eminent citadell and propugnacle of the treu church by hir treu colors , situation and signes from the sinagog of Satan and all Hereticall churchis I haue vith all Christian loue and humilitie vrittin vnto tham à small treatise not as à seducteur by sueit vords to drau thame to my opinion bot as à seruand of God to reduce thame to the rycht vay from vhence by your direction thai haue ignorátly strayit: *For thai be only seducteurs yat vold drau men to follou strange Godds vissing vs to seik Cryst Iesus in the vildirnes and in priuat corners heir and thair and not vithin the glorius tabernacle of his church situat vpon the top of à montane.* Such priuat monopolls and dangerus distractions alltogidder I abhor vissing vith

Deuter.4.
Marc.13.
Luc 17.
Math.24.

Sanct Peter all my cuntreymen *to beuar vith such lieing masters as bringit in sectis of sedition and perdition, and vith Sanct Io. I hartly exhort tham not to giue credit vnto eury spreit bot to try veill if thai be of God.* Vhilk tryall can not be had bot vithin the ark of the church more nor in the generall deluge any sautie culd be found bot vithin the ark of Noah.

Nether go I about thus pointing out the rycht vay, as your enemie to sau zizanie vithin your feild vhillas you be à sleap, bot as your freind I present befor you vhat seid I haue to sau vissing you to turn ouer and try the same vhilk if vithout partiall or preoccupat iugment it sall pleas you to do, you sall nether fynd my doctrin to be zizanie bot yours nor

thã to be your feild bot the feild
of other husband men vho haue
the Iuſt location tharof by attétik
euidents boyth of doctrin and lineall deſcent deryuit from th' A-
poſtles and Apoſtolique men vho
had th' only pouer to locat and
ſubſtitut vthers in thair place:V-
heras you of your recent vſurpa-
tion can produce no teſtimony
bot your auin tuiching your doctrin, hauíg no teſtimony or probation at all for your allegit laufull deſcent as in the 74. page of
this Paræneſe treating of your vocation I haue prouin at lenth by
peremptory arguments, adding in
this place by the vay this much
more nor I haue ſaid in the forſaid
page 74. Yat albeit you culd pro-
duce(as you can not) ſum euident
of ancient poſſeſſion in the perſon

of any one yat hes heirtofor in all
points techit the self same doctrin
yat you nou do, yit you haue so
morgagit and marrit the patrimony pretendit grantit vnto you by
the Apostles your pretendit dona-
tors, by your partiall glosses ād interpretations vsing and vttering
thair vrittes vnto the vorld vith
no les confidence nor if you allone (of all yat euer ves befor you,
presentlie is, or yat heirefter sall
be) had found out thair treu sens
and meaning, and heiruythall you
haue so long lyin out vnseruit or
retourit (to vit à 1500. year ād more) yat as in the former by verteu
of your Proprusiō so in the other
by such manifold Nonentrees you
haue lost all titill ād clame yat you
can iustlie pretend.

    For vhilk cause hauing on my

syid the veritie vhilk seikit no cor-
nars, and in imploying my mynd
to point out vnto simpill ons hou
the pillar of veritie (to vit the
church) suld be discernit from all
vther vsurping yat name I am
bold not in the dark vhen you ar
à sleap bot in the day licht vhill as
you valk to appell you in all kynd-
nes and humilitie not only to ponder my resons vhilk be bot such as
my veaknes can afford, bot also to
permit suir accefs and audience
vnto vthers yat be habill to satifie
you more nor I can vho for so
Good à subiect I dout not may be
mouit to cum vhar you vill and to
confer vith you vpon all matters
cōtrouerted in presence of all yat
lyik to be present. Vharunto me
think you (yat giue out vnto the
vorld so confidently yat you allo-

ne haue the vndouted veritie the
force vharof your aduerſars be
notabill to reſiſt) can not vithout
gret preiudice of your caus diſaſ-
ſent. For if you haue à veritie ſo
veill foundit as you pretend hou
can you refuſe in preſence of the
pepill to put the ſame vnto publict
tryall yat by the licht tharof all
contrarius doctrin may be conui-
cted for darknes and thai confirmit ſo much the moir thairin euin
as the goldſmyth is after, not befor he haue tryit his mettall boyth
vith his furnace and tuichſtone
aſſurit of the fynnes tharof.

Suirly the denyall of this Chriſtian conflict muſt be eſtemit ane
vnchriſtian tergiuerſation and à
matter as ludibrius as if à knicht
yat durſt not amang vther kny-
cghts ſcheu him ſelf in the liſts

vold ftill nottheles giue him felf
out amang ignorants for cheif
champion at all tilts and tourne-
ments. Bot perhaps you vill fay
yat you vold glaidly difput and cõ-
fer bot the Acts of your generall
affemblees and of Parlament muft
not be callit in queftion. as for the
former part of yat fubterfuge I do
anfsr tharúto tuo maneir of vayis.
Firft your generall affemblees tho
thai be generall in refpect of the
realm vhar you ar yit in refpect of
oicoumenique affemblees thai be
bot as à patticular handfull and as
Ariftot in one place fayis of the
numbre of ten, quod fint multi in
domo pauci in foro, yea in refpect
of the faid oicumenique affemblees the moft generall yat you cã
mak is bot in proportion as à flec
is to ane Elephant : yit the decrees
of fuch

of such oicumenique counsalls (as far in maieftie and authoritie exceding your Synods as à gret parlament doth exceid à poor birla court) haue bene oft tymes moderat and difpéfit vith vpon Good confiderations: as in yat vhar it vas oicumeniquly defendit of auld after the counfall of Sanct Paul not to conuerfe, difput or confer vith ane Heretique after the fecond admonition yit vpon Good refpects rhe rigor of yat fentence vas mitigat and oppin difputations permitted vith findry condemnit нeretiques as vith the Donatifts, Arrians, Manicheans, Macedonians, &c. and in the counfall of trent albeit in effect the fame defens vas reneuit yit findry conferances and Colloques haue bene fince yat tyme grantet fpecially

ō

yat of Poiſſy anno 1561.and yat of
lait anno 1600.at Fontanebleau.

Nou ıf theis oicoumenique aſ-
ſemblees(conuocat by ſuch as had
laufull pouer by inſtitution of the
Apoſtles)Vas perſuadit vpõ Good
reſpeꜩs to mitigat ſum tymes the
tenor of thair Aꜩes in permitting
for Chriſtian charitie diſputation
in quæſtions yat thai had decernit
to be out of all queſtion:Vhat reſon can you haue to ſtand ſo pre-
ciſly vpon your points hauing no
Chriſtian realm of your opinion
bot your oune, and no laufull authoritie to cõuocat counſalls nor
to command the conſciencs of
any man.

Morouer in denying indifferét
Conferance or liberty of conſcié-
ce you be contrarius to all vther
Miniſters your felloubrethring on

this ſyid of the ſea ſpecially vithin the realm of France vhar befor liberty of conſciéce vas grantit vnto tham thai did ſtill proteſt thair culd be no Chriſtian charitie nor libertie vhar yat libertie vas refuſit vhatſoeuer politique ordonnance vas maid to the contrar.

And if you can ſuffer to hear hou Io.knox, Io. Villox, Paul Meffenj, &c.firſt began this ſame doctrin vhilk you profes you shall tharby vnderſtand yat thai ſocht no thing at the beginning bot à ſimple libertie of conſcience vithout compulſion or threatning of any perſon vith temporall penalteis, oft tymes remembring yat ſentence of Tertullian. *Odi religionem quæ pœnis exigitur.*and yat of S. Auguſtin *Religio non eſt imponenda ſed ſuadenda.* and no vayis preten-

ding such vniuersall ouerthrou of
Prelats and Ecclesiastique persons
as thai haue sen syne procurit:
thair petitiō being principally to
haue libertie to prech the treuth
vissing no man to adher vnto thā
bot such as thai mycht persuad
vith so forsabill resons of holy scri
ptur as no Catholique Romane
culd ansr vnto : in sign and tokin
vharof Ion knox him self vas content in the touboyth of edinburg
to disput vith M. Quintin kenne-
dy abbot of corsragoll and to resaue and send discourses vpō matters controuerted vnto M. Ninian
Vingzett preist of fam⁹ Memory,
(euin after the Catholique religiō
vas abolissit by Act of Parlament)
the said Io. knox still vsing for exē
pill the promptitud of Sanct Augustin vho neuer sparit at eury oc-

cafion to vritt difput and confer
vyth the Pelagians, Manicheans,
Donatiſts, Circuncellions and all
vther Heretiques of his age: and
aluay holding to his deth yat à
knyght refuſing the liſts in any
place vhar he mycht haue ſuir acces and reces rédrit his querrell ſuſpect and yat à curageux Chriſtian
and treu Paſtor ſuld be redy at all
tymes to giue à reſon of his fayth
tho it ver vith dáger of his lyif leſt
the tender conſcience of the ſimpill ſuld be brangillit and maid
doutfull ſeing him yeild ſo much
vnto any Heretique or Infidell as
to refuſe tham ane equall and indifferent tryall. Laſt of all in yat
it is not defendit amang you by
vrit to anſsr and confer vith Catholiques it is bot à ridiculus excuſe to ſtand vpon verball Con-

ferance vharby in the space of ten dayis you suld more edifie your self and the assistâts nor you fall euer be habill to do vith your pen in ten years tho you suld blek as much paper as be in all the ten Tomes of S. Augustin. So my vel-belouit if you can be contentit ether to render vnto vs legem Ta-lionis, or to follou the exempill of transmarin churches your fellou-sisters or the exemple of the fon-dators of your auin church you can not deny vnto vs nether à lau-full and indifferent Conferance nor à fauorabill libertie of con-science notuythstanding any acts yat you haue maid to the contrar.

As to th' Acts of Parlament maid for establisment of your re-ligion I ansfr tharunto as one vho-ly submitting my self to the laues

and authoritie of my Prince fpecially vnto fuch Laues as be authorifed be folem confent of his
honorabill eftats in face of parlament repéting vith my hart as the
lord knoueth vhatfoeuer I haif in
vord or vork done to the contrary. Yit it can not be vnknouin to
any man yat knoueth any thing
in our eftat yat men intereffit by
actes of parlament this year may
vithout offens the nixt year defyir
ether à mitigatiö or abolition tharof fpecially in matters rinning v-
pon the natur of forfaltur and reftitution as this is vharof I fpek.
For the ratification of your Religion (I vill not fay reftitution be-
caufs it vas neuer in rerum natura
at left vithin Scotlád ether to be a-
bolift or reftord botvithí theis 40.
years) is in effect à forfator of the

Catholique Romane Religion v-
hilk forfaltur may be takin auay
ether by grace or be vay of reduction vhenfoeuer it fall pleas God
yat the Prince and Eſtats fall refaue better information and by yat
fame meanis all actes pronuncit in
your fauor may perhaps be can-
cellat and declarit null and of no
effect: Vharof I fuld not dout if
his Ma.té. (being fo merueluſlie lernit and prudent as he is knouin to
be)culd be mouit to fit doun and
indifferently to hear boyth parteis contending *and then lyk ane
vther Solomon decern the child (yat is
the church of God) not to be vith hir
yat carit no thing for the diuiſion and
deſtruction tharof bot vith hir Yat is
tormented and trubillit to fee the fuord
of feparation thretning the vndoing of
hir tender infant.* fo did Conſtantin

the gret aſſiſt Pope Silueſter the
firſt agans the Macedonians and
Eunomians: So did Iuſtinian aſſiſt Bonifacius 2. Ioannes 2. Agapetus, Siluerius and Vigilius. agans
the Pelagians and Donatiſtes:
So did Carolus Magnus (poſt
tranſlatum Imperium ad Germa-
nos) aſſiſt the afflicted church
and Romane Popes , Stephanus
the 5. Paſcalis the firſt and Gregor the 4. agans Claudius tauri-
nenſis Iconomachus and agás the
Albanenſes, Bagnoléſes and Con-
cordenſes vho all denyit freeuill
Purgatory and the verteu of Ba-
pteſme agans originall ſin *quamuis
fomes peccati per Baptiſmum non tolla-
tur*, diſpyſing the Sacrament of the
altar, Celibat and extrem Vnction
as many do nou à dayis.

And vnto this Chriſtian conſi-
ú

deration I dout not his highnes, his nobilitie and ʃall treu hattit Scottiʃmen ʃall be the more bent vhenas it ʃall pleaʃ tham to remember and reid vhen, be vhom and in vhat form the Chriʃtian fayth and religion came firʃt in Scotland, by hou many gret Princes of our realm it hes bene ratifeit and finally hou long it hes vithout chág or alteratiõ continuit notuithʃtanding all Hereʃeis in vther Realms trouchout the moʃt part of Europe, Afrique ãd Aʃia in ʃum places altering in vther places altogidder aboliʃing all Chriʃtian and Apoʃtolique inʃtitution.

Vhen, be v-hom, and in vhat form the Chriʃtiã Religion came in toScotland.

Our ãnalles teʃtifie yat in the year of our lord 203. king Donald vnder the Pontificat of Pope Victor the firʃt of yat name did reʃaue the Chriʃtian fayth and cauʃit all his nobilles and pepill to embrace the same: Vharof about yat same age Tertullian in his book agans the Icuis semit to giue sufficient testimony *saying yat the verie places in gret Britanny vhilk var inaccessibill vnto the Romans did agknouleg Cryst Iesus.* Vharby no dout he did mean of Scotland seing the Romans tho thai ouerran all the hoill Iland euin vsque ad grampios montes & vltra (vhilk I tak to haue bene the separatiō betuix the Scottis and pictes) yit thair coloneis or conquis did not apperantly farder extend nor vnto ye vall of Septimius Seuerus callit vallum Seueri vharof the vestiges yit Remane extéding the self betuix the firthes of forth ād klyid being near ane hūdreth myles from the said grampij montes. Sanct Chrysostom also in

his fermon vpon the Pētecoſt follouing the vulgar opinion (as
S. Hierome alſo did vharby it
vas affirmit yat of ould our forbears var Anthropophages) ſayis
in this Sort. *The britons vho did ſumtyme eat mens fleſch nou feid thair ſau-
les vith faſting.* and in his Homelie-
vhar he prouis God to be à man he
affirmis *yat in Scotland var churches
foundit and altars erected.* It tendit to
the ſame purpoſe vhilk Sanct Hie-
roſine ſayit of thā vritting to Mar-
cella. and Petrus venerabilis in his
8. book 16. Epiſtle declaring the o-
rigin of diuerſs churchis geuit no
ſmall praiſs to theis of Britāny yat
var not vithin the valls of Adrian
or Seuerus vhilk muſt neadis be
vnderſtud of Scotland for the reſons forſaid. and yat vhilk is moſt
remarquable in this matter is yat

notuithftanding all the mutatiõs
in religion yat fell out and afflicted the parts of yat Iland fubicct
to the Romane Emprors yit in
Scotland thai kneu neuer of any
mutation tharin from thair fidt
reception of the Chriftian fayth
(vh:lk vas in the 203. year of God
forfaid) vnto the year of God 559.
except fo much as vas for celebration of eafter vharin the Scottcs
bifchops follouing too much the
Aliatik form vfit by the quatuor-
decumani and borrouit from the
Ieuis(vho obferuit thair paffouer
vpon the 14. moon) did à litill refift the legat of England callit Au-
guftinus till by lettres from Pope
Honorius thai var exhortet no
more to follou yat Afiatique con-
fuetud.as teftefeis Beda venerabilis in his 2.booK 19.chap. As to the
ú iij

Herefie of the Arrians vhilk fo oppreffit the Realm of England it neuer had actes nor intree in Scotland, nor yit the Herefie of the Pelagians vhilk vas moft dangerus of all the author tharof being ane Englifs má vhom Sanct Auguftin callis *à tranfmarin Peft* and the poet Profper in his verfe de ingratis, termis him *Colubrum Sermone Britannum*. For by the prouident cair of Pope Celeftinus it vas prouidit yat Sanct Palladius vas fend into Scotlád to defend tham from yat damnabill Herefie as teftifeis the forfaid Beda in his firft book 3. chap. and Profper the Poet forfaid liuing in the fame age fayis in his book ad collatorem, *yat ynder the Pontificat of Pope Celeftinus vhillas the holy bifchop Palladius trauellit to hold England (vhilk yas then callit*

the Romane Ile) *to be Catholique he
cōfirmit the barbars tharof yat var not
ſubieƈt to the impyir* meaning the
Scots in the Chriſtian fayth eſta -
bliſſing the ſame alſo in the Or-
cads vhilk of befor var infidells: in
memory of vhilk biſchop Palladius thair is yit à church in the
mernes callit padie vhar his reliques vat keapit vith gret reuerence
and reſpeƈt.

Nether ver our laudabill anteceſſors contentit only to keap the
Catholique Religion vithin thair
auin Realm pure and vndefylit as
thai had firſt reſauit the ſame from
the Apoſtolique Romane ſeat bot
abhorring to hurd vp and to impriſon ſo pretieux à Iouell vithin
the precinƈt of à Realm ſeparated
from all vthers, for yat cauſe thai
did firſt extēd thair Chriſtian cha-

ritie vpõ thair nychbors the auld
Britõs poſſeſſing yat ſame part of
the Ilád vhilk Englis mé nou poſſes as teſtifeis the ſaíd venerabill
Beda in his 3.book 3.chap.by ſen-
ding vnto thair king Oſualdus the
holy Scottis biſchop Ædanus.For
it can not be vnknouin vnto you
yat the auld britons poſſeſſing yat
part of gret Britanny vhilk nou is
callit England thai var ſubiect to
the Romane Empyir and finding
yat the ſaid romans be reſon of ciuill varrs vithin thair auin bouells
culd not ſend ouer legions to defend tham from the incurſions of
the Scottis at lenth thai did vrit
(vnder the Empyir of Theodoſius
the elder as teſtefeis Beda in his 3.
book 13.chap.)Vnto the cõſul Æ-
tius à dolorus ád lamétable epiſtle
ſaying.*Ætio ter cõſuli gemitus Britã-*
norum

norum. Barbari ad Mare pellunt, re-
pellit Mare ad Barbaros & inter hæc
oriuntur duo genera funerum, aut mer-
*gimur aut mactamnr.*Nou after this
pittifull complant finding the Romans culd fend thã no releif then
thai did treat vith the Saxons in
Germany (vho ver Idolators) to
fuccour tham : theife Saxons fend
into England à gret pouer vhilk
vith tyme did expell the moft part
of the faid Britõs calling the hoill
land from thair Captaine Engiftus
Angli or AngloSaxones. So by
proces of tyme vhenas the Anglo-
Saxons by meanis of the forfaid
Palladius and vther holy Catholique preifts var on the vay to be
Chriftians thair king forfaid Of-
ualdus fend as fayis Bæda *ad maio-*
res natu Scotorum cuius miniſterio gẽs
quam regebat Anglorum Dominicæ

fidei & dona disceret & sacramenta susciperet. Missus autem est Ædanus summæ mansuetudinis & pietatis vir. & paulò pòst. Imbuebantur (inquit) à præceptoribus Scotis paruuli Anglorum & cum matribus in studiis & obseruatione disciplinæ regularis initiati erant.

And not only in England our nychtbour Realm did our venerabill antecessors plant and propagat the Christian fayth as it is this day professit at Rome bot also in many vther foren nations vharof Sanct Mansuetus first bischop of Tullos is à glorius vitnes, vhó the auld registers of yat bischoprik affirmis to haue bene aneScottismã. Sanct Kilianus callit the Apostle of Hyperboll in Germany is one other vitnes vhom Beda in his Martyrolog testifeis *about the* 8. *of*

*th' Ides of Iulij to haue cum out of one
of the litill hebrid Iles of Scotland ʋith
his felouis vnto Germany and all alõgſt
the Riuier of Menus to haue prechit
the Chriſtian fayth and to haue bene
crounit ʋith the Diadem of Martyr-
dom in the ſame place. In memory of
ʋhõ thair is yit à ʋerey beautifull abay
in the ſaid citie.* The thrid vitnes is
Bonifacius firſt biſchop of Mayē-
ce properly named vmfredus (v-
hilk is vndoutedly à Scottis name)
this holy biſchop did bring all
friſe ãd many other partes of Germany vnto the Chriſtiã fayth: and
Marianus Scotus in his 2. book re-
membris of the epiſtle vhilk Pope
Gregore the 3. did vrit to the ſaid
Vmphredus and hou by that Pope
he vas callit Bonifacius. and Tri-
temius de ſcriptoribus Eccleſiaſti-
cis teſtifeis him to haue bene of

yat nation vhilk lakit not probabilitie in yat the cathedrall church of the Chanonry of roſs ſeamit dedicat to his remembrance and that yit the commun opiniō thair is yat he vas born in roſmarky. Bot becaus he did once lead à monaſtique lyif in England going thidder for propagation of the Chriſtian fayth tharfor Engliſmen hold him to be thair cuntreyman. The ferd vitnes is Sanct Romuald vho ſuffrit martyrdon in Brabant (as ſayit Molanus in his abrigment callit Indiculus Flandriæ) and is yit honorit thair as ane Apoſtle and his reliques reuerently kepit in the toun of Machlin.

The fift vitnes is S. Colmanus vho vith his felouis paſſing throuchout all Germany vas at lenth martyrd for the Chriſtian fayth vhofe funerall triumph vith his compagnons forfaid IoannesStrabius doth elegantly in Saphique vers defcryue.

Laft Sanct Patricius born befyid glefgo afteruart Patron of Irland and Sanct Fiacre Patron of Brie (eftemit à king of Scotlád fone) vnto vhofe fepultur befyid Meaux vpon the penult of aguft yearly be ane incredibill confluence of deuot peapill vith many vthers mentionat in the martyrologeis of anciéts be moft famus vitnes of the zeall of our antecefsors in propagating the Chriftian Religion as thai firft refauit it and as it is this day profeffit at Rome. Vhofe ardent defyir to lead Monaftique lyif in religius houfes retired from fecular focietie and effars is euident by fo many fair Monastereis erected by tham vithin our Realm vhilk nou to the high dishonor of God and infamy of our nation be all rasit to the grounde the monuments of our Princes, nobills and Parents yea of most holy Martyrs destroyit and thair venerabill reliques cast abrod amang the vilany and dounggills of the streatis geuing me thar by matter to murn and lament vith the Prophet saying. *quis dabit capiti meo fontes aquarum , & oculis meis alueos perennes vt sicut turtur viduus & passer solitarius in tecto possim die nocteque populi mei miserias plangere , & cum Psalmista gemibundus eiulare dicens , Deus venerunt gentes in hereditatem tuam, polluerunt Templum Sanctum tuum, posuerunt Hieriusalem in pomorum custodiam, Morticinia seruorum tuorum dederunt escas*

volatilibus cœli, carnes Sanctorum tuo-
rum bestiis terræ. Facti sumus oppro-
brium vicinis nostris, subsannatio & il-
lusio his qui in circuitu nostro sunt.

And not only did thai erect and
found such magnifique Mona-
sters vithin our Realm bot also
in foren nations leauing behind
tham (to thair auin and thair nations immortall praifs) admirabill
exemples of Monaftik and Religius lyif vharby thai procurit many fair Monafteris to be beildit
vharof ve haue à clear probation
in columbanus vho becaus he vas
born in our hielands boyth Beda
and Marianus callis him *Scotum*
Hibernum or *montanum. This colum-*
banus (as sayis the said authors) caufit
by his laudabill exemple of retired regu-
lar lyif many Abayis to be erected in
France, Germany, Italy: and in Bour-

gögne vnder Theodoric⁹ kïng tharof by his meanes the famus cōuét
Luxouin vas foundit in vhɪlk var ſuch
à nūber of Religius yat boyth nycht ād
day and *hour be hour one part ſucce-*
ding vnto vther thai neuer ceaſſit to ha-
ue ſum in thair queir ſinging Pſalmeʀ
and Hyms to the praiſe of almychty
God, for vhilk caus yat hous vas à
long tyme callit *laus perennis.* Tharefter the ſaid columbanus in the
vay from Bourgonge to Italy as he
did paſs the Appénin hills he cauſit beild the ᴍonaſtery Boben. Lyk
as Sanⅽt Gallus his cuntreimā and
Scoller did foúd that celeber Mo-
naſtry amang the Suiſſes callit yit
Sanⅽt Gall.

To this purpos I culd alleg many more exemples of the pietie of
out predeceſſors in this behalf bot
it may ſuffiſe for all yat in Germany

ny thair be 14. opulent Abayis erected by our natió in vhilk no abbot nor Religius may be refauit
bot of our nation if the tenor of
the originall fundation var kepit:
yit none of thame all is this day
poffeffit by vs bot yat of ratisbone
vhar the rycht venerable dominus
Ioánes albus is abbot.the reft vith
all our priueleges thair ve haue all
loft as folishly ád for as lichtà caus
as Efau loft his birthricht or Adá
his Eden.

  Heir I may alfo to the glory of
God (of vhom all Good giftes
do proceid) and to the prayis of
our forbears ad to the premif-
fes yat as our anteceffors haue bene merueluflie deuot and Religius fo haue thai bene verey lernit. Vharof our cuntreymá and
elegant Poet Sedulius vnder the
b b

Empyir of Theodoſs the younger
ſall ſerue for one exemple. and Al-
cuinus Pædagog to Carolus Magnus fundator of the firſt publict
Scooles yat var in Paris, and the famus Hiſtorian Marianus Scotus,
and Ricardus de Sancto Victore
Monachus , vhoſe Epitaph may
yit be ſene ingrauit in braſin lettres in the Cloſtre of the ſame
Abay. Tellus quem genuit fœlici
Scotica partu , hunc tegit in gre-
mio Gallica terra ſuo, and Io. Duns
born in duns of the Mers callit in
the Schooles l'Eſcot or Scotus ſub-
tilis, and Franciſcus Maronis ſo
much yit remembrit and reſpectit
in Sorbon for his lernit commentars vpon Petrus Lumbardus (alias
maſter of ſentences) and for his
fundamentall beginning of the
ſaid college togidder virh Io. Ma-

ior the licht of his age.all theis var
eftemit vith the oddeft men of
thair tyme for erudition fpecially
in Theologye boyth pofitiue and
fcholaftique tho ve do lauch at the
homlines of thair Latin ftyill euin
as foolish Micholl did lauch at the
homly danfing of hir husband
Dauid) yit vndoutedly the pith of
the fpreit of God may yit be fo fene in thair fpreit and pē yat hardly
fuld ve be habill to vnderftād the
diuyn and delicat traittes tharof in
caife vevhar fo happy as to humill
our felf to ftudy thair doctrin.

Morouer during this tyme yat
the Catholique Romane Religion
did florifs vithin our poor Realm
producing fo many holy lernit
perfons it did alfo produce boyth
at home and abrod Good Stor of
vailliant men and gret captans.

Vharof the manifold rencontres
and set battalls agans Britons, En-
glifmen, danes and pichtes be sufficient arguments : togidder vith
thair incredibill fortitud in Germany vith Carolus Magnus (vho
contracted the first alliance vith
our king Achaius more nor à 800.
years ago :) in France vith king
Charles the 7.in Italy vith Charles
the 8. and Louys the 12.and in Pa-
leftin vith Godefroy de Bouillion:
For vhilk cause sum of thame haue bene erected to the hicgheft
honor yat à subiect in France can
afcend vnto to vit sum to be con-
ftables, sum to be Marefchalls of
France, sum Viceroys of Neaples.
For vhilk fortitud and fidelitie
Paulus Æmilius the French Hifto-
rian fpeking of vs callis vs Gal-
lorum fideles fortes & infepara-

biles amici lyk as ve haue yit yat
honor to gard the moſt Royall per
ſons of the moſt Chriſtian kings
our Scottis gard nychtlie keping
the keyis of thair hous and at all
actions Secreit or ſolemnell tuo of
our Archiers ſtanding by tham as
tuo collaterall knichtes: ane honor
in dead ſo ſignall and ſingular as it
lakit not gret emulation: ane honor acquirit by our fortitud and
fidelitie finding our ſelf in many
hard encontres (vhill as ve profeſſit the Catholik Romane Religió)
and ane honor almoſt loſt at Am-
boiſs by our folie follouing the
Caluinian Religion. Finally ſuch
vas the eſtimation in theis dayis
of the vallure of our laudabill anteceſſors yat Egeſippus in his 5.
book de excidione vrbis Hieroſo-
limitanæ doth compt it for à gret

honor to the Romans yat euin the
Scotis var afrayit to fee thair en-
fenzeis. For theis be his vords. *tre-*
mit hos Scotia quæ terris nihil debet cū
à toto orbe fit diuifa.

All this long and tedius (yit treu
and hiftoricall) digreffion vhilk I
haue maid in declaring vhen, be
vhom and in vhat form the Chriftian fayth and Religion came into fcotland and hou lōg it did continu vithout alteration, vhat vas
the ftudy and cair of preifts and
paftors of yat age, vhat vas thair
behauior or cariage touard the
feat of Rome, and vhat verteus and
valliāt men our Realm did produce during that tyme: all this difcurs
I fay is maid to the effect you may
fee yat tho you be nou vithin yat
realm in poffefforio yit the iuft
poffeffion belongit not vnto you

bot vnto Catholiques Romane
tho thai be bot in petitorio. as alſo
yat all the vorld may clearly vnderſtand yat in our humll petitions
crauing a libertie of cóſcience and
equall tryall of our cauſes befor all
yat lyik to be preſent no thing is
ſocht in the former yat lakit anciét ánd attentik authoritie or yat
you can vith Chriſtian charitie refuſe if you vill ether follou exemple of vther churchis profeſſing
the ſame doctrin vith you or the
exéple of your firſt authors vthin
yat Realm, or if you vill be contentit to do as you vold be done to
vhilk of morall or ciuill curteſie
you cá not refuſe albeit your Chriſtian deuitie did not vrg you tharunto : and in the vther tuiching
conferance you can not refuſe it
(color the matter as you liſt) bot

you render ether your caufe fufpect, or your felf as men yat dif-
fyid fum vhat in your auin ftrenth.
For vhat can be more refonable
nor in the fame Realm vhar you
duell, vhair you haue your auin li-
brareis, conforts, and all other cō-
moditeis of place perfōs and pouer
more nor Catholiques can haue:
and fyne in prefence of all the pepill (vhō you fo deaf vith the vndouted veritie of your doctrin)to
triumph vpon your aduerfars and
bring your faid doctrin to be at
all tyme tharefter out of dout?
Vhat thing more equitable nor to
grant vnto the caufe of god vhilk
in our auin caufes feldom or neuer is refufit: to vit, a fauorabill
permiffion to libell and to intend
à proces of reduction in the fentence pronuncit agans gods treu
religion

religion (vhilk vndoutedly is his caus) pronuncit I say in à iugmēt vhar the professors of the said religion var nether summonit nor suffrit to cum: vhilk form of procedur gaue occasiō once to à mirry man to say yat in scotland god had not only lost his lyfrent for lying year and day at the horn: bot also he vas forfalted and neuer yit vist vharfor and all becaus he vas not permitted to compeir for his intres. Bot I abhor to gest in à matter so deiply rinning vpon our saluation vyth soroufull hart regretting yat in matters of conscience not only acces and audience suld be this vay refusit bot also yat men suld be limited in such high matters vithin the compas of fourty dayis and syne not to haue libertie vithin the said space to defend the eqnitie of thair cause bot vithout all difputation to deny and renunce the fame and to fubfcryue and fueir the contrary. Vhilk form of procedur as it is not vfit in any ciuill matter var the fame neuer fo meá fo doth it lak all exemple preceding : yea the inquifition vhilk you fo difpyis is not for all yat fo partiall and feuer for men thair haue boyth fauorable audience and fufficient tyme to confer, confult and to conclud. and this laudabill exéple me thinhe you fuld glaidly follou left yat men follouing your auin exemple (if at any tyme heirefter à contrary religion fall cú vithin yat Realm)you feall vith fmart the force of your auin laues as many rigorus perfons hes done heirtofor vhofe vnhallouit names I vill not recit fering to offend your eares tharuyth vhilk is not my meaning. Vhat thing mo-

re refonabill then to feik no thing
yat repugnit ether to the lau of
god or deutifull loyaltie vnto our
prince that is to fay to feik no
thing yat can be iuftlie interprit
to be vithin the compas of herefie
or trafon. Vhat thing more iuft
then to cite vs befor ve be accufit
and to hear vs befor ve be côdem-
nit for vho vold proceid vtheruayis agans your felf tho it var bot
in à matter of 40. Schilling you
fuld think (and iuftly) yat you refauit iniury. bot to this hour for
all the lauis maid agans the Catholique Roman religion the profef-
fors tharof haue nether bene cited,
hard, nor yit hes had fuir acces albeit yat hes euer bene their peti-
tiõ lyk as it is prefentlie vnder this
proteftatiõ yat vho of the tuo parteis fall not keip tyme and place
affignit fall euer tharefter be efte.

mit tergiuersators and seductors of the pepill. and heir vnto me think you suld be mouit if you vill ether follou the exempill of ancients or recent counsalls euin of such as you giue out to haue be ne most partiall and Seuer. For the four first Oicoumenique coursalls of Nice, Constátinople, Ephes and Chalcidon kepit this form euin agans the Arrians, Macedonians, Nestoriás and Eutycheans: So did theis of cartage and mileuetum in Afrique agans the Donatists and Pelagiás: So did generally all vther counsalls assembled agans the Manicheans, Luciferians, Angelitis, Anthropomortis, Apollinarists, agans Cerynthus, Basilides, Carpocrates, Hermogenes, valens and the rest. This form vas kepit in thre seuerall counsalls agans Berengarius: and last yat counsall vhilk it

Plesis you to term the bloody
counsall of Trét vas not for all yat
so barbarus and inhumane agans
your self bot yat you var laufully
cited and saue conduits in most
ampill form grantit vy vertue vharof Martin Bucer as atturnay for
the hoill did compeir and ves in
diuers sessions hard befor any sentence vas pronuncit the said counsall knouing full veill the iniquitie and inualiditie of any proces
vbi reus indicta causa iudicatur,
that is to say vbi reus neque per
contumaciam abest, neque perso-
naliter aut per attornatum presens
est. Vhat supplication can be more tollerabill nor yat vharin is socht
allanerly the same form of sayth
and religion vhilk all famus doctors haue professit, all famus cou-
salls haue villit treu Christians to
profes ? yat same form of religion

vhilk our forbears 1400. year ago did firſt embrace : yat ſame form of religion vhilk hes bene euer ſen ſyne confirmit be acts of our parlaments, vharin all our forbears of good memory hes liued and diet till you ād your Coryphe Io.knox vithin this 42. years did perſuad the pepill to follou à contrar doctrin vhilk doctrin if it lead you the rycht vay to ſaluation then all yat vent befor you during the ſpace of 1400.years forſaid neuer heiring tharof muſt be in danger of damnation. Finally vhat petition ſuld be more gratius or acceptabill then to inſiſt for the reſtitution of yat ſame form of fayth and Religiõ yat did ſo bleſſ our lād ād mak it to aboūd in all reſpects far aboue any ſingularitie ordinar yat can be comprehendit in à corner ſo retired from the heat of the ſone ād focietie of other nations. Vhilk bleſſings by degrees decaying in meſure as the Catholique fayth did thair decay vee may infallibilly pronunce the ſaid bleſſings to haue procedit as effeдs from the other as ane cauſe efficient *euin as the flokis of Laban var bleſſed by the preſence of Iacob and the vedouis cruſe by the preſence of Elias: For vnto tham yat deuly vorſchipp our lord thai be bleſſed euin ꝩnto thair dachtubbs as ſayit Moyſes and as ſayit Samuel ꝩho deuly honorit God thai ſall be maid honorabill.*

Nou agans all this authoritie, antiquitie, continuation and benediдion vhat haue you to produce bot the authoritie antiquitie ãd cõtinuation proceding frõ Io. Caluin vhoſe doдri͠ is ſuch as you ſall neuer be habill to ſcheu yat any one mã lernit or vnlernit holy

or Prophan, Orthodox or Heretique, Faytfull or infidell hes bene in
all points of his fentence and opinion : Yea neuer one of thame all
proceding of that fame Cadmæan
progenie of Martin Luther (be
thai Lutherans, Semilutherans or
Antilutherás)yat in all points did
hold his doctrin or did heir of it
befor he him felf fett out his infti-
tuts.

O Mercifuld God vho vold think
yat fuch vanitie and virfulnes culd
be in the hart of má as vith foolish
Roboá to renúce the coúfall ád cú-
panie of all venerabill anciéts for
fum feu variabill neotereans. O
Bernard, ô Gregor , ô Auguftin , ô
Ambrofe, ô Hierom, ô Chryfoftő,
ô Leo , ô Dyonife , ô Anaclet, ô
Paul, ô Cryift Iefus vho did fay to
Sanct Peter thou art à roque and
vpon this roque I fall beild my
church.

church. haue you defauit your A-
poftles? Haue the Apoftles defauit
Apoftoliq̄ mē thair auditors? Haue
Apoftoliq̄ men defauit theis holy
Doctors forfaid? and haue the faid
Doctors defauitvs in thechīg vs to
follou the fucceffors of the faid
Cephas or ftone, and of yat fifcher
of men and firft Apoftle: No No:
ve can not be defauit: For by experience ve knou hou our forbears
and hoill Iland hes bene extraor-
dinarly bleffed fo long as ve var o-
bediēt vnto the feat Apoftolique:
bot as to any benediction follouing vpon this neu doctrin fen it
came vithin our Realm I can per-
faue none bot ane incredibil fteri-
litie boyth by fea and land vharof
ve nead no vther vitnes bot the
hoill aged fifchers and fermorars
of the Realm, togidder vith the di-
molition of magnifique Mona-

ftereis, Abayis, Cathedrall and Pa-
rifs churchis vhilk (var the beautie of our land) as if fum Totila,
Attila or Tamerlan had ouerrun
tham and the Clergie vho did fu-
ftene all neceffiteux perfons vedouis, orphalins, beggars: vho v-
pheld all Hofpitals brigges and
fuch publict and pieux vorks ten-
ding to the vniuerfall feruice of
the Realm, vho finding thair prince in neceffitie vas euer habill and
villing to fupplie him for mentey-
ning his varrs, for tochering his
docthers, for refauig Embaffadars,
for going thair felf on thair auin
charges in Ambaffadry: The Clergie i fay vhilk vas boyth habill ãd
villing to do all theis offices and
more, for the releif of Prince and
pepill, thair be lottis caft for thair
coit, and thai be all damnit to die
and Barrabas is let loofe.

And in this point such as vold
vnderſtand the glory and grace.
Vhilk our Clergie had heirtofor
let him bot behold the viue Image tharof yit extant in theis tuo
moſt nobill verteus and venerabill Prelats.Ia.Betō Archibiſchop
of Gleſgo Embaſſador for his Maieſtie our dread ſouueran lord, and
William Cheyſolm Biſchop of
weſon, vhoſe incredibill prudence
and pietie can not be condinglie
extollit by à pen lyk myne ſo clogged and accabled vith infinit mi-
ſereis. *Tham ve haue from thair youth*
vexit bot culd not vinquiſs tham:tham
ve haue ſold to the Iſmaelites yit in our
famin ve all fynd thair famileis oppin
and thair vndeſeruit kyndnes no thing
inferior to yat of Ioſeph and Ioſes. Finally the more ve haue fynit tham
the more thai haue prouit pure
Gold and the more ve haue affli-

&ted tham, thai ar becum the more
firm and ve the more febill. For
by the glorius vings of thair rare
vertus thai be fo exalted aboue the
rech of all our malitius machina-
tions yat all our furie is turnit in
froth and fome lyk yat of the fuel-
ling feas beating agans adaman-
tin roques.and as all yat ve haue
reft from tham *is bot prt vp in à bot-*
tŏbes bag infinit plages follouing ʋs lyk
the facrilegius AZotiens for ʋfurping
the ark or heritage of the church:fo on
the vther part the faid ʋenerabill Pre-
lats albeit th' one hes not this 40.year
ăd more the other neuer lifted à denier
of is reuenus out of Scotland: yit thair
bafquet ăd oyillcruyfe hes no more falit
nor yat of the ʋedou of Sarepte:yea thai
baue bene and be more hofpitall and fer-
uicabill to thair King and cuntrey nor
all yat vfe any Ecclefiaftique function
vithin yat Realm : Vharin yat of So-

lomon boyth in his Prouerbs and Pre-
chor is verifeit. Benedictio Iuſti quaſi
fluuius inundauit & abundantia Dei
in mercedem illius feſtinauitquia habi-
tacula Iuſtorum benedicta ſunt.

Finally all cair to propagat the
Chriſtian fayth amãg infidells and
all ancient courage by martiall
deids in laufull varrs to reuiue and
refuſcitat the ancient trophees of
our laudabill anteceſſors be ſo for-
gottin yat ve ſeme rether to be de-
generat nor ingenerat of ſuch pa-
rents.For prechors nou adayis may
veill remane in tounes vhar thai be
veill treated and vhar cryſt is alredy profeſſit and thair go about to
mak Monopolls,factiõs and ſchiſmes amang Chriſtians: Bot vhilk
of tham goit abrod amãg infidells
to mak tham Chriſtiãs as did holy
Columbanus, Bonifacius and the
reſt forſaid? or as many holy reli·

gius men do this fame day to Iappon, to Iaua, to Barbary, to Breffill
cuin amang the cruell cannibal-
les: of vhilk religius I did fee in the
laft year of Iubilé 1600. about a 16.
reuerent perfons Iefuites and Cor-
deliers embarque for the fame effect at genoa. bot ve ar fo far from
any fuch refolution as I vold vis at
god yat ve vold only go bot to
the Hielands and bordors of our
oune Realm to gain our auin cuntreymen vho for laik of prechors
and miniftration of the Sacraméts
muft vith tyme becum ether infidells or Atheifts. *Vxores duximus nõ
poffumus ire*. and on th' other part
vho goit to hungary agás the turk
or refpected more the qualitie of
the caufe vhar thai go nor the quã-
titie of thair gages?

Bot leuing this dolorus difcours
of maledictions procurit by our

damnabill defection from the feat Apoftolique I return from vhence I digreffit concluding yat you can not vith refon nether refufe vnto vs à libertie of confcience nor ane indifferent conferance if you vill ether fcheu your felf cheritable, equitable or conformable to vther churches your felloubrethring or vnto the authors of your religion vithin yat fame realme. Befeching you in the mean tyme tak in no ill part yat I haue directed this para- nefe vnto my cuntreymen feing I do offer the fame firft in your aune hâdis to be perufit and anffurit vn- to viffing (if fo var your plefour) the fame mycht rather be by vord nor vrit and tharuythall in prefen- ce af all (if it var poffibill) yat you vold perfuad to the contrar, as per- fons hauing moft entres in this matter. If I haue faid prudétlie you

can haue no íchame ftill t ohold
me your freind: if foolishly vouchaf at left to compt me as your
folish freind and for Chriftiã charitie in charitabill maneir difput
yea defait my doctrin if you may
abftening from all acerbitie of
vords and perfonall contumelies,
*Inueftigantes vtrique veritatem tan-
quã neutri adhuc cognita effet. nihil per
contentionem, neque per lucrum, neque
per vanam gloriam operantes , fed in
humilitate & charitate inuicem alter
alterum fuperiorem arbitrantes , neque
quæ fua funt finguli confiderantes fed
ea quæ aliorum. illuminet vos ille qui
lux mundi eft ne amplius in tenebris pal.
petis , &) illuminatos omni fælicitate
foueat fœcũdetq;,fupplico.Paris the calends of Martij 1602.*

Your louing and obedient freind.
Io. Colville.

VNTO THE
REDAR.

HE difficulty to print
any thing in our *vul-
gar toung on this ſyid
of the ſea nanly in
France vhar our lan-
gage and pronũciation*
ſeamit ſo ſtrange, and vhar the prentars
vſe ſeldome theis lettres k, y, and double
VV, vhilk be ſo commun to vs ſall (I
truſt good redar) excuſe the manifold
faltes and incorrectnes of the ortho-
graphy.

Bot concerning my oune faltes heir
in to much maniſeſted (yit not cõſiſting

ee

in the doctrin yat *I* defend nor in the
matter of this treatife bot in my homly
and inexact treating tharof) *I* can thar
in pretend no fufficient excufe bot by fin-
ceir confeffion of my infufficiency to befech the refpect my good affection not
my gros imperfection and to cenfur the
fingilnes of my mynd as gratiufly as the
myit of the Euangelique vedou vas cenfurit by our lord and mafter, vouchafing
at left to reid me patiently befor thou
reprehend and to ponder me veill befor
you pronunce thy fentence. Laft if the
multitud of allegations brocht in for cõ-
firmatiõ of matters difputed vithin this
treafis, fall feam prolixt and tedius: fuir-
ly in yat alfo *I* muft confes à falt , yit
fuch à falt as *I* haue villingly cõmitted
for auoyding à greter. For the treuth is
yat the commendation in many partes
of fcriptur geuin vnto glaid and plentifull geuers and the exemple of god al-

mychty in Raning doun his quailles and manna so abundantly vpon his famissit pepill, and the Euangelique historie declaring hou cryst our master vold not feid the multitud euin in à desert vildirnes bot vith such largnes as thair restit aluay certane basquetts of superplus : theis laudabill exēples I say maid me purposly to charg the bord vyth so many disches persauing the greatnes of the spirituall famin afflicting my veilbelouit brethring, the rather for that the aduersars dayly deaf tham vyth endles detestation of our doctrin alleging yat ve haue no stoir of sound arguments to confirm the same. For this causs I thocht it culd offend no treu Christian if I suld out of the magasin or storhous of antiquitie, experience and reson produce sum plētifull quantitie for conforting the indigent and confounding the arrogant. Bot to conclud if you canst not allou of this cõsideration I vill anfsr vnto the vith *Allexander* king of *Macedons* vho vrit once in this fort vnto his *Mingnon* Leonidas yat fand falt vyth him for fpending to much frank incens in his facrifices, faying. (Leonidas) frankincens and Myrre vee fend vnto the plétie, to th' end yat heirefter you be no more à Niggard vnto the godds. *Fairueill. At Paris the calends of Martij 1602.*

Your humill feruand.

Io. COLVILLE.

CONTENTS OF
this book.

THAT the ignorance, arrogance and curiositie of this age is greter nor it had bene in any age heirtofor beginning at the 3. page, section. bot to t' end. vnto the 5. page.

That the curius of this age vill not conform thair opinions vnto maximis of holy Scriptur: bot go about to confirm thair said opinions by the said Maximis. ane arrogance anciently condemnit. pag. 5. section finally nou.

That the dum text of Scriptur is no competent Iuge in Matters controuerted pag. 6. section. Agane to decern.

A Notable exempill of Theodose (the elder) Empror hou he did vse the Heretiquis of his age pag. 10. sect. Bot to the end.

Th' occasion mouing the author to vrit this

ff

the Doctors and and counsalls of the church for thair authors wheras thair aduersars haue no authors bot such as trouchout all the said ages haue bene condemnit for Heretiques pag. 136. sect. Nixt let vs.

That all controuerseis falling out tuiching religion sen the dayis of the Apostles haue bene composed and consulted vpon by authoritie of the Romane church as only (at left principally) hauing yat pouer pag. 144.

That in theiss dayis if ve had the spreit of moderation ve suld as much honor and respect the bischops of Rome as the ancient doctors did thair ancient predecessors. pag. 147.

The exempill of the Pop hetis suld tech vs not to renunce the body of the church for the vyces of the Pastors tharof. pag. 150.

The exempill of the Apostles also suld moue vs vnto the same effect. pag. 151.

Vhy thair es euer bene such respect had vnto the Roman church, pag. 155.

Vharfor the treu churc his euer to be estemit in the licht housoeuer sche be obscurit and the Hereticall churchis in darknes howsoeuer thay seme illustrè pag. 157. beginning at this vord finally I vill not.

THE *PARÆNESE* OR
*admonition of Io. Coluille (Laitly
returnitto the Cathòlique Romane
religion in vvhilk he vves bapttesit
and brocht vp till he had full 14.
years of Age) vunto his cuntrey
men.*

OF Academiques the cheif Philosophe Plato (vvho for his deap
knoulege and contemplation in
diuinite vves callit diuine) aboue
all things did rendre thanks vnto
God that he vves born in the dayis of Socrates
out of vvhose mouthe he had resauit so many
fair and frutfull instructions : if this most famus Philosophe florissing in a tyme full of all
Sapience humane did notvvythstanding glorifie him self to haue bene born in the Olym-
piad or age of à Socrates of vvhom culd be
lernit no Science bot humane and morall , the
knoulege vvharof culd bot prefer him in svm

A

Aicademye philofophique: hou muche more am I (being born boyth ignorát and in à tyme fo full of ignorance) oblift vnto the merceis of god vvho hes prouydit for me, not à Socrates bot à Samuel to inftruct me, not in humane bot in diuyne fcience vvharby I am intterit vvthin the Academy of the holy churche, after I have full fonrty years váderit in the vildirnes of my avvin vane opiniós vvthout fear or forfycht, till it pleafit his hevinly maieftie yat in the year of onr lord 1599. in the moneth of October I fhuld cvm to Paris in as vofull and cófortles cafe as the Ifraëlites vver into vvhéas thay fled fró Egypt : for as thai had behind thame thair Enemis, befor thame the read Sea, on ether fyid mótans replenifit vvith ravenus beaftes: So vvheder foever I culd turn my Eyis vves no thing for me bot the fearfull Image of death, My Enemis inuading, my freinds forfaking me.

And as the faid Ifraëlites fand thair deliurance in ane Element Moft to be fearit fo fand I myne in ane inftrumét moft offendit vith me. vvho hauing for the tyme the honor to haue bene Rector of Paris (Vvharby he had fufficient pouer to aueng) yit his pietie fuppreffing all Paffión maid him to pitie and not to perfevv me Vvhenas my kinred and acquentance did ftand far of not caring vvhider I fuld fink or fuim. He vves in this defaftre my Ariadne Leading me out of the Labyrinth of many miféreis: Or rather he vves Vvnto me as that An-

gell vvhilk did côfort Agar fitting in the foli-
tud Leding to Sur , or as à Kynd Samaritan
pouring in my fefterit voundis vyne and oyill,
and ane vther Philip, explaning to me paffages obfcur:vtheruayis I had ftill vvith quene
candaces Enuch red vvithout refolution and
In vane bufeit my felf vvith Sifiphus Rolling
à reftles ftone of blynd zeall vvithout Kno-
lege.

Bot to th'end I hyd not the talent cômit-
ted,nor fchoot vvp vvnder à bufchell the candill vhilk he hes lychted, my deuite to god almychty,to my dearly belouit cnutreymen and
inftructer forfaid is to mak vthers participant
of the benefit refauit: Confiddering yat nou à
Dayis the fnares of Satan be more fubtill and
ménis ignorance arrogance and curiofite mere
groffe,Impudent and dangerus nor thai haue
bene in any Age heittofor, the ampill crookit
vayis Leding to perdition being al moft innu-
merable yit all hauing fum apperance to be
Straicht and treu and all crying and contefting
cryft to be hear, cryft to be thair, and eury
one going about to eftablifs his doctryne by
arguments dravin out boyth of humane and
diuine fcience. In Such doutfulnes and def-
perat confufion vvhat courfs can fimpill ons
follovv? or hovv shall thai certenly knov
vvhar Cryft and his verite is all ftanding fo
doutfull and aubiguus.

For if in thus vnholy age one fhuld be re-
foluit to follovv the moft holy then shall fum

obiect yat holynes is a verey incertane mark
for yat the most holy vver bot sinuars Seing
all flesch be includit vnder sin and yat thair is
none yat doth good no not one : vhich assertion or stübling blok thai go about to proue
and illustre by exemples follouing, imputing
polygamy vnto the patriarches, vvnto Noah
drunkinnes, vvnto Lot incest, To Movses,
incredulite, To king Dauid adultery and ho-
micid : Euin as if mē shuld abstene to imitat
and follovv the faythfull brigand be reson of
his brigandry, or the teares of S. Peter and of
the Magdalene for his denyell and hir debau-
chit Lyf preceding: or as if the yeall of S. Paul
vver to be dispysit becaus he fand à lavv in
his membres repugning to the lavv of his spreit
and becaus the euill yat he vold not yat
he did. By the self same reson Noah mycht
haue refusit to haue interit vithin the ark
becaus in it vver includit vncleane beasts
vith the cleane : and S. Paul to have ioynit
him self vvith the vther Apostles becaus one of
thame vves à Iudas. Agane if one shall resolue
to follov antiquite Thay shall allege Cain the
reprobat to be eldar nor Abel th' elect and Esau
elder nor Iacob, and Ioseph and Beniamin to be
the Youngest of all the tuelf trybes yea the
Deuill and sin to be most ancient yit not to be
follouit? Euin as if on th' vther part thair lakit
exemples Vvhar the Eldest brethering vver
bestbelouir of god and most to be follouit of
men (as Vver Sem and Abraham) or as if

one should say god and goodnes vver not
more anciẹnt nor Satan and Sin. ᴌaſt if one
vvill proteſt to follovv famous counſalles and
doctores it ſhall be arrogátlye affirmit that Doctores vver bot men and Coũſalles bot aſſemblees of men ſubiect to errores: As thocht thẹy
vvho neuer ſhal haue the honour to be doctores of the church nor pouer to conuocat oicu-
cumenique or generall counſalles vver exempt
and vovid of all errour.

　　Finally novv adayis ſuch is our deplorable blyndnes and boldnes that vve be not
content to infer or gather our concluſions
vponẹ enunciations or antecedentes expreſlie ſet dovvn in Scripture (albeit vve brag
much of expres vvordes) bot vve vvill have the ſcripture à ſequell or Servant to our
vnattentik antecedenres. as for exemple. Obey
your Princes euin theis that be throvvart or
peruerſs. and of paſtores. do vvithout contradiction vhat thay command . Theis tvvo pre-
ceptes be expreſly commáditin holy ſcripture
yit vve vvill ᴃot ſtudy to leuell by this infallible ſquair our fond and fallible opiniõs vvhilk
go about vnder pretext of cõſciéce andcõmun-
velth to ſchak of the moſt neceſſar and ſalutar
yok of all ſubiection ciuill and Eccleſiaſtique not being content to render our ſelf and
our paſſionat opinions captyue vvnto theis ſacred oracles. Bot vve be bold aneuch vppon
our auin maximis or antecedentes (vvhilk be
that Princes and Paſtores peruerting Iuſtice

A iij

and Religion may be difobeyit and degradit) to gather, cite, vreſt and throvv vnto our purpos all ſcriptur ether ſpeking directly or indirectly of th' one or vther dignite Inlykmancir in that affirmatyue, Emphatique and moſt piththy propoſitiõ Regiſtrat in the ſacred protocoll of the holy Euãgell *This is my body,* ãd in that negatyue propoſition (This is not my body bot à mark or ſigne tharof) our partialite and preſũptiõ is to mvch manifeſted, in that ve go about to falſifié the finger of god leading the pé of the bleſſed Euangeliſtes and to verifie the imagination of man, vvhilk in expreſs vords ſhall never be fovnd in Euangeliſt, Prophet nor Apoſtle. To be ſchort ſic is our damnabill induration that Vve Can admit no principall or ſondament of religion bot theis of Protagoras vvho did allovv every one of his diſciples to eſteme that moſt trevv vvhilk to thair opinion did appear moſt probable : No ſquair or reull bot the leſbyã of lead vvhilk mycht be bovvit and applyit to any form or figur.

Agane to decern in queſtiõs of Religiõ cõtrouerted Vve can admit no Iuge bot the dum lettre, vhilk is ane paradox ſo abſurd and vithout exemple preceding as to this hour by antiquite it can not be verifeit vhar the actor and defender pleading at any bar or court have bene iugit allanerly by Vvrittin lavves. Morouer ſeing it is of neceſſite requirit that not only the parteis pleading bot euin the meaneſt membres of all courtes ciuill or criminal

yvnto the bedalles, fergeants, domfteres and
ifcheres shuld have iugment and difcretioun in
fum mefour albeit the procefs vver bot of à
fous or fchilling: Vvhat folie is it in the mater of faluation to admit à Iuge Vvhithout iugment or fens. Bot let Vvs heir confidder the
practife that hes beine obfervit Vpon this fubiect heirtofor in all politique gouernemen-
tes fathfull and infidelle. Did thay Vvho fo
much eftemit the lavves of the 12. tables a-
mang the Romans , or thay vho reducit the
hoill lavves in one Cod or volum only admit the faid lavvis for competent Iuges? And
Amang the Hebrevvis Vvhar the blefled lord
god him felf Vves Lavvmaker Vves thair not
Iuges eftabliffit to Iuge and difcern Vpon all cō-
troverfeis that culd fall out?and albeit it be faid
in one place(*fearch the fcriptures*)that is no com-
mandement to declyne all vther Iuges bot the
fcriptur,becaus that cōmanding our childring
diligently to ftudy the lavves Vve Vvis thame
not to contēm all vther Iuges nor to denye any
decifition of lau bot fuch as thai thair felf shall
collect of the faid lavuis : as alfo in ane vther
place of fcriptur it is faid *(tell the church.)* by
Vvich Vvordis ane vther Iuge nor the fcriptur
is euidently defignit. Heirvvihall it can not be
denyit that the church is to the fcriptur as the
pilot to the Rodet,the mafon to the lyne The
Magiftrat to the lavves.for as during the tēpeft
it aualit no thing to haue Vvithin the fchip ftoir
of Rodares except thai be gouernit by the hand

of the steirsmam or pilot:And as to beild à hous
stoir of Lynes,squaris,stone and tymber disor-
doritly heapit vvp heir and thair serve for no
purpos except the mason vse his art in disposing
tharof:And as millions of Codes and digestes,
of actes of covnsall or parlament or vhat soe-
ver laues Imperiall or municipall can never
decyid à proces nor pacifie parteis contending
except the magistrat by viue voyce decern se-
cundum allegata & probata:Evin so the rodar
and compas, the lyne and squair of the holy
scriptur and laues contenit tharin except thai
have the church to be steirmam,masson and Iu
ge thay of thair self shall neuer pacifie parteis
contending in fayth and religion,more nor the
compas allone can gyid the Schip or the lyne
allone beild the hous. And agane albeit evry
one Imbarquit have for sautie of his lyf à speciall Intres to see the sthip vveill gouernit yit it
shuld be boyth presumpteus and perrelus if
contemning the ordinar Pilot and Marinelles
evry one shuld put to his hand to sett the compas,cast the lead, Hold the helm and steir the
roddar:and albeit evry one of the familie have speciall resons to see the hous cōmodiuslie
beild yit shuld it be boyth à fectles and confusit
vvork if evry one of the houshold should play
the Architectour or mason:Euin So in the schip
of Crystis church tosted this day so dangerou-
sly to and fro by so many turbulent vyndes
and vaues of herreseis,and in the fabrique of
his mysticall hous if evry one Shall presum

and

and vſurp the gouuernall and lyne of the bleſſed ſcriptures,in ſuch rakles côfuſion can be no
beilding vp bot breking doun, no ſautie bot
ſchipurak.

And vhar it is allegit that by ſcripture vee
muſt iuge of ſpreittes and parteis contending
vpon queſtions of ſcripture:yit yat being granted it doth not neceſſarly follou that the ſaid
ſcriptures be competent iuges : for adhering to
our former ſimilitudes vithout the gouuernall
the ſchip can not be veill gouernit,nor vithout
the lyne or ſquair the hous deuly perfyted:yit
the ſteirman is callit the gouernor and not the
gouernall, the maſſon the beilder and not the
lyne or ſquair : and this compariſon doth hold
in all exemples of the lyik nature: for behold
vhen you compt vith comptares not thai bot
you be callit the comptar: vhen vith your money you buy any thing not the money bot you
be the buyar.and yit more ſpecialiy,you can nether hear,ſmell nor taiſt bot by meanis of your
eares, noſe and toung,yit you be callit the hea-
rer,ſmeller and taiſter and not thai.Euin ſo albeit by the moſt cequall lyne and leuell of the
ſcripture the churche doth iuge betuix orthodox and hereticall opinions, yit Sche not the
Scriptur only ar to be eſtemit laſull Iuge:for as
ſayit the Apoſtle ſche is the pillar and fondamēt
of veritie: vho if ſche ſhall not vith hir holy hãd
ſteir ad gouern the Chriſtian barque ſo miſerá-
rably diſtreſſit vith ſo many contrarius fluxes
and refluxes hereticall and ſchimaticall vee

shall be of neceſſite oueruhelmit vith the vehe-
mentnes of ſic erronius inundations, and if ſche
shall not apply vnto vs the iuſt leuell of verite in this voſull varietie vee muſt remane no les
confuſit, indiſpoſit, diſordorit and vnapt for the
myſticall fabrique of the hous of god as confuſit materialles of ſtone and tymmer ſcatterit
abrod hear and thair be vnſitt vnto à materiall
fabrique of the hous till thai be collected, placit ad and poliſit by the cunning handes of the
skilfull maſſon.

Bot to the end the madnes of this age vhilk
vill not ſubmit thair ſelf vnto ſuch as vithin the
church be deuly authoriſed vith Apoſtolique
ſucceſſion (lyk as in ancient ages all contro-
uerſeis in fayth ver ſubmitted to the doctores
and connſalles poſſeſſing the ſame places) may
be euidently vinquiſit I vill befor I inter into
my matter produce only one exemple of the famus Emprieur Theodoſe the elder ſo much
praſit by S. Auguſtin, Oroſius and the Poet
Claudian.

Theodor.
Caß.in the
Tripartit.
Hiſtory.

This ſacred éprour ſeing in his dayis the church
pitifully vexit by the hereſeis of Eunoni⁹, Nouatius, Macedonius and Arrius did call vpõ Nectarius biſchop of Cõſttiãnople vhar for the ty
me he remanit crauing the ſaid Nectarius opiniõ vhat cours ves to be holdfor pacifeing theis ſchiſmes. Nectarius (not preſuming to much
of his lerning as men vithout lerming in theis
dayis do) did conſult vith Agelius ane vther biſchop and vith Siſinnius à lector. Nou this Siſin-

nius being the od man of his age for erudition
and eloquéce |gaue this aduys faing that fo long
as the parteis forging and foftring neu doctrin
had libertie to vrit and difput thair culd be no
hoip of concord bot rether of greter fchifmes and factions,affirming the only vay to pacifie all ves to caus matterres controuerted be
fubmitted to the cenfur of the churche in re-
forming and reducing all vnto and by the
voyce and authorite of the fathers vho had bene anciétly admitted for autétik doctorstharof:
for fo faid he fuld the curiofite of reftles branes
be brydelit by the felf fame maieftic viche had
confundit all heretikes from the afcenfion of
Cryift Iefus.The bifchop Nectarius lyiking veill
of this aduife did inform the Emperor tharof
vifling him call vpon the cheif herefiarches and
ringleadars of the factius and to ask of thame
if thai vold ftand to the decifion of ancient,do-
ctors vho did floris befor thair neu opinions ver
hard of and ver for that caus to be eftemit indifferét iuges in that thai had neuer fene nor hard
any of the parteis contending , and in cafe the
faid nouators fuld refufe this moft refonable
fubmiffion the Emperour ves folicited to hold
thame manifeft côtradictors and impugnars of
the authorite of the fathers ãd of the primityue
church. To be fchort the fchifmatiqs ver cited
and ftanding vp befor the Emprour he did ask
of tham vhat opinion thai had of Ecclefiaftique doctors namly of fuch as had vrittin befor
theis neu queftions ver controuerted? Vharun-

to at the first with gret modestie thai auſuerit
ſaying thai did eſteme the ſaid ancientes gret
preceptors and pedagogs of the church. Bot
the emperor àgane demãding if thai vold ſubmit thair neu opiniõs to be cenſurit by the writ-
tes of the ſaid anciets, then that began to dout,
ſum refuſing, ſum granting ſimpliciter, ſum grãting and refuſing conditionally : Vhaꝛupen
amang tham ſelf did aryis ſuch confuſion and
clamour, ſum affirming, ſum denying ſum diſtin
guiſing that by thair inſolidite and incertenty
the ſolidite and certenty of the Catholique
church ves manifeſted and the ſaid Emperour in-
terponing or conioyning his imperiall authorite vith the ſpirituall did conclud and decern
vith Tertullian traitting this paſſage of S. Paul
flee from ane heretique after he be once or
tuyis admoniſit in vhilk traittie the ſaid Tertullian doth aduyſe treu Catholiques not to diſ-
put vith Heretiques by expres text of Scripture
bot to reduce tham to the ancient tradition of
the church and doctors tharof and from the
ſaid church and ancients to reſaue the treu ſens
and interpretation of the ſcriptur and of all
queſtions cõtrouerted vithin the church according to the laudabill opinion of Origenes vho
doth affirm that only to be reſauit for vndou-

Occaſion mo-
uing the au-
thor to vrit
this ſmall
treatiſe.
ted verite vhilk in no point doth differ from
ancient Eccleſiaſtique tradition.

Bot Seing in theis latter dayis thair be no
emprour to practiſe the counſall of Siſinnius albeit the curioſite of this tyme brangilling all the

fundamentes of treu religion had more nead
tharof nor euer heirtofor:in so much as Simpill ons be cast into such incertentie that hardly
can thai resolue vhidder to follou antiquitie or
nouetly,science or ignoráce,ordor or disordor,
it is thatfor the deuite of eury one in particular
to supplie this generall defect to his pouer(be it
neuer so meam) by studeing to edifie the ignorants and by expressing his charitable affection
ether by vord or vork. For vhilk caus I not putt
vp (as the lord knouit) vith the suelling spreit
of curiosite,contention or malice, nor corrupted by lucre or auarice do vnto the glory of my
gratius lord god , benefit of my cuntrey men
and satisfaction of such as ether dout of or de-
tract my conuersion simpillie and sensibillie sett
doun my popular opinion in this behalf declaring hou I my self ves clearit of all theis doutes
and brocht by goddes grace to knou on vhat
syid the verire ves to be found.

After I had red in the Apostle Timoth.1.and
3.chap.the church of God to be callit the fundament or pillar of verite I thocht it necessary
to serch out vhar this pillar ves to befound
that being assurit tharof I suld no more dout of
the verite beildit tharupó,esteming it à matter
presumpteiis, preposterus and absurd to think
that eury priuat man must first knou the verite
befor he knou the church and by the said verite to discern the treu church from the fals:
Seing S.Augustin him self ves not aschamit in
expres vordis to confes that he had neuer bele-

uit or knouin the Euangell for Euangell (albeit it be the vndouted verite) except the authorite of the church had first moued him tharunto. The holy father doutlefly did confider hou impoffibill it ves to eury one in particular of him felf to penetrat and rip vp the latent fecreittes of this verite vharin is comprehédit fuch deap and deantie treafors of vifdome, vich gaue not only occafion to ancient Doctors of the primityue church to fpend fo much tyme and ftudy in explaining tharof bot euin the Apoftles thair felf if thai had not bene firft affifted by the celeftiall commentares of Cryifts auin viue voice and fecondly vith fupernaturall affiftáce of his holy fpreit after his moft glorius Afcenfion thai had neuer bene habill to haue comprehendit the deap of that infcrutable profundite for manifeftation vharof the holy fpreit ves fpecially boyth promifit and fend vnto tháme.

That the fens of Scriptur is not fo facill as many fuppo-ne.

Sanct Hierome in his firft book agans the Pelagians doth complene of the Heretiques of his age vho to drau the pepill to thair opinions ver not afchamit to affirm that the Scripturs ver eafy to be vnderftud of childring, vemé and idiotes. to this effect vritting to Paulinus theis be his vordes. *The only art to vnderstand the fcriptur is that vhilk eury one doth ¦vendicat or vfurp euin to the doting cloone*, Skolding *drab and babilling* Sophift: *of the Scriptur (*Sayis *he) thai all prefum and pratill, teching befor thai be tacht.* of vhilk

August. 2. booc Confeß. chap.25.

presumpteiis arrogance if vee shall truft S.Auguftin, S.Hilar, S. Epiphan and the faid S.Hie-

rome all hæreſeis haue precedit vhenas **eury** Hilar.2.booĸ
one interpreting the Scriptur after his auin ple- *of the Trinit.*
ſure perſuade him ſelf to haue foúd out the vn- *Epiphan.*7.
douted verite. Bot the moſt venerable fathers *Syn.Seſs.*6.
did not tak vpon thame to vnderſtand the ſcri- *Hieron.* 2.
ptur till thai ver firſt veill inſtructed by ſuch as *Galat.*
had ſufficient vnderſtanding tharof. So ſant
Hierome glorifei s him ſelf to haue **lernit** the
holy Scriptur vnder Gregor Naziazen and di-
dimns. So Sanct Baſilius Sequeſtring him ſelf
from all ſecular ſtudy and ſocietie did ſchoit
him ſelf vp in ane monaſtery full 13 Yeares paſſing his prentiſschip in the ſcriptur and ſouking
vp the treu ſens tharof out of the bleſſed paip-
pes of ancient approued doctors and not of his
auin priuat imaginations as too many do nou
adayis.

Moreouer in the auld teſtament **vee read** not
that all ver doctors and interpretors of the **lau**
bot à feu did exerſe that function: and in the
neu teſtament vheras Sanct Paul doth inſtitut
degrees vithin the church aponting ſum to
be Doctors, ſum Prophetes. &c. tharby the A-
poſtle doth manifeſtly inſiuuat the ſens of ſcripture not to be patent to eury one. Tertullian
alſo in his preſcripſions. chap. 14. doth eſteme it
for ane euident mark of hereticall churches
vhar thair is no difference of ſex or office nor di-
ſtinction maid in reding holy ſcriptur, and vhar (to
vſe the ſaid authors vordes) Catechumens or intrants
vithin the church think thame ſelf perfyit befor thai
be inſtructed, vhar vemen be ſo bold and inſolent

that thai dar presum to tech, disput, contend: vhar he
that is to day diacon is to morrou Lector, and to day
preist tomorrou Laique or secular, and vhar Laiques
exerce and vse the office of preist and Sacrificateur.

Agane if it be the part of the Phisitiã and not
of the patiét to try the sincerite of medicamē-
tes: if the steuart and not eury houshold man
suld oppin the stoir hous and distribut the vit-
talles for eury one of the familie in particular:
if the master and marinelles not eury slumme-
ring and seaseik passinger suld sound the deap:
direct the cours and gouern the schip : Hou
much more is the tryall of the Metaphysicall
Medicin and distribution of the celestiall food
of our Saüles conteanit in holy Scripturs and
gouernement of the schip of the church proper only vnto tham that vorthely haue passit
thair degrees in that spirituall facultie and be
laufully aponted dispensators and steuarts of
that celestiall familie and finally be masters and
marinelles ministeriall vithin the mysticall barque of the holy church aud not to eury child,
voman or idiot?

Besyid this vee see by dalye experience not
only in liberall sciences bot in artes mechani-
que hou base soeuer thai be that mé haue nead
to lern diligently certane yeares befor thai be
habill to tech and thai must pass thair prentis-
chip befor thai be mad maisters, and ve see
that thai vho presumes to do vtheruayis be
estemit bot arrogant and impudent: if so be
vhy suld not the lyik (if no more) tyme and
                                                    study be

study be imployit in Theologie befor vee presum any gret perfection thairin seing sche is
the quene and mistres of all vther sciences bot
vee as thai say in Latin entre in and defyill vith
vnueschin feet the pure Sanctuary of hir Scripturs euin the first year, moneth or day that vee
can spell or read any thing in our vulgar toung
as tho vee nedit no pilot or pedagoge : being
thairinto lyik the folisch butterflees vho desy-
rus of lycht flee headlong to the candill and so
burn thair self not knouing the inconuenient
ioynit vith the lycht vhen it is not deuly and re-
spectiuly vsit: So heady ferss idiots beleuing
the beames of holy scriptor can not burn teme-
rar braues thai flee thairunto vithout fear or
forsicht not considering the maiestie thairof
bot folischly trusting thair self capable of any
thing thai can curiuslie consait, incontinent thai
tak on and teche befor thai be instructed, thai
interprit, disput, distinguis conclud, prech and
pen befor thai can veill reid the rudimentes of
vther inferior sciéces much les attenit vnto any
perfection in this science of sciences, and heirin
thai do resemble such as cüming to pass à dàge-
rus sea do hyir à barque ad furnis the same vyth
cöpas, rodar ad all such necessares, bot thinking
pilottes and marinelles to costly and superfluus
in that thai thair self haue sum knoulege in that
art hauing lernit sum generalities thairof. as to
knou the arthes, pointes of cöpas, babord and
sterbord, lof ad lie: Bot the nicht cüming, the sea
suelling, the storm incressing and the licht of

C

moone and starres extinguisit by force tharof,
no dout such temerite can not escaip vntymus
repentance:euin so thai vho be imbarquit in the
veak veschell of thair auin fond imaginations
presuming, nottheles to saill the sacred seas of
holy scriptur vithout perfyit pilotes and peda-
goges can not escaip sum notable schipurak
ether by dasching thair self vpon sum roque of
rebellion or by ruuning in sum botomles golf
of hereticall sect or schisme.

S. Angustin in his first book of Christian
doctrin. 6. chap. speiking vpon this matter agās
the foolhardines of sum in his age doth say in
this sort:thai be desauit vith manifold obscuri-
teis and ambiguiteis vho raschly read the scriptures taking oft tymes one thing for ane vther
and in ane vther place the said father doth affirm the holy spreit not to haue vnaduysitly couerit or maid obscuir the scripture to the end
thai suld not by too much familiarite or faci-
lite becum contemptibill. bot Ireneus as most
ancient so is he most euidét in this point saying
in his 2.book chap. 27. agans Hereseis that the
scrpturs abound in infinite mystereis of diuyne
Sapience and that thai schyne vith inspekable
maiestie contening so many variable Dialectes
so many obscuyr phrases,parables,tropes,figu-
res vith so many clauses vhilk at the first seam
contradictorius or repugnant.

The scripturs then be difficill in tuo respectes,
one in respect of the mater vharof thai treat,
that is to say of the most highe mistereis of crea

tion, Incarnation, Regeneration, Predeſtinariõ
of the Sacramĕtis, Angelles, of the moſt bleſſed
vnite ãd trinite, vith many vther ſupnaturall ſe-
crcittes. Agane the ſtyill of the ſcriptur rĕdres it
difficill: for not only paſſages ãd clauſcs tharof
vhilk be indead obſcuir bot euin ſuch as ſeã verey p'ane oft tymes cã not bevndeiſtudvithout
aſſiſtãce of the ſelffame grace vhilk did deuyiſ
and dyit thame as ſayit Solomon in the 9 of
the book of Sapience. O *lord vho can knou thy
sens or meaning except thou ſend thy ſſreit from
aboue:*

　Morouer no mã can deny bot that aue mer-
uelus iugmĕt and experiĕce is requirit to knou
vhat places be litterally vhat figurariuly to be
interprit. Heiruythall the ambiguus phraſes of
Scriptur doth render the ſame difficill : as vhen
vce reid in S. Io.8. *Thou vho art thou ?* I *the beginning vho doth ſ̸pek vnto you.* and in Matheu the 11.
he kneu hir not till ſche brocht to bed. and to the
Corinth. 1 chap. 15. *vhat ſhall thai do that be bapte-
ſit for the dead or for dead.* and to the Epheſ. 3. *that
the manifold viſdome of God may appear by the
church vnto Princes and poteſtates in places or perſons aboue &c.* and in the firſt of Peter the 3. In
*the vhilk cũming vnto the ſſreittes impriſonnit vho
beleuit not attending the pouar of God in the dayis of
Noah.* Siclyk imperfyit phraſes producis gret
difficulte as that in the 5. to the Romans. *as by one
man ſin vnto all men ſo by the Iuſtice of one iuſlifica-
tion of lyfe vnto all men:* vhat in that hoill period
or clauſe thair is no verb copulatyue to abſo'ue

the sentence, and the same difficulte doth aryis
of phrases spokin after the Hebreu fasson as in
the 118 Psalm. *my saull is euer in my handes.* aud
in the Euangell. *vho vold saue his saull let him lo-
se it.* Siclyk be sum phrases Ironique or spokin
in derision as in Genese 3 *Lo Adam as one of hys
knouing Goed and bad.* Thair lakit not also most
exquisit and quik antiphrases or spechis hauing
à contrarius sens as in Iob 1. vhar it is said *that
he sacrificed daylie for his childring lest thai suld bliß
God,* and in ane vther place the said Iob speking
to God. *I haue not sinnit yit my Ee remanit in bitternes* And yit agane vnto God. *thou knoweth that
I haue done no thing vickitly.*

Bot of sentences at the first face seaming cō-
tradictorius the Gretest difficulte of all doth
arys as in Exod. 20. *I am the lord God strong and
Ialous visiting the iniquiteis of the fathers vpon the
childring vnto the thrid and fourt generation:* vharunto that of Ezech 8. apperit directly contrar
vhar it is said. *the sone shall not bear th' iniquitie of
the father.* And in the lordes prayer vee pray the
lord *not to lead vs in tentation:* Yit Sanct Iames
sayit that God tempted *no man.* and Sanct Paul
to the Romans. 3. *vee beleif (says he) that man is
iustifeit by fayth vithout the vorkes of the lau.*
contrary vayis Sanct. Ia. chap. 2. sayit. *you see
then that man is Iustifeit by vorkes and not of
fayth oniy:* yea Sanct Paul in this matter seamit
to be contrarius vnto him self saying 2. Corinth. 3. chap. *all fayth vithout charite to be no
thing.* seing charite is à vork commandit by the

lau. Item Exod.20, Honor *thy father and mother,*
&c and Matth. 23. *Call no man in this erth father.*
and in the same Decaloge. S*anctifie the saboth,*
and in the 12. of Matth.*the Preistes vithin the tem-*
pill did violat the saboth not committing any cryme.
Item *à litill you sall see me and à litill you sall not see*
me. Item in Iob.*in my flesch I am assurit to see God*
my Redemptor. and in 1. Corinth. 15. *flesch can*
not inherit the kingdome of God. Item in the 26.
of the Pruuerb. Ansuer not à fooll according to
his folie: and in that same place ausuer à fooll
according to his folie. Item Iohn 10. the father is
greter nor I, and Iohn. 4. the father and I be one.
Item Io.11 the void ves maid flesch and Malach.
3. I am God and am not chāgit. Itē Marc.15. vee
read that thai vho hang on the cross vyth
Cryist did blasphē him: yit in the 23, of Luc. it is
said that only one of tham did blasphē him. Itē
in one place, my flesch is vercy food, aud in ane
vther: flesch profited no thing. Item in the epistle to the Hebrēues it is said yat vithout effusion of blood is no remission of fins: yit in the
Evāgell vee reid that Cryist boyth did remit and
gaue pouer to his Apostles to remit sins vhar
thair ves no effusion of blood.

Theis phrases ambiguues, figuratyue, Ironique, antiphrastique and at the first seaming cō-
trarius gaue no small matter of studeis vnto
famus doctors preceding, uhose tedius trauel-
les and incredible labors scheu euidently yat
thai haue bene too stupid and vane in taking such endles panes vpon matters so plane

Matt.9.2.
Luc.5.20.
Luc.7.27.
Io.20.23.

C iij

orelles vee too arrogant esteming difficulteis so facill: for explaning vharof none be more busy to vritt paraphrases, annotations, commentares and commun places nor thai yat mak
the ignorant pepill belcif the scriptur to be
so plane and none persuad more the necessitie of prechors, nor thai do: vhilk suirlie ver
all superfluus if the sens tharof ver so euident
and patent as thai imagin. And moreouer if it
ver so Sanct Peter ver much to be blamit vhenas he doth say yat in th'Epistles of Sanct Paul
sindry things be difficill to be vnderstud vhilk
the vnlernit and incostat peruert as vther scriptures to thair auin perdition. and not ouly S.
Peter bot sindry other disciples merit iust re-
prehension vho in the 6. of Iohn did say. This is
ane hard spech vho can hear him.

By Knoning the treu church vee shall knou the verite äd treu Pastors and by thame be resoluit of all doutes of cō-science.

Theis difficulteis so dangerus vnto the vnlernit and inconstant (as Sayit Sanct Peter in
the place forsaid) maid me diligently to serch
out vhar the treu orthodox Catholique, Apostolique church suld be that by hir I mycht vithout
danger knou yat vihilk adheriog only to my
priuat opinion I culd not vithout fearfull däger
presum to knou: to vit to knou the veritie (vhar
of sche is the pillar and fundament) the laufull
Pastores, treu sens of the verite and of all questions this day controuerted. for if it be treu
(às it can not be vith reson denyit) that of the
primityue church and Doctores tharof vee haue resauit the cataloge of the canons or bookis of authentik Scriptur (vhilk be the vndou-

ted verite) by vhat reson can vee refuse to
resaue the treu sens and interpretation of the
said bookis and of all questions ryfing tharupon of the laufull, lineall and vndouted successors of the said church rendring vnto thame
the lyik honor, respect and credit vhilk our laudable forbeares euer from the dayis of king
Donald (vho regnit à 1400 yeares ago and'resauit the Christian fayth as it is this day professit
at Rome by meanes of Pope Victor the fyfteint
bischop from Sanct Peter)did giue vnto anciet
churches preceding : vharunto if vee suld vith
Christian obedience bou out stubborn hartes
vee suld clearly vnderstand all theis ceremoneis
vsit in the Romane church in the seruice of God
vihilk do seam vnto many (as thai did once to
my self) so ridiculus Idolatrus and abfurd to
be nottheles most decent, necessary and salutar
ornamentes, full of consolation, Good exemple
and prouocation vnto humilite and holines,
and such as be (as one of the ancients did say)
benefices vnto men malefices vnto the deuill
and Sacrifices vnto God.

Bot in respect all Heretiques heirtofor haue
boyth arrogated vnto thame self the treu sens
of scriptur and name of the treu church it shall
be necessary for auoyding of prolixite to mak
mention only of such markes as be peculiar
and propre only to the treu church omitting
such as be commun boyth to the treu and fals.
Ireneus in his dayis did much complene in his
S. book agans Valentinus vpon the impudent-

nes of Heretiques vho bragging of the treu sens
of Scriptur vnineffected vyth gloses and traditions of men did also brag that vith them ves
the treu church and treu successors of the Apostles : and the lyik impudence doth Lactantius
regret of the Heretiques in his dayis vho (sayis
he) did more confidëtly vse the name of Christians and treu church nor the Christians thair
self. and befor Lactantius Sant Cyprian in his 4.
book of diuyn institutions. doth say of Noua-
tian that as apes not being men did notuythstanding contrefait the gestor of men so Noua-
tian not being of the church ves not aschamit to
vsurp the name tharof blaspheming the treu
church and calling hir hereticall: and Hilarius in
his book to Iouinian⁹ doth inlyk maneir lamët
yat the Synagog of the antecryst suld vendicat
the name and pouer of crystes church. Sanct
Augustin in his Book to Constantin August
doth obiect the self same impudenee agans the
Donatistes, and Sant Bernard in his 66. sermon
vpon the Cäticle doth declare yat in his age ver
sum calling thair self Gnostiques and Apostoliques vho (as that allegit) had only reuelit vnto
thame the treu sens of Scriptur after the same
had bene hid from the knouleg of ages preceding: and theiss Gnostiques albeit thai vold specially be callit Apostoliques yit thai did Scorn
and mok all vther euidence of Apostolique succession except of thair doctrin lyk vnto sum
of yat same humeur in this deplorable age,
vhose preposterus opinion in this bealf I remit
to be

to be refuted Heirefter in the article of Apostolique fucceffion.

Then to th'end theis falflie vfurpit titilles
defaue not the ignorant caufing thame tak the
vyfe of Putefer for Sufanna and Samaria for
Ierufalé, I vill produce four peculiar markes of
the treu church vhilk the moft fimpill foull in
the vorld may eafaly fee only to apertene to
the church of Rome and hir adherentes and
not to any vther church impugning hir.

And as to fuch as vold haue found doctrin
and fincer miniftration of the Sacramentes to
be infallibill marques of the treu church, fuch
men be pitifully abufit:for theis be not the propre marques of the church quarto modo as fay
the Logicians feing all Heretiques yat haue bene heirtofor haue chalengit as much or more
that prerogatiue as did the vndouted orthodox
church. Yea this day euery Hereticall fect doth
bitterly contend one agans one vther to haue
only the honor of theis tuo markes. Tharfor
vee muft fynd fum vther markes more certane
and fpeciall to th'end vee may euidently fee
vhilk church this day contending vpon this
point fuld be preferrit vnto the reft. Vhence
then fall vee extract the faid infallibill marques?
not of the brane of any party contending: for
lyik as to the making of of à perfyit circle vee
muft haue à firm and immouable centre : fo to
find out theis marques deuly as aperteyneth to
th'end no party contending haue iuft caufe of
exception thai muft be deriuit from fuch equall

*Soūd doctrin
and fincer mi-
niftration of
the facramēts
be not infalli-
bill marques
of the treu
church.*

D

and clear fundaments as all contendantes fall agree vnto. For this cause vee fall extract thame partly out of the Symbol vhilk generally all Chriſtians this day vſe collected (as Sanct Auguſtin doth affirm) by the Apoſtles thame ſelf: Partly of theis Symboles vhilk ves gatherit by ancients in the moſt famus counſalles of Nice and Cöſtantinople more nor à 1300.years ago. In the Symbol of the Apoſtles the church is callit holy and Catholique, in th' other tuo ſche is callit one and Apoſtolique. Vharupon I do gather four marques ſo proper and peculiar to the treu church yat churches Hereticall can not vithout manifeſt impudence arrogat the ſame as thai do the vther tuo of ſound doctrin and ſincer miniſtration of the ſacramentes.

Four infallible marques of the treu church.

Then the firſt mark is to be holy: vhilk is not to be vnderſtud yat all being vithin the church be holy and iuſt: becaus yat the church vhilk in the Grec is callit Eccleſia hes hir name from vocation or calling vharby it is certane yat thair muſt be as veill vnholy as holy vithin hir, conſiddering yat many be callit and feu elected to holines and iuſtice. For this cauſe in Scriptures the treu church is deſignit vnder the name of à grange or barn in vhilk be boyth corn and caf: Sche is callit à feild in vhilk the poppill and tares grou vp vyth the Good grane: Sche is callit à nett vihilk reſauit both Good ād bad fiſch: A vyneyard in vhilk be both ſour and ſueit grapes, frutfull and vnfructfull vynes: A flok in vhilk be boyth goattes and Scheip, Rouch and

The firſt mark of the treu church is holines.

rent, fcabbit and hoill: To ane hous vharin be Vefchelles of gold and Siluer, of tree and erth, fum to honor and fum to dishonor, and to the ten virgins of vlhilk as many ver foolifch as vyife. Tharfor in the treu church fo long as fche is militât heir in the erth the bad be mixit vyth the Good feeing it is only the church triumphant in the heauin vhar all the membres be Good lyk as all the infernall menzee be leud. Thé the treu church is not callit holy in refpect thair be none in hir bot holy ons bot in refpect none can in effect be holy houfoeuer thai haue outuart apparence of holines except thai be cóprehendit vythin hir. Euin as à gret army is callit braue, puiffant and riche, not becaus eury one of the army in particular haue theis qualiteis bot becaus the better part and moft vorthy perfonis tharof be fuch: Euin fo the treu church frô the better part not frô the greter is callit holy. Vharunto is agreable yat of Sanct Matheu 13. vhar the chunch is callit the kingdome of heauin not yat all vithin hir be heritores of yat kingdome bot becaus none can inherit heauin except he be firft comprehendit vythin the church.

And vhar as it is faid of the church in the cátique of Solomô you art (my darlin) alrogidder beautifull and thair is no fpoit in the, yat is meant properly of the church triumphât vhilk in the fame chaptor is faid to be crouned by hir fpoufe: Bot if vyth S. Gregore vee fall apply theis vordes to the church militant then the

D ij

church sayis the said holy doctor may be callit
fair and spotles becaus the elect membres tharof by inherent grace be pure befor God and
be not defylit by the societie of the reprobat,
and albeit no iust nor holy man be faltles befor God yit he cessit not to be holy becaus by
his vouis and vill he doth Supple the defect ād
febilnes of his force and faculty obseruing à
daylie Cleannes (as Sayit the said holy father)
vhenas by his teares he doth daylie vesch avay
and confes his smaller sins and doth abstene
from the greter.

*S.Grego.*18.
Eccles. dog-
mat.

Greg. vpon
the 4.of the
Cantiq.

Nether is it impertinent to call hir sancta id
est sanguine Christi tincta vhilk is to say sprink-
illit vyth the blood of Cryist becaus *vyth his pre-*
tius blood he hes vaschit auay hir sins and hes so loued
hir yat he hes geuin him self for hir , yat sche mycht
be sanctifeit and purgit by his blood from the vorkes
of deth. and for this cause Sanct Augustin vpon
the 85 Psalm.dot affirm yat all the faythfull be
callit sanctes.

*Apocal.*1.
*Ephes*5.
*Hebrew.*9.

Thair be also many vther resons vhy the
church suld be callit holy , as for yat sche doth
institut nor prescryue no reull in doctryne or
maners vhilk is vnholy : by th' one forbidding
all infidelitie and by the vther all iniquitie, hauing also vithin hir ane holy Sacerdoce or preist
head vhilk neuer hes bene altogidder depryuit of sum secreit assistance of the holy spreit(as
heirefter in the auin place sall be moir planly
delectarit) in so much as tho sche seam bot as à
barn or stak vharin doth appear no thing out-

v ardly bot caf and ftra: Yit being threfchit, fcha-
kin and riddillit befor the vynd of treu tryall
thair fall alvay be found in hir à heap of Good
corn vhilk no vynd of vanite nor tempeft of
tribulation can fcatter or blau avay. And albeit
as fayit the prophet it doth appear yat Satan hes
fchorn the feild of the church ād vēdagit the vynes tharof ād yat God doth bot glane after him
ād only gather fum feu grapes: yit is not his nūber fo fmall bot yat he boyth hes hād throuchout all ages of all kynd perfons and in all places fufficiēt ftoir of holy ons vythin his church
defigning no other limite or marches to his in-
heritāce bot from the fone fetting to the ryfing
tharof. and this inheritance by the ancients is
pertinently comparit to gold or filuer vhilk in
the mynes is not found all pure and perfyit bot
couerit and mixit vith many filthy materialles,
yit the myneres and meltares do not for all yat
vilany difpyis the defylit lignot bot doth
put vp the fame efteming it a mettall moft rare
ād pretieux Naming the hoill myne or pitt tharof not after the name of the huge montans of
other contemptible matterialles couering or
compaffing hir bot à myne of gold.

Bot omitting all theis fignifications of holi
nes vhilk all properly do apertene to the Ca-
tholiq̄ Romane church I adher principally vnto
yat fignification vhilk bringit vith it fuch fpe-
cialite as can not be applyit to any vther Chriftian church bot to yat of Rome vhilk is yat
amang the Latins by theis vordes (fanctum ef-

ſe , to be holy) is vnderſtud as much as to ſay
to be firm and ſtabill, difficill to be inuadit or
violat at leſt vhilk nether ſuld be inuadit or
violat. So the ciuill lau doth call the rampartes
and fortications of à ſtrong citie , the Tribuns,
treſors and tempills tharof holy things becaus
none may, at leſt none ſuld moleſt or incom-
mod theme. Euin ſo no thing being more auguſt magnifique or venerable befor God and
amang men no thing more firm and ſtabill nor
the church of God, of Good reſon ſche hes ever
had the titill and addition of holines , for vhat
can be more firm and ſtabill nor yat vhilk is de-

Io.17.
Matth.7.
Marc.16.
2.Corint.2.

dicat by and to Cryiſt *from vhom by force no thing
can be abſtracted yat his father had geuin vnto him
She is beild vpon ſuch a roque as nether rane nor
vynd increßing can dimoliß nor the portes of hell
preuaill, hir fundation being ſo ſolid (as ſayit the
Apoſtle) yat one vther fundation can no man lay
then yat vhiik is aliedy layid to vit Ieſus Cryiſt.*
Reſting vpon this fondation thair nether is, ves
nor ſall be pouer or policie yat can defait hir.
for as ſayit S. Io. Chryſoſt in the Homilie of his
expulſion. Tom.5. ſche is more durable nor the
erth ād as durable as the heuin, becaus hir root-
tes be feſſinnit in boyith heir hir membres militant and aboue hir membres triumphant. Morouer that of Sanct Math.28 vhar our bleſſed
ſauior doth ſay yat *he ſall be vyth his Apoſtles to
the vordles end*:theis vordis of neceſſite muſt be
relatiue vnto thair ſucceſſors and to the hoill
church ſucceding as veill as vnto the ſaid Apo-

ſtles ſeing thai culd not liue till the vorld ver
édit:By theis vordes I ſay The church is not only declarit to haue ane vndouted holynes boyth
in doctryn and lyf (houſoeuer ſche be traducit
or sklanderit) and that becaus Cryſt Ieſus be
verteu of his holy ſpreit is vyth hir to the con-
ſommatiõ of the vorld, bot also hir firmitie and
permanentes is expreſlie confirmit in yat no
term is ſet vnto hir bot the latter end of all
ages. The church then is ye land Vhilk the lord
hes ordenit to left for euer, vharof the prophet
doth ſay. *thou hes foundit hir vpon hir ſtabilite and* Eſay. 60.
ſche ſall not faill vorld vythout end: and ſche is the
kingdome vharof it is vrittin. *Hir kingdome ſall*
command eury vhare. of vhilk the prophet ſo oft
cryit. *The pepill and kingdome yat ſall not ſerue the*
ſall periß.

Vharupon I gather for concluſion of this article. That church *vhilk nether foren enemis nor*
fals brethring culd neuer to this day altogidder defait Cantiq. 6.
remaning terrible lyk ane army veill renged in battall: Pſalm. 28.
That curch vhilk may ſay vyth the Pſalmiſt:hou
oft from my youth haue thay inuadit bot culd
not vinquis me. That church as ſayit Iuſtin⁹ Martyr in the collogue agans Triphonius : Vhilk as
the vyne the more you ſned hir the more ſche
is frutfull : That church as ſaid Hilarius in his
book de Trinitate, vhilk triumphet the more
ſche be tred vpon : That church vhilk can not
ſink more nor the palm and abydit the fornace
lyk the fyne gold, euer floriſſing houſoueuer
ſche be forcit is to be eſtemit holy in this pro-

per fignification of holines contening firmite and perpetuite. Bot amãg all churches that this day ftryue for the prerogatyue tharof only the Romane church may produce attentik teftimoneis of this firmite agans all fortons euer fince the tyme yat th' Apoftle Sanct Paul vritt his Epiftle vntho thame vhilk nou is near à 1600. year. During vhilk tyme nether infidell Paganes by thair fearfull tormentes, nor Tyrans by thair Barbarus perfecutions, nor Ieuis by thair obftinat oppofition, nor fchifmatiques by thair factius feparatiõ, nor Heretiques by thair pernitius cõtradictiõ and inuectiõ euld neuer be habill to extinguis the lycht of this Romani lamp nether by thair flicht nor micht: vheras other fects and monopolles going about to fupplant hir and all Herefeis lifting vp thair hornes aganes hir for the moft part haue periffit befor thair doctrin ves veill plãted: and if any of thame haue fum feu ages indured: the patience of God almychty in yat behalf and his longanimitie hes euer recompenfit thair obftinat induratio vyth the more fearfull punitions often tymes to the Eyis of the vorld vharof vee haue the notable exemples of Simon Magus to the terrour of the beholders by euill fpreittes moft violently lifted vp in the air and tharefter throuin doun all rent and difmembred: of Manicheus flain quik by the king of Perfians: of Mõtanus vho patt violent handes in him felf: of Arrius vhofe bouelles braft out at his fundamét to the extreme horror of the affiftants and of

Neftorius

Egefip.3.book 3.chap.
Arnob. 2. book agans the gentils.
Eufeb.5 book hift.chap.16.
Athanaf.1.
Ruffinus, Euagrius.

Neftorius vho ves eatin vp vyth vermin. In ſum: all Hereſeis and Heriarches yat have impugnit the Romane church be ſuch as ſayit Sanct Paul as cã not lõg induir bot Sche (as Sayis one of the ancientes) is tne beautie of the firmament vhilk ſchynit perpetually: and hir Enemis be bot cometes conceauit of terreſtriall vapores vhoſe flam ceaſſit hou ſone thair groſ aliment beginnit to faill. Sche is one indeficient flood vhilk being continually nuriſſit by the lining ſpringes of the holy ſpreit can not dry vp: thai bot brookes or burnes vhilk do ceas hou ſone the ſtorm or tempeſt is ouerblouin. To this purpos Sanct Auguſtin uritting vpon theis vordes of the 97. Pſalm: Thai ſall turn to nooht as doth ruſching vatteris, ſayer. Be not aſtenied to ſee the ſmall brookes ryis and rummill for à vhyill for that is bot à ſp it vhilk rouſchit avay and can not leſt: Many Hereſeis (ſayis he) haue rored and run mychtely bot thai be nou as running vatteres paſt and gone and in ſuch ſort dryit vp as if ancientes had not maid mention of thair names hardly had vee knouyn yat euer any ſuch perſons had bene, this much Sanct Auguſtin. Contraryvyis it is certane yat the church Catholique Romane hes continuit euer glorius as veill in perſequution as in proſperitie ſen the dayis of th Apoſtles vnto this hour profeſſing and obſeruing that ſame fayth and form of diuyne ſeruice vhilk this day is obſeruit: vhilk albeit the enemis tharof can not villingly grant yit the moſt impudét of tham all muſt

2. Timoth. 3.

E

be forcit to confes yat the matteres moſt reprehendit by thame vithin the ſaid Romane
church, ves brocht in and begŭ near à 1200 year
ago, vhilk is à longer tvme nor câ be prouin yat
any Hereticall church hes indurit. Heiruythall
it is to be conſidderit yat vhen Martin Luther
maid defeċtion except in the church of Rome
and hir adherentes ves no religion in the vorld
bot Paganiſm, Iudaiſm, Mahometiſm and the
dregges of Neſtorianiſm in Grecia bot no man
can be ſo effronted as to ſay yat the church of
Cryiſt ves amang any of theiſs ſeċtes: and tharfor of neceſſite it muſt follou yat ſche ves ether
at Rome or no vhar. And ſuirly as this marque
of holines ſigniſieng ane euident perpetuitie is a
marque moſt infaliible ſo doth it infallibilly diſ-
cernšbetuix the orthodox and Hereticall church
for ſince Theobutes and Simon Magus firſt
Heretiques vnto Martin Luther ſum 200 Hereſeis hes ruſchit and repleniſſit from bank to bra
lyk inundatiôs of ſpeit vatters, vharof ſum haue bene mentenit by moſt michty patrons as by
Emprors, kings and cunning mé vho vrit and
publiſt innumerabill bookes in ſuch ſort as humane raiſon vold neuer haue thocht yat ſuch
doċtryne culd haue bene ſuppreſſit: yit by the
admirabill prouidence of God thai be ſo extin-
guiſit yat thair reſted thirof no memory at all
as is befor ſaid: lyk as no dout ſall eum to paſs
vpon all hereſeis modern vho lyik to yat vhilk
Gamaliel doċtor of the lau did ſay of Theudas
and Iudas of Galité Schiſmatiques vho ſeduſing

Act. 5.

much pepill to follou tham ver deſtroyit and
thair pepill ſcatterit. So thai vho this day follou
the lyik ſchiſmaticall humour houſoeuer‹thai
run and rore,thai bot abuſe thair ſelf if thei at-
tend any better firmitie or fin nor vther of the
lyik humour haue had heirtofor. Vharupon to
be ſchort I collect and conclud yat holynes in
all the ſignifications tharof namly in the laſt
(vhilk is moſt proper) is only proper and peculiar to the Catholique church Romane and to
hir adherentes and to no vther yat hes aban-
donit hir.

The ſecond marque of the church is to be
Catholique or vniuerſall. the° vhilk Sanct Auguſtin interpreting in his 131. Sermon doth ſay
yat to be Catholique is to be deffundit throuch
the hoill vorld and not to be comprehendit in
ſum feu corners as Schiſmatique churchis be.
And this vniuerſalitie vee fynd to be threefold
to vitt of places, tymes and perſons. To proue
vniuerſalite of places the Pſal. ſayit:thair ſound
ves hard throuch all the erth and thair vordes
vnto the end of the vorld. and in Sanct Marc
laſt chap·The Apoſtles be commádit to go and
tech th'Euangell throuch the hoill vorld.

The vniuerſalitie of tyme is no les euident in
yat by attentik hiſtorieis the church may be
prouin to haue viſibilly continuit from Adam
vnto this hour inſomuch as hir beginning ves
at the beginning and hir diuturnite ſall be ſo
long as the vorld ſall induir for God hes foundit hir to leſt eternalɉy ſaying in the 28. of Math .

*The ſecond
marque of
the church is
vniuerſalite.*

I _fall be vyth you to the vorlds end and in the 21. of_
Luc. This generation (meaning of the church) fall not
paß till all things be endit.

And yat the church doth comprehend all
kynd of perſons of vhatſoeuer eſtat, condition,
age, ſex or nation thai be cf is verif it by Sanct
Paul. Rom. 10. _Saing yat in hir is not any difference_
betuix Ieu and gentill, circumſition and prepuce, bar-
bar and grec, bound and free, maſle and femelle, bot
Cryſt is all in all, the lord of all, plentifull vnto all
yat call vpon him : for vhoſeuer callit vpon his name
fall be ſaue. And agane: _you hes redemit vs vyth thy_
blood furth of all nations, trybes, tounges and peapill
and hes maid of vs à Kingdome vnto God and sanct
Peter Act. 9. _of à treuth (ſayis he) I do perſaue yat_
God is not ane excepter of perſons bot yat throuchout
all nations vho ſeruit him and doth iuſtly by accepted
vythout exception.

Act. 9.

The multitud and viſibili-tie of the church pro-uin.

Thé if the treu church be diſperſit trouchout
all places continuing from all ages and compód
of all kynd of perſons, nations, eſtats &c. It ſeamit à glory laking Good ground to oſtend or
brag of ncunes or ſeunes. For ſo did the Donatiſtes, agans vhem Sanct Auguſtin, ſayis yat thai
robbit Cryſt Ieſus of his dignitie ſeing it is vrittin: _in the multitud of pepill conſiſtit the aignite of à_
Prince and in feunes tharof he is dishonorit: Seing
alſo Cryſt hes had and euer ſall haue his heritage from end to end of the vorld: in ſuch ſort as
vho vold abſtract from him the honor of yat
multitud acquirit in the multitud of his merceis thai bot abſtract thair ſelf from the infinit

multitud of his inheritance, vhilk being comparit to the sand of the ɩɩ a he can not content him self vith à small handfull of such as haue chosin to thair self singular opiniens repugning to the generall consent of all attentiue antiquitie (as heirefter in the auin place sall be goduilling declarit.) Vho vyth the Psalmist do all agre yat copiosa est apud eum redemptio (yat vyth Cryst thair is à copius abundant or larg redemption.

Eunomius theheretique desyrit his auditors nether to respect multitud nor antiquite: bot Basilius the gret in his first book agãs the said Eunomiusestemit him vnhorty to be hard much les to be ansuerit vnto: the said father affirming it ane matter most absurd to yeild alyk reuerēce, respect ād credeit to ane hādfull of rebellius, recent, busy branes and to ane venerable multitud of ancient obedient and reuerend persons defendars of the Christian fayth agans infidelitie and liuing and deing in Christian obedience vnto Cryst Iesus and vnto such as he hes aponted his Vicarres and Vicegerents vythin his church.

And vnder this generalitie is comprehendit the subaltern marque of visibilitie. A mark indeed housoeuer it be impugnit yit veill establissep by many passages of holy Scripture. For in Math 18. command is geuin to hear the church and to complene vnto the church. Vhilk commandements seing thai ver geuin vnto Christians to induire for all ages, thai do necessarly

E iij

proue à perpetuall vifibilitie of the church, vnto vhom vee fuld in vane fpekį or cōplene if fche ver not fubiect vnto our fenfes. It is treu yat vee fpek, pray and complene vnto God vnfeing his inuifible maieftie becaus he his à fpreit inuifible   Bot to Imagin the church(vhilk is ane affemblee of bodies and not of fpreittes) yat vee can fpek and cōplene vnto hir as vnto à thing inuifible it is ane abfurdité neding no anfuer and ane Herefie neading much hellebor. Suirly the Royall Prophet ir his 18. Pfalm ves of ane vther opinion fpeking of the church and faying yat God had placed hir in the fone yat fche mycht be manifeft. and Sanct Math. 5. callis hir à citie beildir vpon the top of ane mōtane vhilk *Efay. 2.* montane Efayias and Micheas forfpak, faying. *Miche. 4.* Yat in the latter dayis the montaue of the hous of the lord (meaning of the church at and after the firft cumming of Cryft)fall be preparit vpō the top of the mōtās ād fall be exalted aboue all vther hilles, and all nations fall refort and much pepill go vnto hir: and this is the hill vhilk king *Dan. 2.* Nabochodofar did fee cutt out of the quarry vythout handes and from à litill ftone to grou vnto ane huge montane and to haue vifibilly filled the hoill vorld: in vhilk montane after the interpretation of Daniel the lord of heauin(after he had brufit all vther kingdoms) rafit vp à *Bern. 6. ferm.* kingdome for him felf to indure for euer vhilk *vpon the Cā-* fell not be diffipat nor geuin to any vther pea-*tiq.* pill. Sanct Bernard citing this place agans the Heretiques of his tyme mentening the felf fa-

me abfurditie of inuifibilitie doth fay. Go too
fayit he, be you fo mad as to beleif the ftone of
the church cutted out of the montane vythout
handes an l maid à gret montane to be fmud-
derit vp in your caues and corners?You ar(fayis
he)defauit,and tharfor let no Chriftian fall frō
this montane : Bot if fedufars sha'l fay vnto
Chriftians (as once the deuill faid vnto Cryft)
if you be the fone of God fall doun: (Vhat foeuer paffages of holy Scriptur thai can alleg follouing the fraud full exemple of the deuill)let it
not entre in the hart of à Good Catholiq to cō-
fent more nor Cryft did vnto fuch impofturs,or
defauers. and if one fall fay : Lo Cryft is hear,
Cryift is thair : Cryift him felf admonifis vs
not to giue credite.and if thai fall allege yat he
is in the defert or in the fecreit corners of the
hous,go not out fayis Cryft nether follou tham:
and the refon is becaus the head naturall is not
bot conioynit vyth the naturall body nor Cryft
the head myfticall of the church Bot vith and
in the fame church and no vay in or vith thame
yat eftablifs vnto thair felf particular fectes and
fotieteis repugning to the vniuerfall body of
the Catholique church: from vhilk vhofoeuer
doth feparat him felf he is not to be eftemit Catholique bot ether Heretique or at left Schifma-
tique becaus he doth chofe to him felf fingular
opinions contrar the vniform,ancient,and laudable confent of the vniuerfall body of the
church.

Bot to mak this matter yit à littill more

plane I do infift in maneir follouing, fayrg: yat in fo much as all the partes of this militant church be vifible and in fo much as in the church vee muft haue fayth proceding of hea-ring(as fayis th´Apoftle)vee muft haue preching of the vord and prechors, miniftration of Sa-craméts,collection and diftribution of almeffe, places to convene,&c. fuirky to fay yat all theis circumftances(for the moft part fo neceffary as vhar thai be not thair can be no church) be in-uifible ver too abfurd and impudent:and if thai be not inuifible,the church muft neads be vifi-fible.

3.King 19. As to yat vhilk is allegit of Elias comple-ning yat he allone of all the church did remane: the feabilnes of yat argument can not be bot clear to the fimpilleft faull in th vorld yat vill vythout partialitie read yat text,vharin it is ma-nifeftly faid yat God had referuit à 7000. vho had not bouit hair knee vnto baal: Vhilk nvm-ber culd not be inuifibill at left one vnto one vther houfoeuer thai ver feparat from publict focietie by the tyrannie of yat tyme, except vee fuld prefuppofe yar thai ver all blynd. Agane it is certane yat the Propher Making yat com-plant ves in Samaria vhir bv meanis of bloody Achab and Iefabell the church had no oppin exercife of religion at yat tyme and fo his com-plant ves bot for the church at Samaria not for the hoill church Iudaïque feing yat evin at the felf tyme thair ves à florifing church at Ierufa-lem vnder Good king Iofaphat as is manifeft by the fame the same Hiſtory. Bot geving ád not grãting yat the church had bene vnuiſibill to Eliah it doth not tharupõ neceſſarly follou yat ſche ves altogidder inuiſibill:ſeing the Prophetes did not ſee all things bot only ſuch as pleaſit our lord reueill vnto tham.::for Ehſens who had the ſpreit of Elias doubtlht vpon him ves not aſchamit to ſay and this ves hid from me. ^{4. Kings 4.} ^{chap.}

Item it is à verey poor argument to ſay the church hes bene or is vnſeene:ergo ſche is vnuiſibill or may not be ſene. For thar be many things vee ſee not vhilk notvythſtanding may veill be ſene.as for exemple.Ve ſe not the money.Schot vp in a box not the child in the mothers vomb yit thai be things verrey viſibill vhen impedinenrs be remouit.

And vhat thai ſay yat the accident vhilk aualit or takit place in one membre or part of the hoill takket place or at leſt may tak place and fall vpon the hoill membres. Bot the accident of inuiſibitie hes fallin vpon ſum partes of the church as vpon yat of Samaria. Ergo. Vh irunto I anſuer firſt yat in arguments à poſſe ad eſſe the conſequent avalit not nixt the propoſition not being ſimpliciter treu is to be ſimpliciter denyit. for experience techit the contrar often tymes in partes of one nator as veill as in partes of different natour.For exemple of partes of different nateur be the body and Saull vhilk Ioynit togidder mak the hoill man: Yit the accident of deth fallit in the one and not in the other.and in partes of one nature lo the eyis

F

and eares as vther orgãs of our senses be of one corporall nature: Yit blyndnes vhilk fallit to the eyis can no more fall vnto the eares nor deafnes can fall vnto the eyis Bot if I suld grãt the proposiriõ to be treu yit the assumption ver manyfestly fals:for it sha'l neuer be prouin yat ether the church atSamaria or any vther part of the Catholiq church hes bene so inuisibill bot yat thai haue bene sene one to anevther secreitty being secretty schoot vp as thai did publikly hauing publik liberty.ãd vhar thai yit go about to iuggill saying yat the treu church consistid in the elect,and vee nether seing nor knouing vho be the elect that for the treu church cã not be sene.Euin as if vee ver valking amidds à gret court of Ducs, Marquises, erlles, Barons and Knyghtes,and suld Imagin vee did not see any of thame becaus vee kneu not vhilk of tham thair king loued or hated: ver not this à vyise argument to proue thit court to be inuisible.

Suirly in this friuolus and fond assertion I haue such compassion vpon my former partialite in alleging this poor argument yat I knou not nou vhidder to be Hiraclit or Dimocrit yat is to say vhidder I suld lauch or lament the same: for granting vnto me the benefit of this fond distinctiõ thẽ sall no thing be visibill vnto me nether in church nor markat,my freindes my foes,my parentes,my Prince,yea the authors of this chimer by the self same gyges ring suld be inuisible to thair inuisible flok. and morouer if it be treu yat logicyãs say,yat things contrarius haue

contrarius raifons or confiderations then fuld
it follou yat as the elect is inuifible becaus vee
knou not vho be elect:So the reprobat vhom
vee knou to be reprobat muft be vifible.and fo
confequenily the deuill and fuch reprobat foull
fpreittes fuld be more vifible nor men.

Bot if no vther thing can moue the defendars of this phantaftik reuerie of inuifibilitie
(repugning fo much to fens,raifon ād fcriptur)
to quyit and renūce the fame:at left me think
that fuld be difgulted tharof for yat it doth allu-
terly tak auay thair auin church and all obediē-
ce tharunto.For if it be treu yat the treu church
is compond of the elect vhilk be inuifibill becaus none fee or knou vho be elect:Then thai
thair felf not knouing vhidder thai be elect or
not if any man fall agknoleg or obey thame he
bot abufit him felf to knou or obey yat vhilk
nether he y at is vython nor thai yat be vythin
knouit certenly to be the treu church:Vharin I
can compare tham to no thing fo much as vnto
the folish Atheniens reprehendit by Sanct Paul
for yat thai erected ane altar to the vnknouin
God:Euin fo thai vold have vsto agnouleg a-
māg thame à treu church vhenas thai thair felf
do fay yat the treu church is inuifibill and vnknouin becaus no mā knouit vho be the elect.

·Bot hear I pray the indifferent redar confider vharfor this fubterfuge of inuifibilitie producing fo many abfurditheis ves inuented.
Vhilk ves for yat the lait enemis of the Romane
church finding yat thai culd not fcheu vh ir

thair chnrch ves befor Marin Luther at left befor Io. Hus, Ierome de Prage and Viklef, tharf-
for as one deap drauit on ane vther and as
the haching of a ferpenis egge can bot produce
ane vther of the fame kynd: So to excufe the
defect of this moft neceffary and requifit retour
of euident fucceffion frem th' Apeftles day is
thai haue, fleing Scylla fallin into Caribdis as
all felflykares and louars of thair auin priuat a-
ctiós and opiniós haue done heirtofor. So Cain
to couer his murther, difdanfully askir at God if
he ves the kepar of his brother:fo the vnnaturall biether of Iofeph vent about to color his
vickit vedition vnto the Ifmaëlite by à fhamm-
les lie alleging vnto thair venerabill father yat
the youth ves deuorit in the vildernes tearing
His coit and tramping it in the blood of à goat.
So our gret grand father to qualifie his originall
inobedience vesnot afchamit to imput the falt
to him yat vas faltles fayirg to God The voman vhilk you gaue me for my help did perfuad me.

Nou to put ane end vnto this fecód mark of
vniuerfalitie let vs indifferetly cófideer vithout
fead or fauor to vhat church this day profeffing
Chriftian fayth may the fame be moft Iuftlie at-
tributed. Is thair I pray you any of thame all except the church Catholique Romane yat can
exhibit attentik teftimoneis tharof vythout in-
termiffion euer fen th' Apoftles day is? vhilk of
thame all impugnirg hir hes bene and is prefently difperfit trouchout all natiós of the vorld

as fche has bene and prefently is.vee fee yat all
abandoning hir be lyik vnto creuling ferpents
vho vfe not to creep far from thair cauerns.and
if vee fuld grant yat Herefie ver allvhar as the
veritie is alluhar, yit as fayit Sanct Auguftin the
veritie is fo alluhar yat novhar fhall be fund in
hir any difference vheras Herefeis fcarfe can be
fund onely i'; ane vther in tuo cũtreyis, collegis
or cõuentiõs For this caus the faid S.Aug cõparit herefeis vnto ferments or fuedding, of the
vyne vhilk ly ftill inutilly inthe place vhar
thai be fned of, and the treu church he cõparit to the root and ftok vhil's ftill extending hir
branches bringit furth in deu feafon grapes in
abundance Euin fo the Catholique church Romane hes extendit hir beautifull branches from
the fone ryfing to the fetting tharof: Amãgs the
Turcks,Perfians,Tartars,Pagans:For fche is not
comprehendit vithin Itay,France,Spane,Al-
many,Polony,Syrie,Armeny,Ethiop,Egypt,
and in vther places vharof vee fcars knou the
names bot euin in the neu fund vorld (fpecially
vhar the Potent king Catholique doth regne:)
on the Orient Tharof all the Indes (vhilk ver
once fubiect to the Kings of Portugall nou vnto Spane)obferue the form of the curch Catholique Romane:vpon the Occident the Ameri-
ques : Touard the north, Iappon : Touard the
fouth Brefill.and not only in theis neu fund landes bot euin in fuch nations as haue abiurit all
Romane obedience thair be many yealus Catholique Romans the number tharof increffing

F iij

daylie,as in England,Scotland , Denmark , and
Hollãd.For vhik Caus vythout impudent per-
tinacitie it can not be denyit bot yat this second
marque of vniuersalitie of persons, tymes and
places is allanerly proper vnto the Catolique
church Romane and hir adherentes and to no
sect impugning hir.

Bot agãs this mark of vniuersaliti thair be yit
tuo ordinar obiections: by th' one is said yat it
cã be no certane mark of the treu church vhilk
hes the name of à litill troop,flok or handfull in
respect of the aduersars tharof, lyik as the vay
leading to lyf is said to be strait and narrou and
feu to entre tharby and the contrar larg and
ampill and many to pass yat vay. Item yat thair
be many callit feu elect, as alsovee be forbiddin
to follou the multitud vhilk for the most part
is inclynit rather to vyce nor to verteu.Heirũ-
to I aussr.Yat thair be not only one bot many
larg vayis leading to perdition and gret multi-
tuds yat go thidder (seing perdition is boyth in
thingis forbiddin and permitted in the former simpliciter in the other vhenas things lan-
full be abusit) vheras thair be bot one vay to
lyf so strait ãd dificill as feu can entre tharby : it
is treu also yat multitud is not aluay to be follouit since the most part is not alvay sene to be the
best part : yit the scriptur doth call the church
the multitud of yame yat beleue not in respect
of infidelles vhilk beleif not al,vho hes euer in
nũber excedit the faythfull as much or more
as the ten trybes did exceid the tuo,or the body

of Gedeōs oſt the handfull of 300. vhilk lay not
doun on thair vombe to leap the vatter, bot in
reſpect of heretiques, vhoſe number nor perpetuite neuer ves comparabill vyth yat of the treu
church vhilk tho ſche be in reſpect of all vther
trees' vhilk be infinit in number) only lyk that
one tree of lyf vhilk ves in Eden yit in reſpect
of the rottin branches yat haue fallin from hir
ſche is à gret deall more plentifull and larg nor
thai all: For (as is heirtofor ſaid, thai fallin g ly
ſtill and conſum, bot ſche doth yearly bud and
bring out neu bourgeons in place of the vithe-
red, floriſſing lyk à frutfull palm planted by the
riuier ſyid. For this cauſs ves ſaid to Abraham
(father of the faythfull) yat his ſeed (meaning
of the faythfull or church) ſuld be as innume-
rable as the ſtrars of heauin or ſand of the ſea.
and in the 7. of the Apoc. the Euāgeliſt did ſee of
all the tribes of Iſraëll or of the Hebreu church
aue hūdreth fourty four thouſund cōprehēding
vnder yat finit nūber à nūber infinit, ād tharefter à gret multitud of all nations, trybes, peapill and toungs vhilk culd not be nummerit all
cled in vhyit garments and careing palm branches in thair hādes, ſignifiég heirby the church
vniuerſall vnder grace.

By th' other obiection thai alleg yat in ſaying
Catholique or vniuerſall Romane is includit à
contrarietie in reſpect Rome is bot à particular
place. I auſuer. yat thair is no more contrarietie
nor incongruitie in ſaying Catholique Romane
nor in ſaying Catholique Apoſtolique. For if

the vniuersalite of all persons may be pertinet-
ly limited vnder the compass of tuelf particular persons: vhat absurdite to comprehend the
vniuersalitie of places vnder the name of one
principall place seing boyth holy and prophane vrittars haue vvih out offens vsir yat phrase
of speking, th'one calling the vniuersall impy-
rd the Impyir Romane, the vther (namly S.
Paul in the first to the Romans) calling the vniuersall fayth annuncit throuch the holl vorld
to be the Romane fivth. Then if the vniuersall
Christian fayth by so famus ane auth or as Sanct
Paul may be callit the vniuersall Romane fayth
Vnitie the 3. mark of the church. vhat falt is to call the vniuersall faythfull or
church vniuersall, the vniuersall church Ro-
mane?

The thrid mark of the treu church is vnitie:
vharby sch ois discernit from all excomunicats
yat be cut of from hir vnitie and frô all schisms
and sectes yat haue disvnited yair self from hir
vniform societie: Vhilk sectes being evry one
discoformable to one vther the treu church remanit all vhar one and conform to hir self.
Vhirof the bryidgrome sayit in the 6. of the can-
ticke: *My doue is one, sche is one vnto hir mother.*
and this vnitie ves also signif it by that seamles
coit of Cryst mentionit in the 19. of Sanct Io-
vhilk had no pach nor peice and vhirupon vn-
deuvding the same the Soldats did cast loittes
for fulfilling the prophesy. lyk as the Mosaicall
or dônance cômanding bot one lamb to be eating for the pasouer in evry familie ves à figur
boyth

boyth of Cryſt Ieſus the only Immaculat lamb
and of the vnitie of his church in vhilk he vold
haue no diuiſion. agreable to yat of th Apoſtle
4. to th' Epheſ. ſaying: *one body, one ſpreit as you
ar callit in one hoip of your vocation.* thatby meaning yat as many membres mak bot one body,
and as all theis mébres be gydit vyth one ſpreit:
ſo all Chriſtian mébres mak bot one Chriſtian
church and ſuld be contentit to be gydit vyth
one ſpreit yat thai may ſay, think and accord in
one, and vyth one mouth and hart, in one forme
of fayth and religion (houſoeuer thai differ in
habits) vorſchip and adore one threefold vnitie
and onefold trinitie. Vharupó I do collect. That
yat church vhilk is lyik theland of of one langage mentionat in the xj. of Geneſe, in vhilk
one Cryiſt, and one reull of Religion is obſeruit
and vhar thair is bot one hart and one kynd of
exterior form amangs the hoill multitud of the
beleuars (I gather I ſay) yat only to be the treu
church Catholique.

Bot amangs all churches Chriſtian contending for the ſaid prerogatiue only ſall this conformable vnite be found in the Catholique
church Romane: vhilk being compód of ſo many particular churches ſo largly ſpred throuch
the vorld and amangs ſo many nations of different mynds and maners: yit in hir god is not only adorit in one ſort euin to the meaneſt rites ād
ceremoneis tharof bot almoſt evry vhar in one
tong or langage thai pray and prais God: in ſo
much as ane infidell cumming from the fardeſt

part of vorld and feing evry vhar this conftant
conformitie he fall incontinent vnderftand the
faid Romane church to haue this vndouted
vnitie.

And morouer if at any tyme different opinions in ceremony or fubftance interuene
amang the mébres of this church, The authors
tharof captiuating thair auin iugment after rhe
reull of the Apoftle do ever giue obedience vn-
ro the facred oracles, cannons and decrees of
generall or prouinciall counfalles pronuncit v-
pon matters controuerd. Vhilk vyth my Eyis I
did fee in the year of Iubilee 1600. at vhilk tyme fum of the moft lernit and Reuerend Iefuites and Iacobins difagreeing vpon the prefcien-
ce of God did fend thair deputes veill inftructed vnto Rome fubmitting thair felf and all
thair opinions to Ecclefiaftique cenfur: and follouing the laudabill exemple mentionat in the
5. of the Acts vheras the primityue church prefented thair temporall trefors befor the feit of
Sanct Peter (vho in the 10. of Matheus Euangill is callit the firft of the Apoftles)euin fo thai
laying thair fpirituall threfors at the feat of Clement the 8. Sanct Peters holy and moft Clement fucceffor did humill thame felf and obté-
per vnto his fentence returning home veill ac-
cordit and cótent lyk as in the year immediatly
follouing the controuerfy yat ves betuix fum
inglifs Iefnites and Preifts (not for any matter
of fayth bot for chofing ont of perfons moft
capable to be fend in England for reefta-

h leſſing thair of the Catholique Romane religion) ves by conſent of boyth parteis remitted
to his holines determination.

Bot this vniform vnitie and Chriſtian obe- *No vnite a-*
dience ſall not be found amangs any ſect this *mang tham*
day vendicating the name of the treu church. *yat h aue abâ*
For thai diſaſſenting one from ane vther boyth *donit the Ro-*
in ſubſtantiall and ceremoniall pointes vill not *mane church*
ſubmit thame ſelf one to ane vther conténing
the iugment of any bot of thair auin fautors and
follouars, vharby vithin thair auin bouelles thai
be more vexit and vinquiſit then thai be by the
Catholiques. Vhilk Sáct Ambroſe and Epiphanius prouis to haue chauſit vnto the Arrians,
Eunomians, Macedonians aud Marciones. Lyk
as vee may ſee the ſelf ſame contrarietie in our
age. Behold Martin Luther hes moſt ſatirikly
ſcharpit his pen agans the Anabaptiſts, Zuinglius, Caroloſtadius ad Æcolympadius: and thai
vho vill be callit no Lutherians bot proteſtants
vrit bitterly agans Luthers doctrin : Agane
Ioachimus Veſtphalus , Heſſutius , Caſtalio,
Caſanouius, Molineus, Morellus vex Io. Caluin
moſt mychtely, and the ſame Caſtalio, Brentius,
Smedelinus and Sindry vthers Inuad Theodor
de Beza. In ſome being deuy dit in infini t ſectes
thai ſo vrangill and virie thair ſelf yat thay can
giue no greter argument vnto the vorld of thair
erronius doctrin nor by this vnchriſtian alter-
cation, vhilk is ſnch yat hardly ſall you fynd any
one of theis ſectes altogidder cóform to the ſelf
at the leſt vhilk doth not vſually cháge ſum one

opinion or vther according to the circumstance
of tyme ioynit vith sum neu curius conceptiōs
interuening. For vhilk caus it is reported yat
Georg Duc of Sax suld haue said yat he kneu
full veill vhat his nychboris of Vhittenberg did
trust yat year bot vhat thai suld beleif the nixt
year no man culd knou becaus thai ver so subiect in that be half to mutabilitie. And of this de-
plorabill diuisiou vee haue most manifest exéples vithin our ile of gret Britanny vhar betuix
the Englis and Scottes Protestantes thair be no
littill disputatiō of the supremacy of the church
of the authoritie of bischops, of habitts and holy dayis: yea in ether of the said kingdoms the
Protestants disagrees amang thair self: as in England the Prelats and puritans, and in scotlād
euin the ministres amang thame selfs haue had
much to do first for abolition nixt for restitutiō
of bischops: yea in Geneue (thair lydian stone)
the Ministres lak not sum intestin canker of cō-
tradiction seeing Mousieur de Perot the second
Ministre of that toune dois hold firm and fast
agans Theodor Beza yat the bischops of Rome
haue greter prerogatyue nor any other, and yat
the bischops of Geneue vho ver naturall lordes
of yat toun ver most iniustly expellit. For this
caus this day it is cum to pas vhilk Hilarius in
his age did complene vpon as of à matter most
misetable saing yat thair be as many faiyths as
thair be defferent desyrs as many doctrins as
maners, as many occasions of blasphemy as
thair be curius hedes. Bot thair querelles be the

quietnes of the church : for vhen as thai ftryue
one agans ane vther thai bot confirm the fayth
Catholique Romane, and it fallit vnto thame as
vnto vandring pilgrims vho ftraying once frome the hie vay (becaus thai did fcorne to haue
any gyid in a paith appering fo eafy to hold)and
feking according to thair particullar phantafeis
fum one fum ane vther crookit by vay thai err
vnperfauing thair error till by fum notable in-
conueniét that be forcit to confidder the fame:
euin fo the nouators of this age flyding out of
the Catholique ftreit of holy church and refu-
fing hit to be thair gyid tyning once the ftring
vay of treu religion eury one according to his
auin curiofitie doth find out fum od and extrauagant by vay being only feffinnit by the tailles
lyk Sáfons foxes and careing thair vythall burning fyir brandes thai run defperatly to burne
and deftroy the ryip corns of the Catholique
church Romane according togidder in nothing
almoft bot agans hir euin as Pilot and Herod
did agans Cryft Iefus : for lyk the forfaid foxes
thair heades or opinions be fett into findry arthes vhilk Sanct Auguftin interpretis to be one
euident mark of herefie, and as Rupertus fayit
thai eat vp thair auin tounges vhen as eury one
of tham doth impung his fellouis and condifci-
pills opinion yea oftin his auin Mafters, as Me-
lanchon did Luthers , Zuinzius Melanchons,
Caluin Zuinglius , Seruet Caluins. So thai
being contradictorius one to ane vther thai be
all deftitut of the charecter or mark of vnitie.

Thai fall thé do veill and vyflie both for thair reputation temporall and Saluation eternell ty-muflie to leaue theis tumultuus vatters of con-traction, theis obstinat alters of opposition and this confusit Babell of discord and disunion re-membring yat obedience is the best victim yat ve can osfer and vnite vyth tham vnto vhom ve au obedience à most euident argument yat vee be vnited vnto him yat is the author of vnitie and concord, vhilk in one of the most excellent Canticles of degrees the Psalmist cô-parit vnto sueit oyntment distilling from the head of Aaron (hie preist) vpon his beard and bordors of his garment, and to the deu falling from the hill hermon doun into the valleyis of Sion , saing morouer yat our lord hes commádit his blessing to abyid in this vnite for euer. O then that the beard and garments (that is to say Potestats, Princes and pepill of this age) vold susfer this blessed Balm and diuyne Deu of vnitie slyid doun vpon thame from the Mi-nisteriall head and hill of the church and yat thai suld vyth as gret kyndnes resaue as he vold kyndly and clemently (follouing his name and naturall) Ministre the same vnto thame as one seiking the conuersion of all and confusion of none. O yat thai vold patiently lyk the Lost scheip induir to be bound and brocht home from thair vandring in the vildernes of thair partiall opinions vnto the glorius societie of the nynetie nyne yat neuer strayit : or rather yat thai suld be so happy as to return not bound

nor compellit bot of freuill as did the forlorn
sone to th'end the fatt calf of reconciliation, ꝗ
the banquer of benediction and Musicall in-
strumêts of absolution micht be prepared and
presêted vnto thame to thair particular saluatiõ
and generall Ioy of the hoill familie of the
church yat vyth one voyce vee micht all glorifie the celestiall father becaus thai ver once lost
and nou be found. Otheruayis to spek indifferently if thai fall continu disunited vythout and
vithin as thai be it sall be hard for thame to proue befor indifferent Iuges yat thai be so much as
treu membres much les meriting to haue the
honor andi dignitie of the hoill body of the
church vhilk can no more be vithout vnitie nor
fyir vythout heat and vatter vithout humidite.

By the fourt mark the church is callit Apostolique vharby is not meanit yat the Patriarches and Prophets be excludit, seing the church
did not begin at the Apoles bot at Adam being
foundit vpõ the doctrin boyth of Prophes and
Apostles: For vhat the Apostles prechit to haue
cum yat the Prophets did Prophecy suld cum.

The 4. mar: k
of the churc b
is to be Apo •
stolique.

Morouer that church only suld be estemit
Apostolique in vhilk ve fynd not only thair doctrin bot also à laufull continuall succession of
preisthood or bischops euer from the dayis of
th'Apostles to our age. And agane the doctrin
of th'Apostles doth consist boyth in thair traditions and vrittings vho vndoutedly did pro-
pone and vse many rites, ceremoneis and formes for planting, vattring and confirming the

church and consciences of men vhilk nohuar
vee fynd vrittin. For vhilk caus Paul vritting to
the Thessal. exhortet thame saying. Stād ād hold
the traditiōs yat you haue lernit of me ether by
my sermon or by my Epistle. by vhilk vordes he
declarit euidētly yat he vold his vordes suld haue
as gret credit as his Vrittis: Yea apperātly more
in so much as he doth name tham befor the
other: vhilk consideration seamit to be veill
groundit in so far as Sanct Hierosm in one
epistle ad Paulinum speking vpon this subiect
sayit yat thair is much more pith in vords nor
in vrit: for proue vharof he doth alleg yat of
Æschynes vho being in the Rhodes à banist
man did hear the pepill read yat inuecty-
ue orason vhilk Demosthenes did vrit agins
him: at the hering vharof vhenas he did persaue thame meruellislie to prais the art and elo-
quence of the said Demosthenes, then Æschynes
after sighing à lytill did say vnto thame: My
freinds vhat if you had hard the beast him self
pnūcing theis verds? meaning thairby yat his viue voyice had geuin thame much more matter
of admiration then that cnld haue by reading of
his vorkes. And agane by Sanct Paul 1. Corint.
11. it aperit yat by vord he did institut the form
hou the supper of the lard suld be administrat
Epist. 118. cap. 6. saying the rest (meaning of the said supper) I sall
dispose at my cumming. Vharupon Sanct Au-
gustin vritting to Ianuarius taketh occasion to
say yat the same form vsit in his dayis in ministration of this blessed sacrament (vhilk differit
no thing

no thing from yat vhilk this day is obferuit in
the Romane church)ves by vord inftitut by S.
paul to remane for euer as à patern inuiolable.
and yit in ane vther place the faid Apoftle.I cō-
mend you my brethring yat in all things you
keap my precepts as I haue left tham by tradi-
tiō.and laft to timothe.2.epift.chap·2. vhat you
haue hard of me befor many vitnes yat report
to the faythfull vho be habill to tech vthers. of
vhilk vords it is moft clear (as ancient Irenee
lōg ago hes collected) yat rhe primityue church
ves inftructed in many pointes of religion
aud rites by th' Apoftles vhilk thai neuer did
vritt,bot gaue thame by verball traditiō to thair
fucceffors by vhom from hand to hand thai
haue bene knouin and fuld be continuit fo lōg
as the church Apoftolique can left.

For this caufe vhofoeuer vold profes him
felf to beleif à Catholique Apoftolique church
he muft not only beleif ãd refaue vhat the Apoftolique church hes beleiffit and refauit of thair
vritts bot alfo vhat fche beleuis and refauis of
thair traditiōs vnurittin by thã. vtheruayis vee
fall be brãgillit and maid incertane in the cheif
points of our fayth. Nether did the anciēt Heretiques (as the Arrians and findry vthers) differ more in any point from treu Catholiques
nor in this yat thai vold refaue no Ecclefiaftique
tradition houfoeuer it ves authorifed vyth antiquite bot groudit thã felf fcrupulufly only vpō
the text of Scriptur.Vheras Good Catholiques
knouing boyth traditions and vrittes to haue

*It is ane He-
refie ancient-
ly condemnit
in the Arrias
to admit no
thing in the
church bot
the bair text
of fcriptur.*

H

procedit from one fontane of the holy fpreit
ād to haue bene both brocht vnto vs equally by
one canall and conuoy of the holy church thai
reuerently vyth the Theſſoliens obſerue boyth
the one and vther ād obſeruing merit the prais
Forſaid geuin by the holy Apoſtle vnto thame:
vhilk prais ve reid not in any place of holy Scri
ptur to haue bene geuin to any yat did contem
theis verball traditions. Sanct Hilar. in his book
to cōſtan. Auguſt. Vhenas one ſaid to him yat
he vold haue no nev thing Said or eſtemit for attentik yat ves not vrittin in the text of ſcriptur,
replyit ſaying. My freind ſay rether thou vilt haue no neu Medecin agans neu poyſon, no neu
punition agans neu inſurrection, no neu con-
ſultations agans neu treaſons, no neu varrs agās
neu ennemis. and Athanaſius ſpeking of this
purpos, vhenas out of Thëognoſtus, Dionyſius
Allexandrinus and Origines he had prouin a-
gans the Arrians the ſone to be of one eſſence
vyth the father: Behold (ſayis he) vee haue verifeit our opinion or ſentence by vniform conſent and tradition of the fathers from hand to
hand delyuerit from predeceſſors to ſucceſſors: Bot you Diſciples of Cayphas vhom can
xou exhibit to be authors of your opinions bot
your ſelf.

And this gaue occaſiō to Theodoretus in his
firſt book. 8. chap. to ſay yat the Arrians ver cō-
uict by not vrittin vordes Chriſtianly vnderſtood. For vhenas the ſaid Arrians did reiect the
vord conſubſtāriall becaus it ves not to be foūd

in Scripture, then Athanasius and the bischops
Catholiques assisting did refut that heresie by
testimoneis of the fathers vho had resauit the
same vord consubstantiall by Apostolique tradition. Vee knou also yat Eluidius the heretique
by passages of Scripturs did impung the immaculat virginitie of the blessed Virgin Marie lyk
as he Donatists did the Baptism of infants: Bot
S. Hierome did refut th' one and S. Augustin th'
other by Ecclesiastique tradition,

The vse and necessitie of traditions is declarit.

And of this Apostolique Ecclesiastique tradition vndoutedly such is the authoritie yat not
only is it vnto the self bot euin vnto the hoill
scriptur as à tuichstone: for as the fyne gold can
not be discernit fró the fals bot by the said stone: No more suld vee haue knouin vhat scriptur
ver atentik or vnattentik if thai had not bene
tuichit vyth the lydian stone of the church: be
reson yat in the Scriptur the self vee fynd not in
expres vords any catalog tharof, for vhilk cause, vee must of necessitie seik the same elsuhar
and seiknig it elsuhar ve sall neuer fynd certéty except vee yeild vnto Ecclesiastique tradition: for vhenas you say yat the vndouted asseur-
ance of all matters pertening to fayth and saluation is contenit expreslie in holy scripturs
and I agane not finding in hoy scripturs this ca-
tologe distinguising books canonique from
apocryph you perrell to much the authoritie of
theis canonicall books. O bot you vill say (as I
my self sum tyme did most impertinently) that
by the pouer of the self same spreit you knou

By tradition of the church is Knouin v-hat books be canonique v-hat Apocry-phe.

H ij

his ftyill in theis yat be attẽtik and yat you'tharby haue incorporat à greter certéty nor the authoritie of man can giue vnto you. if fo bee you
arrogat vnto your felf allone and to your fpreit
Imaginatyue (after the maneir of th Anaba-
ptifts) yat vhilk you refufe to giue to the hoill
church as tho neuer one of the church had bene illuminat vyth yat fpreit befor you. or as tho
in thair approbations thai ver bot men appro-
uing by no greter varrand nor humane, and yat
you in your approbatiõs be more nor man and
fo'pofleffit vyth the holy fpreit as if you culd
not be defauit in yat vhilk you refaue for affeu-
rance.   And thus puft vp by the bellifs of your
priuat prefumpteus Imaginatiõs you vold haue
your fcience to be our lantern and lodftar, pronuncing all vthers yat be not of your opinion
to be bot ignorant obftinat perfons altogidder
depryuit of the lycht of the holy fpreit:albeit it
can not be deneyit bot yat ancient Doctors and
counfals of vhom vee haue refauit the cataloge of holy fcripturs haue bene by many degrees
more illuminat nor you vyth the fame fpreit,
vharof thair pietie,antiquitie and doctrin ioynit
vith the verteu of fo many miracles fo far exceding any perfection yat can be perfauit in you
be vitneffis admitting no exceptiõ : Vheras you
of your fpeculatyue infpiration haue no other
teftimony bot your ouin,vhilk is boyth fufpect
and partiall. Be contentit then to fubmit your
variable apprehenfions vnto thair venerable
authoritie and your rakles temeritie vnto thair

reuerent traditions consideering vyth your self yat your priuat certenty is manifeſtly detected to be full of publict incertenty in yat all ſectes impugning the Apoſtolique church Romane doth arrogat the ſelf ſame peculiar prerogatyue of the holy ſpreit as you do. Vharin I pray vith my hart our gratins lord God to pardõ you 4.Kings 6. ſeing you vatt not vhat you do. For lyk the king of Syrias ſoldarts vho vent to dothaim the hous of Eliſeus to haue ſurprifed him being preuented vyth blyndnes thai ſtrayit to Samaria amãg thair enemis : So you intending to inuaid the hous and head miniſteriall of Cryſtes church you bot go blyndfold to your auin perdition, and perſeuering in this perrinacitie in taking vpon you by your ſecreit illumination to knou the ſtyill and method of the holy ſpreit in diſcerning ſcripturs you fall vnuars in the damnabill errors of ancient Heretiques of vhom ſum vold haue all matters in fayth and religion prouin by expres vords of ſcriptur as the Arrians and Donatiſts (of vhom in thair auin place.) Vthers vold admit no books of Scriptur to be attentik bot ſuch as ſeruit moſt to confirm thair errors. For this cauſe Carpocrates and Manichæus did condem the hoill auld Teſtament: Cordon and Cerynthus all the Euangelles except yat of Lucas: lyk as the Seueriãs reiected the Actes of the Apoſtles: the Ebionites all th' Epiſtles of Sanct Paul, and the Alogians ſaid yat the Apocalvps ves bot ane figment of cerynthus. So thair ves neuer one of the Canonicall books culd eſcaip ⸗

the allſeing Eyis of theis lunatiques vho reiecting ancient tradition did beild vp vnto thair
ſelf à Babell of thair auin Imaginatiue illumination. Bot the viſdome of God hes prouydit à re-
mede agàs ſuch buſy branes inſpyring the ſucceſſors of his Apoſtles the ancient Paſtors and
Doctors of his church to leiſ vnto vs in Regiſter
à iuſt catalage tharof to th' end yat any queſtion aryſing tharupon vee may haue recours
to the protocoll and not to particular inſtru-
ments of parteis contending : vhilk cataloge
vee reid inſert amang the acts of the counſall of
Cartage vhar S. Auguſtin ves preſent à 1200.
yeers ago, and in the Epiſtle vhilk holy Innocé-
tius vrit vnto Exuperius. chap. 6. lyk as the famus counſall of florence à 150. ago did allou
the ſame by commun conſent of all the Grec,
latin, and Armenian legats aſſembled tharunto
and laſt of all the celebre counſall of trent hes
boyth repeted and ratifeit the ſame cataloge.

Auguſt. 7.
tom. agans
creſcentius 1.
book 13. cha.

For this cauſe vee admit the Canonique ſcripturs affirming tham vndoutedly to be ſuch albeit the cataloge tharof be not expreſſie mentionat in holy ſcriptur, be reſon yat by laudabill
conſuetud euer ſince the dayis of th' Apoſtles,
thair ſucceſſors frô hâd to hâd haue by traditiô
reſauit and reputed tham to be ſuch: Vhilk did

Auguſt. 4.
tom. of con-
ſent of the E-
uange. 1. book
1. chap.

moue Sanct Auguſtin to affirm *yat ancient tradition ſuld determin and deſyne vnvrittin vereteis and
apoint the canon of the ſcriptur.* Lyk *as in ane vther
place the ſaid holy father ſayit yat the* Euangells *pu-
bliſit, vnder the names of* Sanct Thomas *and* Eartho-

lome Apoſtles and of Nicodemus Diſciple by verteu of the ſame tradition be reieɛted, and theis of Marc and Luc be reſauit albeit thai ver nether Apoſtles nor Diſciples bot did only vritt vpon report and relation of vthers.

Vee ſee then yat in moſt principall heads of Religion vee be forcit to adher vnto ſuch traditions as in ſcriptur vee haue no particular mention tharof. and heirin for ſatisfation of ſimpill ons I vill be yit à littill more ſpeciall: Behold no ſcriptur doth ſay yat three perſons mak one Godhead, yea the name of perſon(at leſt applyit vnto God) is not to be fond in any place of ſcriptur not yit the name of the bleſſit trinitie, nottheles vee ſay that be three perſons and à trinitie, not becaus the ſcriptur ſo ſayit bot (as ſayit Sanɛt Auguſtin) becaus the ſcriptur doth not gane ſayit and becauſe ve haue ſo reſauit thame frome the Apoſtles and thar ſucceſſors.lyk as Dionyſius Areop 4.chap.of his Hierarchie ād origenes in his 5.book 1.cha. teſtifies the baptiſm of childring to be traditiue and not of the text of ſcriptur vhilk ſcriptur ſeamit to exclud ſuch as haue not the aɛtuall vſe of faith as much or more frō baptiſm as frome the Cene as apperit by the vords of Sanɛt Philip to the enuch in the 8.of the aɛts ſaying if you beleif no thing can ſtay the to be baptefit and by that of the Euangell vho beleuit and is baptefit fall be ſaue: by vhilk and many other paſſages of Scriptur aɛtuall fayth or beleif ſeamit to be ſo neceſſary in baptiſm yat it ſould alvay precead the

fame': Bot the nouators of this age difdaning
to refaue this cuftome by tradition thai alleg
childring neu borne to be faythfull throuing
fum paffages of fcriptur impudétly and vnap-
ly to that effeét as vhar it is faid by our mafter
in the Euágell fuffer littill childring to cum vnto me:euin as if to cum vnto Cryft and to be baptefit by him ver all on thing or as if he did
baptis all that he fuffred to cum vnto him vharas ve reid not in fcriptur yat euir he baptefir a-
ny perfon.in this fame fort thai throu alfo yat
of the firft.Corinth.7.chap.Yat the feed of the
faythfull be holy tharfor fay thai childring
vhilk be the feed of the faythfull muft neads be
faythfull.ane incógru⁹ and abfurd cóclufió : for
all things yat be holy be not faythfull mor nor
all that beleif be holy:lo the deuill beleuit fayis
S.Iam.2.cha.ãd yit he is not holy:ãd vee reid in
the fcriptur that tépills, altars, orisós yea kiffing
fum tyme be callit holy yit fuch things can haue
no fayth.and morouet to fay(as fum do)yat the
fead of faythfull men be aétually fayt hfull is
as extrauagant as to fay yat the fead or childring of lernit men be aétually lernit men hou
fone thai be borne vheras the one ãd vther haue bot the aptitude or difpofition to the one and
vther qualitie.and laft if Childring be aétually
faythfull vhy ar thai not as veill admittit to
thair Cçne as úto thair baptifm.As to thair fubterfuge cóparing baptifm to Circomcitió it is
yit moft feolifch of all for if thai vill aftriét me
to the ordinar tyme of Circumcition thai muft
be alfo

be alſo aſtricted to the Sex yat ves Circumcidit
to vit the maſles allanerny and ſo thai ſuld baptis no femelle childring. Thus the nouators
to eſcaip the neceſſitie of tradition thay bot
mask thair former errour vith ane vther more
intolerable and ridiculus, aſcryuing to infants
yat vhilk thair age and the ordinance of God
almychty doth not permit vnto tham(at leſt
ordiinarly): euin as to hyid the obſcuritie of
thair church vharof no teſtimony can be found
befor the year of our lord 1520. thair lyik the
ſubtill ſepia truble the clear fontans of the holy
ſcriptur vith thair vgly ink of inuiſibilitie to
the end no man ſuld perſaue thame being inuo-
luit vithin theis ſophiſticall labyrinths.

Theis and many vther incongruiteus thai fall
into vho vill not yeild vnto Apoſtolique traditiõ bot in preiudice tharof vold vreſt and thrau
the ſens of ſcriptur otheruayis nor the nature
thirof and vniform conſent of ancients vill
permit. Bot heir I returne to the matter.

The beleif (vhilk Sanct Auguſtin in his 10.
tom. Sermon 115. de temp. affirmit to haue bene
maid by the Apoſtles ſelf) and vnto the analo-
gie and proporti õ vharof all vther ſcriptur ſuld
be leuellit and interpreted: yit nether in the A-
ctes of the Apoſtles nor in no vther place of
ſcriptur can ve read yat Symbol or beleif as it is
collected and confeſſit in Chriſtian churchis.

To be ſchort novhar ſall it be ſcheuit in the
text of ſcriptur vhar vee be cõmandit to chang
the ſabbath day(vhilk ves ſatterday)in the ſon-

1

day follouing, bot vee haue in the Decalog à
precept directly commanding the said Saboth
to be obseruit ād the vther sax dayis be designit
for our labour. Novhar sall vee fynd the supper
of the lord callit à Sacrament: Novhar any com-
mandemēt to resaue the said supper fasting bot
rether if vee suld follou the exēpill of our blessed master to resaue it after supper. Yea sum-
things be expreslie forbiddin by the text of Scri
ptur vhilk notvythstāding vee may vithout offens vse as to eat of blood and things suffocat
vhilk in the first counsall of the holy Apostles
ves expreslie defendit ād forbiddin, and all theis
cōsuetuds and rites partly not vrittin partly forbiddin by tradition vee be bold to obserue because the church hitherto hes obseruit the same
euer since the dayis of the Apostles vhose traditiōs if you vold more particularlie see you may
reid Origenes in his 5. homel. vpon Numeri.
Tertull. de corona militis. Athanas in his book
of diuers questions. Basill. in his book of the ho-
lyghost. chap. 28. and 29. Sanct Hierom agās the
Luciferians: Bot Sanct Augustin most of all doth
planly say *yat thair be many things vhilk nether cā
be found in the vorks of the Apostles nor in the coun-
sells of thair successors vhilk notvythstanding being
obseruit by the hoill church ar to be estemit as recommendit vnto vs by the said Apostles.*

*Aug. 2. book
cap. 7. of the
Baptism of
childring.*

*The contēnars
of traditions
do not vith-
stāding vse
many both
new id auld.*

Bot heir I cā not meruell aneuch at thair partialite vho so much impung traditiōs seing thai
thair self follou many auld traditions vith the
Catholiqus and yat vhilk is more intollerabill

diſdaning ſumtyme to follou traditions recommendit vnto vs by ancient authoritie thai vill
follou thair auin traditions laking all authoritie
approbation or commendation bot thair auin,
as by thair Pſalm books prentet at Geneue is
manifeſt,in vhilk be comprehendit thair neu
formes of prayer,preching,faſting, Sacraments,
buryall,excommunication, abſolution, viſita-
tion of the ſeek, election of miniſtres elders and
decons, punition of offendars and diſciplin of
thair church.all vhilk formes be inuented by
thair ſelf and can not be red nether in holy ſcriptur,nor ancients.

And yit thai be ſo inconſederat as to obiect
for execrabill in vthers the ſelf ſame things v-
hilk thai think tollerabill in thair ſelf.Yea more
nor yat thai vſe and vſurp à gret many of things
vhilk thai condem in the Catholiques chãging
only the names tharof and not the natur.as for
exemple thai vill haue no biſchop bot ſuperin-
tendents:no Cathedrall chaptors,bot Preſbyte-
reis:no preiſts bot eldars:no Dioces bot Prouin-
ces:no ſenzeis bot Synodall aſſemblees: no Ar-
chebiſchop or Mitropolytan bot moderators:
no Officialls bot Commiſſars.

No handfaſting bot contracting:No dene ru-
rall bot viſiteur:no curſing bot excommunica-
tion:no aggreging or reaggreging bot firſt ſecõd
and thrid admonition.no forcing of mens conſcience bot confiſcation of Goods, impriſon-
ment and baniſment of ſuch as vill not conform
thair conſcience to thair appetit:thai vill not

The enemis of the Roman churche vſe many conſuetuds tharof changing only the names and not the nathor.

haue Catholiques to refufe difputation to any mã in matters of fayth and religiõ tho the fame be ratifeit by actes of generall counfalls and Imperiall edicts, bot vhar thai haue authoritie it muſt be treafon ãd herefie to dout or to demãd difputation in matters of thair fayth and religion ratifeit only by thair generall affemblees and acts of parlament.

Thai vill haue no altar vharupõ to celebrat the bleffed memoriall of the deth and paffiõ of our bleffed fauior bot à tabill: No fayth to eat ãd drink really his bleffed body ãd blood heir on erth vnder the fpece or form of bread ãd vyne as he did teſt in his latter vill, bot à fayth to eat ãd drink the fame really in the heauins cõtrary to his vill and teſtament, as if he had not force aneuch to fulfill his promis heir on the erth except by force of thair fayth afcẽding vp to heauin his infirmitie ver affiſted: thai vill not grant Good vorks to mercit, and yit thai exhort all men to Good vorks and confes yat at the latter day our lord and Maſter fall cum and rendre to eury one according as he hes done, Good or bad: thai vill not haue glorifeit Sancts in heauin to pray for tham, bot men lyik thair felf thair fellou membres and brethring yat be not yit glorifeit vith the garland of immortalitie thai vill haue to pray for tham. and fpeking of the dead thai vill not haue vs to fay vhom God affolzie or ab folue, bot the lord be vyth thame (à defyr full of dout and directly agans thair auin doctrin vhilk condemnit all prayer for the dead:) Thai

vill not call the blessed Eucharist of the Catholique church à sacrifice bot thair communion
must be callit à sacred or holy action: thai vill
not suffer Catholiques yat can not read to vse
beaddes for remembrance of vhat prayers thai
haue said vhat rested to be said, bot in thair
church such as cã reid be suffreit to haue strings
or marks in thair books to the end thai may
begin vhar thai left and so go on till the Psalms
or prayers aponted for yat tym be endit: Thai
can not auay to see à Crucifix yit thai commãd
to hear hou Cryst Iesus our blessed master ves
Crucifeit, as tho our eyis gaue not quikker im-
pressions vnto our hart nor our ears can do according to yat of the Poët. *Segnius irritant animos
dimissa per aures, quàm quæ sunt oculis subiecta fide-
libus, & quæ ipse sibi tradit spectator.* or as tho it
ver idolatrie to see yat vhilk Sanct Augustin desyrit so much to haue sene to vit his master and
redemer in the flesch: vhilk Ioyfull aspect since vee can not in this corruptible tabernacle inioy vee suld be glaid daylie to see at lest in por-
trait hou he suffrit, yat by the ministry boyth of
eyis and ears our frosin hartes may be inflãmit
to loue yat inspekable loue yat so villingly did
losse his lyf for our saik: and heirin I beleif I may
vithout offés affirm yat the most part of the youth vithin the realm of Scotlad nether knouit v-
hat is à Crucifix or vhat it is to be crufeit and all
becaus thai neuer did see the pourtrait or repre-
sentatió tharof. Thai vill haue no holy dayis bot
the saboth yit none must vork vpon veek dayis

aponted by tham to thair preching (at left during thair feruice) Thai vill haue no fafting on
fryday as did the ancients, bot thai allou to faft
on funday vhilk the ancients did condem.

Thai can not auay vith the faft of lent vhilk
all Chriftians, fuld obferue (as fayit one of the
ancients) becaufe it vas inftitut in imitation to
our pouer of the faft of fourty dayis vhilk our
bleffed mafter indurit in the vildirnes and ves
prefigurat by yat of Moyfes and Elias reiecting
the fame becaus vee be not habill to faft fourty
dayis as he did , euin as if vee fuld not imitat his
loue, patience, obedience, humilitie and chafte-
tie vith other his moft laudabill exemples (vhilk
he him felf gaue vnto vs to imitat faying I giue
vnto you my exemple) becaus ve can no more
attein to his perfectió in tham nor in his fafting:
bot in place of this Chriftian imitation thai vill
inftitut fafting· vpon thair auin fond imaginatió
minaffing the contemnars tharof vith all punition temporall and fpirituall.

Thai vill admit no interdictions after the Catholique Romane faffon , bot fuch as Remane
obftinat contradictors vnto tham is debarrit
from thair prayers and facraméts. Thai vill not
haue generall counfalls to merit the name of
the church, yit in the Actes of thair generall af-
féblees thai vfurp yat qualitie faying the church
hes decernit &c. Thai difdane the vords of binding and loufing in the Romane church, yit thai
profes to excómunicat and abfolue: Thai fcorn
to heir that the Catholique church can not erre

in matters of fayth or that simple men suld beleif as sche beleuit, yit the most ignorant amang
thame must grāt and sueir thair articles of fayth
to be vythout all error and thai must be beleuit
vhidder men vnderstand tham or not.

Thai vill not haue Catholiques to fynd falt
vyth prophane persons violétly intrusing thair
self in functions, faculteis and possessions Ecclesiastique Romane: Bot if any man amang tham
be he neuer so qualifeit sall inter in to play the
minister and to lift vp thair stipends vithout ad-
mission preceding, incontinent he is declarit à
seducteur, à Shismatique, à sacrilegius person, à
volf inuading the flok, à vyld boar vasting the
vinzard of Cryst Iesus and à theif yat hes entred by the vindo and not by the door.

Thai despyis all acerbitie of vords yit the pops
holynes must be callit the Antechrist, Rome the
Synagog of Satā, the Romane Clergie successors
to Iudas and all Catholiqne Romans obstinat
Idolators. Thai abhor all cruelty yit strait commandements most be publesit prohibiting lo-
gein, meat or drink to be geuin vnto thair contradictors. thus vsing in the premisses ād in many vther points the self fame things vhilk in Catholiques thai condem I meruell not à litill of
thair inconsideration and of mens simplicitie
vhilk is so miserably abusit bot most of all is to
be meruellit hou thai can vythout schame obiect so frequétly the contumely of cruelty agās
Catholiques perseuing the said Catholiques so
bitterly as thai do vyth imprisonment, proscri-

ption, confiscation of thair Goodds (Yea vyth famin, if the clemency of our gratius souerane and compassion of the pepill did not impesch thair furie) suirly for my auin part I besech God yat men suld on the one and vther syid go about to establis Religion by no seueritie bot vyth all sueitnes specially thai vho laking laufull vocation can haue no laufull authoritie to punis vthers.

Teiching vocation.

For thair be bot tuo sorts of vocation or calling and nether of thame can theis nouators iustlie acclam, seing the ordinar vocation must be from tham yat haue the ordinary pouer, to vit from such as can exhibit euidét testimoneis boyth of doctrin and descen t or successió Apostolique: and this kynd of ordinar calling thai lak except thai vold say yat Io. Viclef, Io. Hus, Hierome of Prag, and Martin Luther thair predecessors had the same becaus for the most part thai ver professit preists and graduat Doctors vharby thai had pouer to institut vthers as thai thair self ver ordinarly institut. Bot thai must vnderstand yat as the defection of thair said predecessors in preching and defending damnable doctrin repugnant to the obedience and dignitie of thair institutars togidder vyth the senté-ce of degradation iustlie pronuncit agans tham did sufficiétlié degrad and depryue tham of all ordinar degree or function vhilk of befor thai had obtenit: euin so thair successors succeding in thair vyce ád cótumatiusly perseuering tharin be comprehendit vnder the self same censur
of de-

of degradation. For as à deputie contrauening
the tenor of the patent of his deputation fche-
uit him felf ipfo facto vnuo*thy of fuch credit
Euin fo fubaltern deputations maid by the faid
deputye los thair force and effect vhenas the
perfon fubaltern or mediat perfifted in the vyce of the immediat deputie . and agane if it be
treu(as it is indead) yat fuperiors hauing pouer
to bynd or erect haue alfo pouer to loofſ àd de-
iect fpecially vhen the partie erected vnto any
dignitie doth difpyis or Inuade the dignitie of
the erecter:fuirly thair predeceffors haue forfalted any prefermét thai haue had of the church
of Rome lyk as thai thair felf haue done by
thair opiniaftte obftination agans the faid feat
Apoftolique as alfo by thair voluntar and vickit
abnegation contenit in the confeffion of thair
faith prented and put vp amang the actes of
parlamét vharby thai deteft abiure and renon-
ce as things damnable and idolatrus all benefit
office and charg proceding from the authoritie
of the church Romane,by vhilk oppofitió and
renuntiation forfaid thai manifeftly depryue thair felf of all ordinar vocatió if thai or thair
predeceffors hes had any. As for extraordinar
vocation thai haue as litill refon to vfurp it
feing yat kynd of calling hes euer bene accum-·
paneit vyth fuch extraordinar giftes as gaue fufficient authoritie and credit to thair calling , as
vith irreprehenfibill holines of lyif Ioynit vyth
extraordinar miracles:Bot thair lyf rendring no
extraordinar licht nether of extraordinar holi-

K

nes nor miracles thai haue no reson to vſurp
the honor of extraordinar calling.I am not igno
rant vhat ſubterfuge thai vſe in this point alleging thai tech no neu doctrin crauing neu o-
peratiõ of miracles ſeing thai tech only the doctrin alredy confirmit ſufficiently by the miracles of Cryſt Ieſus and his Apoſtles.vharunto
I anſsr yat albeit it ver treu yat thai did tech only the doctrin of Cryſt and his Apoſtles vncor-
rupting the ſame vyth thair auin gloſes and neu
interpretations repugning to the ancient inter-
pretatiõs of the fathers yea oft tymes to the text
of ſcriptur.yit in ſo much as thai Impũg the Paſtors vhilk only haue the euidence of Apoſtolique ordinar ſucceſſion , of neceſſitie thai muſt
fortifie and confirm thair extraordinar oppoſi-
tion vith ſum extraordinar miracle. Euin as the
prophets did vho albeit thai techit no lau bot
yat of Moyſes confirmit long befor vith glorius
miracles Yit in reſpect thai did reprehend the
ordinary Doctors of the lau and ſuch as ſat in
the ſeat of Moyſes thai did qualifie thair moſt
inſt thretnings and reprehenſions by miracles
meriting gret credit and authoritie.

Bot in reſpect this matter of vocation doth
merit à ſeuerall diſcours I delay the ſame to
ſum vther place more propre and conuenient
returning vnto my purpoſs and affirming that
the miniſtres thair ſelf in moſt things vhilk thai
vſe in thair church thai follou ether old or neu
tradition or at leſt interpretation vhilk be not
expreſlie contenit in holy ſcriptur:For as is afor

said in thair baptifm the baptefing of childring
and in thair communion to refaue it fafting and
not after fupper is by tradition,in the decalog
the chang of the faboth day is alfo by tradition, lyk as the vords of parents and adultery
muft refaue interpretatió: yea morouer vee fuld
not knou the bleffed volum of holy fcriptur to
be fuch if by tradition it had not cum to onr
knoulege.nether is it à Paradox to fay yat the
books of prayers pennit and prented in Geneue be no more in expres vords in fcriptur contenit nor the Roman matin books be.Vharun-
to thai aufsr indirectly vhenas thai fay all yat be
contenit in thair books ether to be fcriptur or at
left not repugning tharunto:becaus thai aftrict
Catholiques to expres vords and thai as preui-
legit perfon muft be licenuiat fo thai may fcheu
the matter or fundamét of thair forms to be includit any vay vithin Scripturs : Bot thai muft
vnderftand that the matter and fundament of
vords differ as much from expres vords as the
fondation of a hous and à finiffit hous or as the
matter and form vhilk be fo different in natur
as that à naughty form rendrit à Good matter
to be naughty : behold the moft delicat fruitts
refauing once the filthy form of putrefaction
or the beft venifon yat can be viffed conuerted
once in vernim becum bot contemtibill notuy-
thftanding thair former fynnes:or to fpek more conueniently to this matter:behald the puritie of theis paffages of holy fcriptur vharupon
Arrius,Donatus,Eluidius and other Heretiques

did found thair errors ver bot vitiat and defylit by the heretical forms yat thai ver partially throuin vnto resauing cõtrar thair nator by the filthines of the said forms sum infection as clear fontãs infected by repair of filthy beastis or pretieux stones staned by sum contrarius accident be not preseruit by thair singularitie from such inconuenients vhen th u chanse to fall. and suirlie that be giltie of this partiall preuarication or collusion vhosoeuer doth cite, apply, throu, or interprit holy scriptur not according to the mynd and tradition of the most ancient, most holy and most lernit fathers bot according to the mynd ãd plesuir of sum priuat modern persons vho to aduance thair auin priuat credit go about to mak the holines and doctrin of the said fathers to be suspect and odius.

Bot to th'end I may once absolue this section of traditions I only add theirs manifest passages follouing. first of Sanct Ignatius Bischop of Antioch ane author of the same age vith the Apostles vho in the year of our lord 38 goirg to be martyred did exhort all churches by vhilk he vent to diminis nothing ef Apostolique tradition vhilk he vißit tham for the more securitie to put in vrit. Nixt of Tertullian ane author of the first age after the Ascension saying in his book of fasting yat the solennell institutions ver eikkit to the fayth ether by scriptur or by tradition of the eldars.

Thridly of Eusebius bischop of Cesaree in Palestina ane autor of the second age after the Ascension saying in his books of Euangelique de-

Manifest passages of anciets prouing traditions vnurittin.

Of Ignatius Euseb. Story Eccles. 3. book 3. chap.

Euseb. 1. book 9. chap. demonstra. Euangel.

monſtration _yat the Apoſtles applying thair doctrin
to the eares of many hes conſignit or left thair ſaid doctrin partly by vritt partly vythout vrit as à certane
lau or cuſtum vnurittin._ Ferdly Sanct Baſill biſchop
of Ceſaree in Cappadocia à 1230. years ago in
his book of the holy ſpreit chap. 27. ſaying _of the
doctrin yat is obſeruit vithin the church ſum tharof
vee haue by vritt in inſtruction, ſum by ſecreit tradition of the Apoſtles, yit boyth th'one and other haue
alyik force in_ Religion, _nether is thair any hou ly till
ſo euer he be exerciſed in the laucs of the churck yat
can deny the ſame._ Fyftly of Sanct Epiphanius biſchop of Salamin in Cypre à 1220. years ago
ſaying in his book agãs Heretiques, in this ſort.
_Vee be forcit to vſe traditions for all things can not
be drauin out of ſcriptur, and for this cauis the holy
Apoſtles haue left vs ſum things by tradition, ſum
things by vrit._ Saxtly of Sact Chryſoſtom archibiſchop of Conſtantinople about à 1200. Years
ago vritting vpon the ſame text of Sanct Paul, 2.
to the Th.ſſal. 1. chap. (vhar the Apoſtle com-
mandis tham to obſerue his traditions reſauit
ether by vord or vrit.) the holy father ſayit th⁹.
_it apperit (Sayis he) of this text yat the Apoſtles haue
not left vs all by vrit bot yat that haue recommendit
many things vnurittin: tharfor ve think the tradition
of the church is vorthy to be beleuit: It is à tradition,
Inquyir no farder._ Laſt of all S. Auguſtin biſchop
of hippo in Afrique in the ſame age vritting a-
gans the Donatiſts in this ſort. _The Apoſtles to cõ-
fes the treuth (ſayis he) hes vrittim no thing of this
matter bot it is to be belenit yat this cuſtome hes ta-_
K iij

kin *his beginning from thair tradition, as thair be ma-*
ny things vhilk the church vniuerfall obferue vhilk
notuithftanding of Good refon is to be thocht commã-
dit by the Apoftles albeit thai be not vrittin.

Vhy Sanct
Auguftin
callit the tuo
teftamẽts tuo
papes.

Theis be teftimoneis fo manifeft as it ver fu-
perflu⁹ to produce any more:yit I knou thai vill
alleg to the contrar the felf fame S.Auguftin in
his 3.traittie vpõ the epiftles of Sãct Iohn faying
yat the tuo teftaments be the tuo Papes of the
church out of the vhilk vee fuld fook the milk
of holy hiftoreis:vharby thai vold conclud yat
the faid father vold feclud all tradition yat ves
not comprehendit vithin the faid teftaments.

Bot the aufsr heirunto is eafy to fuch as vill
read the place forfaid vharin the holy father
makit diftinction betuix the milk and folid
meat contenit in the tuo teftaments, by milk
meaning Cryft in his humilitie, by folyd meat
meaning Cryft as he his equall vnto the father,
affirming that the facred hiftoreis of his huma-
nitie and diuinitie ar to be foukit out of the
papes of the tuo teftaments the one for milk th'
other for folid meat:vilk vee alfo confes to be
treu : Bot to infer heirupon yat Sanct Auguftin
by theis vords dois condem all vnurittin traditions ver not only to condem him felf vyth all
the venerable fathers preceding him bot alfo
to condem the faid tuo infallibill teftaments or
pretieus papes out of the vhilk vee may fouk (if
ve be not fenfles) the milk of Apoftolique and
Ecclefiaftique vnurittin traditiõ by the Apoftle
faying in one place. 1. Timoth. 3. chap. ẏat the

church is the pillar and fondament of veritie
(vharby all hir tradition and ordonnances vrittin and vnurittin be confirmit to be autentik:)
and by the same Apostle in ane vther place 2.
Thessalo.1.chap.commanding thame to keip his
traditions vhatsoeuer vrittin or vnurittin as is
aforsaid.morouer theis traditiõs haue seruit for
cheif veapins vharvyth the holy ancients haue
voundit all Heretiques to this hour For Anciét
Ireneus vsit the same agans the Heretique Valentinus : Tertullian agans Marcion : Origenēs
agans Celsus:the counsall of Nice agans Arrius:
Basilius agans Eunomius and Amphilochius:
Sanct Hierom agans Vigilantius,Iouinianus and
Luciferianus : Cyrillus Allexandrin agans Ne-
storius:Proclus bischop of Côstantinople vritting to the Armenians:Theodoretus in his Po-
lymorph agans the Heretiqus of his tyme:Sanct
Augustin agans the Donatists,and Iulian:Leo,
Gelasius and Iohn bischops of Rome agans Eu-
tyches:the Saxt Synod vsit this tuo eggit veapin
agans the Monothelites:the seuint Synod agans
the Iconomachs:Beda the venerable vsit the same vritting of the varietie of the cours of the
Moone : Peter of Cluny did the lyik agans the
Henricians and Petrobrusians : Sanct Bernard
agans Peter Habailardus : Euthemius agans the
Heretiques of his tyme:Finally all holy vrittars
vnto theis dayis haue vsit the same for most pi-
thye and peremptory arguments agans all herefeis and Heretiques.
    Bot I do not so insist in defending the neces-

Not only tra-
dition bot al-
so expres scri-
ptur prouit
Catholiques
opinion in
cheif contro-
uerseis.

sitie and authoritie of Apostolique and Ecclesiastique tradition as if the hoill glob of the Apostolique church Romane suld succumb if thai
ver denyit: becaus expres scriptur doth confirm
thair doctrin in points most cõtrouerted, vhilk
I proue by theis feu testimoneis foilouing. vhen
in the beleif it is said by degrees yat *Cryst our bles-*
sed master ves crucifeit, dead, bureit and therefter des-
cendit to the hell, tharin the fayth of the Catholiques isProuin to be orthodox or autentik vho
deny his descéding ether to haue bene befor or
in bot after his deth Agane vhen it is said indefi-
nitly in the same beleif: I *beleif the communion of*
sancts: doth it not proue the Sancts militãt and
triumphant to haue à mutuall communion? bot
vhat communion can vee mortall militants haue vyth theis immortall glorifeit triumphants
bot vhen by our reuerent voues ad prayers ve
supplie thã to interceid for vs throuch his meri-
tes and passion vharby thai be alredy glorifeit
knouing yat thai vnderstand our estat in yat it
is mentinat in the fyftent of Luc yat thai reioyis
at the conuersion of sinnars: and on the other
part vhenas the said membres triumphant do
commemorat or offer vp our orisons and almes
deadis as ve reid partlie in the tent of the actes
in the history of Cornelius, partly in the 8. of
the Apocalyps that thai haue done. Vhen it is
said in the 2. of Machab. 12 chap. (Vhilk book
Sanct Augustin doth numer amang the Canonicall) *prayers for the dead to be holy and helthfull,*
vho can deny bot such prayers be necessar? vhé
vee reid

vee reid Sanct Ia.5. Yat the preiſt ſuld be callit vnto
the ſeik to auoynt yame in the name of the lord and
to pray for tham, doth not this text command vnction to be conioynit vith prayers in the laſt article of lyif vhen our ſeiknes is ſuch as can not
be curit? Vhen vee reid in the.5. to the Epheſ.
Matrimony to be à gret ſacrament, vhy ſuld vee cō-
dem tham yat this day affirm the ſame? vhen ve
read. 1. Corinth. 7. chap. Yat he doth veill yat Ioynit his virgin in matrimony, bot yat he doth better vho
ioynit hir not and vhen vee reid 2. of Timoth. 5.
If young vidoues yat be conſecrat vnto offices of the
church ſall Marye thai incur damnation violating
thair former vow:is it not euident yat our mother the holy church hes drauin out the doctrin
of celibat or auouit virginitie out of the pure
fontās of holy ſcriptur, Vhen vee reid. Peter. 5.
many things to be in the Epiſtles of Sanct Paul difficill to be vnderſtand:and in Io.the 6. Many Diſciples
to haue ſaid to Cryiſt, vhenas he himſelf did ſpek,
This is à hard ſpech vho can heir him? Yea ſum Diſciples to haue left him for the hardnes of his ſpech and
the verey Apoſtles thame ſelf to haue ſaid in one
place, ſpek vnto vs planlie and not in parables. in
reſpect of theis ſpechis vhat Hereſie is it to ſay
yat the ſens of ſcriptur is ſum tymis difficill:vhē
vee reid Philip. 2. Yat God ſall rendre to eury one
according to his varkis:and 1. Corinth. 9. Evry one
ſall reſaue his proper reuard according to his labor.
and Matth. 16. Since vee be commandit to vork onr
auin ſaluation and Math. 25. vhen it is ſaid Yat at
the latter day it ſall be rendrit to evry one according

L

to his charitie and almes deades to the indigent: doth
it not follou ꝗat Good vorks be meritorius? vhē
it is said. Yat the fin agans the holy spreit sall neuer be
forgeuin in this vorld nor in the vorld to cum and in
the 1. Epistle of Io. 5. chaptor. Yat thair is à sin
vnto deth vhilk suld not be prayit for. ād agane, Yat
thair be sum sins not vnto deth: is it not manifestly
prouin sum sins to be morta¹l, sum veniall , and
sum heir in this lyif sum after this lyf forgeuin?
Vhen in Io. 3. it is said except vee be regenerat by
vatter and the holy spreit vee can not inter in the
kingdome of heauin, is not tharby declarit the ne-
cessite of baptism vnto saluation? vhen vee read
in the 8 of the Acts , Yat the Apostles layid thair
handis vpon thame yat ver alredy baptesit, is not
tharby the imposition of hands vsit in the Romane church vnder the name of confirma-
tion m ost euidently establissit? Vhenas as vee
reid to the Thessaloniscen. chapit. forsaid the
Apostle to commād tham to obserue the traditions
lernit of him ether by his sermō or vords and agane in
the 1. Corint. 11. yat agans the contērieux he doth obiect
only cōsuetud or custum saying vee haue not such cu-
stome nor the church of God. Be not the authoritie
of vnurittin traditions tharby euidently confirmit? vhar to Timothe the church is callit the pillar
and fundament of veritie, and, in the 18. of Matt. Vho
disdanit to hear hir let him be to the as ane ethnik or
Publican: doth not theis passages vrg to beleif as
the church beleuit and to be assurit sche can not
err? Vheras in the 4. of Genes. God sayit vnto
Cain vhy art you angry ād vharfor doth you cast doū

*thy visage: if you do veill fall you not refaue it, and if
you do euill is not fin or punition at thy port: bot thy
appetit fall be vnder the and you fall reull ouer it.*
and in the 15. of Ecclefiafticus (vhilk book albeit Io. Caluin affirm to be doutfull yit feing in
the 3.counfall of Cartage 47.canon it is rekkinnit amang the canoniques as the Epiftles of iames and Iud vhilk ver alfo once douted vpon
and yat Sáct Auguftin in his book of grace and
freeuil chap. 2. doth vfe this fame paffage to
proue freeuill I produce the fame for autentik
fcriptur) Iefus the fone of Syrach in the faid
book faying in this fort. *God at the beginning did
conftitut man and left him,in the handes of his auin
counfall:He gaue vnto him commandemẽts and precepts faying if you vilt keip tham thai fall conferue
the:he hes fett befor the fyir and vatter to vhilk of the
tuo you vilt put out thy hand: befor man is Lyif and
deth,*Good *and bad,vhat plefit him fall be geuin him*
Vheras in the 30.of Deuterõ.Moyfes fayit to the
pepill *I call the heauin and erth to vitnes yat I haue
fett befor your Eyis lyif and deth,curfing and bleffing
chufe tharfor lyf yat you ãd your fead may lyue.*Vheras to the fame pourpofe.1.Corinth.7. chap.it is
faid. *vho being firm vyth hym felf doth in his hart
conclud not of neceffitie bot hauing pouer vpon his
auin vill,&c.*Doth not theife clear paffages proue the doctrin of freeuill to be orthodox and   Matth.16.
attẽtik?Vheras ve read yat Cryft our mafter firft
reuelit vnto Sanct Peter Yat *he ves Chrift the fone
of the leuing* God the other Apoftles efteming
him bot ether Elias for his yeall vnto the obfer-

L ij

uation of the lau, or Hieremias be reſon of his
holynes, or Io. Baptiſt becauſe he prechit the
doctrin of baptiſm as Iohn did, or ſum prophet
becauſe he propheceit of things to cum. Vheras
ſpecially *pouer ves geuin to him to bynd and louſſe
and promis of the keyis of the kingdome of heauin*:
Vheras *For him only Chriſt payit tribut , him only he
cauſit valk on the vatters, him only he did recõmẽd to
cõſirm the fayth of his brethring, of him allone he tuik
pleſour ſo oſt to demand if he louit him, to him allone
he ſaid thryis ſead my ſcheip, vnto vhom allone chãging his name he gaue one of his moſt famus namis
calling him Cephas: vnto vhom of all th' Apoſtles he
apperit firſt after his glorius Reſurrection and befor
his deith to him allone did fortell the ſame and the ma
neir of his deth, Finally vheras in expres vords in the
10. of Math.Euangill he is callit the firſt of all the Apoſtles:* is not the ſupremacy of S. Peter by theis
paſſages and by many vthers (vhilk God villing in à traittie à part I ſall ſum day collect)
moſt clearly confirmit. Vheras in the firſt to the
Romans *the Apoſtle doth ſo extoll thair fayth yat he
ſparit not to call the fayth vniuerſall or Catholique
prechit thruch the hoill vorld to be thair ſayt* : Vhat
Hereſie or offens is it this day to call the vniuerſall church of the faythfull vnder the venerable
name of the Romane church vhilk nou profeſſit no vther form of fayth nor yat vhilk the Romane church did profes vhenas the ſaid Apoſtle
did commend thame.

　　　　To be ſchort vheras *in expres vords it is ſaid:
this is my body and agane except you eat the fleſch of*

Io. Laſt.

Io. 13.
Io. Laſt.

Io. 6.

Ane euident
probation of
reall preſence.

the fone of mã and drink his blood you fall not obtene eternell lyfe. and agane *my flefch is verey meat and my blood verey drink* doth not theis expres teftimoneis moft clerly proue the eating and drinking and reall prefence of Cryfts body? and vheras in this reall manducation the gros apprehenfions of the Capharnaits is reprehendit by theis myfticall and deap fpechis of our blefſed fauior faying: *it is the fpirit yat quinkkinnit:the flefch profitet no thing:* and agane,*my vords be fpreit and lyf, bot thair be fum of you yat beleif not:* by theis vords (I fay)is not the difdanfull derifion of fuch as falfly imput Cyclopique Anthropophagie or eating of mens flefch vnto Catholiques manyfeftly elidit and couicted? for theis fcoffing mokars grofly imagening (as did the Capharnaites) the naturall and carnall body of Cryft fo to be eatin naturally ad carnally yat his flefch is torn and his bones brokin after fuch fort as Poëttes did fayn the geat Polyphemus and as ve knou the barbarus Brefilians to eat men and vemen,and tharuithall lyik vnto naturall Philofophors diftrufting all doctrin vhilk agreit not vith naturall fens or raifon thai be pitifully defauit ether ignorantly or arrogantly preferring(contrar the doctrin of Cryft) fens vnto fayth and flefch vnto the fpreit.For if I fuld fay vyth theis Sacramentars yat by my fayth I afcend vp vnto heauin and tharby am conioynit vith Cryft and fo doth eat his flefch and drink his blood:in doing all this vhat haue I done repugning to naturall raifon feing the

verey infidell Philofophors confes the heauins
to be the habitation of the goddes and yat by
our vouis and eruift affection ve be conioynit
vyth tham and no otheruayis:Bot on the vther
part if vith the Catholiques Romane I fall fay
yat I do eat à bread defcending frō heauin prefigurat by the Hebreuis Manna,the food of angells geuin by God vnto men , à graip confauit
in the vynetree of à virginall vomb, hauing no
preffoir bot à potence or crofs, no veshall bot à
bleffed naturall body, no canall bot his facred
fyid hāds and feit,,no fum bot the force of the
holy fpreit to mak me dronk vyth yat celleftiall
nectar :A flefch prefigurat by the immolation of
Ifaak and eating of the pafchall lamb,and ane
Innocent calf killed for me and vs all prodigall
childring,and in one vord ifI fall vyth Catholiques affirm the bread to be changit in the
flefch of Cryft and the vyne in his blood,the
philofophors fall lauch,fens and naturall raifon
fall raige and repung: tharfor in this manducation of Catholiques vee haue nead of fayth and
fpreit,in the other manducation of the facramē-
tars(Cheiflie theis yat follou Io.Caluin,it fuffe-
fis to follou the grofs opiniō of fens and flefch.
vee read yat the Difciples of Pythygoras had
fuch refpect and reuerence vnto thair maifter
yat it vas fufficient probation amang tham in all
thair difputations to fay,ipfe dixit(he hes faid it
and vho douted tharof(houfoeuer thair auin o-
pinions ver contrarius) ver expellit out of his
pædagogy:bot thai in theis dayis vho vill only

Dogma datur Christianis, quod in carnem trãsit panis & vinum in sanguinem: quod non capis quod non
vides, animosa firmat fides, præter rerum ordinem.
Sub diuersis speciebus, signis tantum & non rebus, latent res eximiæ, caro cibus, sanguis potus, manet tamẽ
Christus totus, sub vtraque specie. A sumente nõ can-
cisus, non confractus, nõ diuisus, integer accipitur: Su-
mit vnus sumunt mille, quantum isti tantum ille, nec
sumptus consumitur. Sumunt boni sumnnt mali, sorte
tamen inæquali, vitæ vel interitus: Mors est malis, vi-
ta bonis, vide paris sumptionis, quam sit dispar exitus.
Fracto demum Sacramento, ne vacilles sed memento
tantum esse sub fragmento, quantum toto tegitur, nul-
la rei fit scissura, panis tantum sit fractura, qua nec sta-
tus nec statura, signati minuitur. Tantum ergo Sacra-
mentum veneremur cernui, & antiquum documentũ
nouo cedat ritui, præstet fides supplementum, sensuum
defectui.

As to yat vhilk is allegit out of the first Corinth. 11. chap. Vhar the body of our lord is callit
bread: Vharupon if thai vill infer yat thair can
be no thing thair bot bread may I not as veill
infer yat thair can be no thing thair bot the body of our lord seing our lord him self did call
the bread his body. This mycht be ane sufficiẽt
ansuer to ane argument so insufficient bot yit I
vill be more speciall in declaring vharfor the bo
dy of our lord is callit bread by th' Apostle. First
becaus Cryst him self and his blessed body is in
many places of scriptur so namit: as in Ieremie
11. vhar it is said let vs put the tree to his bread: Vhar
by the tree the cros and by the bread Cryst or

his bleſſed body vas prefigurat according to the
opinion of all th'ancients:and in the Euangell
Cryſt is callit *the bread vhilk deſcēdit frō heauin.*
Bot in the tabill of out lord I remember not to
haue red the body of Cryſt to haue bene callit
abſolutly bread bot euer vith ſum adiection, e-
ther demõſtratiue, relatyue, or explicatiue:as in
the paſſage of Sanct Paul forſaid vhen it is ſaid:
Vho eated of this bread, and agane, the bread
vhilk vec brek,and in the 6.of Iohne,the bread
vhilk I ſall giue you is my fleſch. and as all the
ancients doth affirm the holy ſpreit vſit to loyn
theis adiections yat vee may vnderſtand that by
yat he ſpekit not of commun bread bot of ſum
miſticall bread or myſterie comprehēdit vnder
the form of bread. Secondly the Apoſtle calling
the body bread he ſo ſpekit becaus the linia-
ments and form of bread and not of the body
be ſene,euin as he callit the blood nether blood
nor vyne bot à coop becaus the contening coop
is more patent to our Eyis nor the contents tha-
rof:thridly in the ſcriptur oft tymes things be
namit after thair exterior form: So the braſin
ſerpent vas callit à ſerpent ſo the Angelles var
callit men appering in the form of man. Laſt
of all it is à cõmun cuſtum in ſcriptur to retene
or keap the ould name in things changit from
one form or natur to ane vther:ſo vyne is callit
in the Euangill à graip or berry, ſo the deuill is
yit callit Lucifer, ſo man is callit clay,ſo the rod
of Moyſes ves callit à rod vhen it vas no rod
bot à ſerpent : and this I fynd alſo confirmit by

Numer.21.
Geneſ.18.and
19.

ane vther auld hym afcryuit to Sanct Ambrofe
vhar it is faid. *Paulum profers tu docētem, panis no-*
men imponentem, corpori dominico:Moyfen ego refe-
rentem virgæ nomen in ferpentem,pari modo replico.
Mos eft frequens Scripturarum,rerum vt præteritarum
voces dent præfentibus:Homo humus nominatur, vi-
num vna appellatur,dæmon Lucifer vocatur,fat hæc
fanis mentibus.

Laft vheras in the place forfaid th'Apoftle
doth pronunce fuch as eat and drink vnvorthe-
ly to be gilty not of bread or vyne bot of the
body and blood of Cryft Iefus, tharby he doth
manifeftly point out vnto vs no commun bread
bot the body of Cryft to be eatin in this blefled
Sacrament.

Then to conclud this fection if you fhall fay
vith he Capharnaits, this is ane hard fpech, I
vill anfuer vyth Cryft yat flefch heirin profetit
no thing yat is to fay yat carnall raifon can no
more comprehend this nor fche can cōprehend
à creation of all things of no thing,à conception
and generation vythout carnall copulatiō preceding,à corporall afcenfion vithout violence,
or à refurrection of body and bones conuerted
in duft and afches if you fall fay vith Sanct Tho
mas yat you canft not beleif except you fee, I
fall yit anfuer vyth our blefled fauior yat thai be
blefled yat beleif and haue not fene.and if you
falt (as did the Virgin Marie)aftoniet exclame
faying hou can this be feing I knou not à man?
as if you fuld fay yat you canft fee no naturall
apperance or likliehoid yat the bread fuld be

conuerted in ane reall body: I anſuer vith the
Angell yat it behouit the holy ſpreit to ſurpriſe
or poſſes the and the pouer of the moſt high to
ouerſchaddou the, otheruayis you ſall no les
dout of thy creation, ſaluation and reſurrection
nor of the reall preſence. Morouer you ſuld not
misknou yat fayth hes no praiſs or merit vhar
humane raiſon may proue the ſame, ād yat mo-
deſt Chriſtians in matters of fayth ſuld content
thair ſelf yat thai be ſuch vndemanding vhy or
hou thai be ſuch lyk as S. Paul being rauiſſit vnto the heauins kneu he ſau Cryiſt bot vhidder he
did ſee him corporally or not corporally he nether kneu nor inquirit.

Bot returning to the matre I hoip I haue by
argumēts preceding clearly ſcheuit the doctrin
of Catholiques in cheif heads of Religion controuerted to be infallibilly confirmit, by expres
text of ſcriptur lyik as heirtoſor by euidēt probation I haue confirmit the ſame by euident teſtimoneis of ancient fathers. For vhilk cauſe
ſeing expres text of ſcriptur and authoritie of
Doctors notvithſtanding the diſtance of tyme
and places vhar and vhen thai did vrit, to vit
Tertullian and Sanct Auguſtin in Afrique: Hilarius in France: Ambroſius, Leon, Gregorius in
Italy: Io. Chryſoſtom. in Thrace: Theophylact
in Myſia: Io. Ephraim, Io. Damaſen and Sanct
Ierom in Syria: Baſilius in Cappadocia: Origenes, Cyrill and Athanaſius in Egypt: ſeing the
four principall Oicumenique counſalls, to vit
of Nice vharin did aſſiſt 150 biſchops: of Ephe-

se vharin did assist 200. bischops:of chalcidon
vharin did assist 630.bischops:Seing I say boyth
scripturs,fathers and counsalles do spek, vrit ād
conclud in questions this day controuerted as
the Romane church presently doth,sche must
be vndoutedly the treu church Catholique.and
vho vold haue à clearer demonstration of hir
present consent in doctrin vyth yat of the primityue church. let him read the book callit the
Augustian cōfession vhilk(being collected out
of all Sanct Augustins Tomes)euidently prouit
yat same form of sayth and Religion vhilk nou
the aduersars of the Romane church so biterly
doth impung to haue bene vsit in the said doctors dayis à 1200.years ago or more.

Of Apostoli-
que succession
vithout the
vhilk in the
primytiue
church all do-
ctrin vas su-
spect.

Nou lest the abondance of this subiect force
me more and more to digress I begin to spek
as I haue promisit of Apostolique succession yat
is to say of the laufull lineall successiō of pastors
frō th'Apostles dayis vnto this present age:vhilk
lineall succession vhar it is not conioynit vith
the doctrin of th' Apostles thair can be no
church Apostolique. Bot the enemis of the Romane church laking this marque do reiect it as
à thing not necessar as did the Arrians and Donatists vho dispysing all doctrin yat culd not be
cōfirmit by expres text of scriptur thai culd not
abyid to hear any man spek ether of traditions
or of laufull succession of bischops. Bot this
marque of successiō vee suld the more villingly
resaue for yat thair is not almost one of the holy fathers vho has not estemit it amág the most

Lib.4.ca.63.

principall marques of the church. Firſt Irenæus
vho ves nixt the Apoſtles dayis} did agknouleg
the ſame ſaying. the treu knouleg (or mark of
the church) is treu doctrin and the ancient ſtat
or dignitie of the church obſerued throuch all
the vorld by ſucceſſion of biſchops cōtinuit vnto our tyme. and agane the ſame Irenæus com-
māndit to obey only ſuch biſchops as haue thair
ſucceſſion euidently deſcending from the Apoſtles, vho vith the grace of veritie (or treu doctrin) haue reſauit the certane ſucceſſion of Epiſcopat: all others vharſoeuer thai be eſtabliſſet
he holdet for ſuſpect. And Tertullian not long
after him ſpeking agās the Heretiques of his tyme. I vold (ſayis he) thai ſuld ſcheu me by vhat
authoritie haue thai cum to licht (or to authoritie, let thā produce the originalls of thair churches: let thame ſcheu the ordor (or lineaʼl deſcent) of thair biſchops by ſucceſſiō deſcending
from the beginning in ſuch ſort as thair firſt biſchop can exhibit ſum Apoſtle or Apoſtolique
perſon (yat is to ſay placit and perſeuering vith
th' Apoſtles) to be his author and predeceſſor, as
the church of ſmyrna can exhibit Polycarp placit by S. Iohn and the church of Rome Clemēt
placit by S. Peter. this much Tertulliā. and Origenes almoſt in the ſame age vith Tertulliā ſayit
in this ſort. In reſpect (ſayit he) thair be many
yat beleif thai think as Cryſtians ſuld think and
yit ſum of tham hold opinions different from
former biſchops: in ſuch difference let the Eccle
ſiaſtique preching Ioynit vyth ordinar ſucceſſiō
preſcryuit

Lib.4.ca.43.

Tertull. in the
præſcriptions
agans Here-
tiques.

Origen in the
proem of his
1.book callit
periarchon.

prescryuit by th' Apostles and continuit to our
age be aluay obseruit, For yat is only to be estemit vndouted veritie vhilk in nothing disagreit
vyth Apostolique tradition. Sanct Cyprian hauing respect vnto this laufull and lineall successió doth affirm the Church to be vhat PopeCor-
nelius vas not vith Nouatius vho culd produce
no euidét of Apostolique succession. Sanct Hierom vritting to Pope Damasus doth for this
same caus highly extoll the laudabill successió of
the Bischops of Rome saying. I spek vith the suc
cessor of Sanct Peter and vith the disciple of the
crofs, and follouing none bot Cryst by communion or consent I associat my self vith your bea-
titud yat is to say vith the chair of Sanct Peter.
Vpó yat roque I knou the church to be beildit:
vhosoeuer out of yat hous doth eat his paschall
lam is prophan, and vho beis not found in yat
ark during the deluge sall perifs. and à littill after. I knou not (sayit he) vitalis, I despyis Miletus,
I compt not much of Paulin⁹ (vho haue no laufull successió loynit vith thair doctrin) bot vho
gatherit not vyth Damasus he scatterit, for he
yat is not of Cryst is ane anticryst. Sanct Augustin in many places doth agkouleg this note of
succession in expres vordis pronúcing such to
be out of the church as separating thair self fró
thair ordinary successiue bischop do ether establis thair self or any vther to be Prelats, Pastors
or bischops. and vritting agains the epistle of
Manicheus 4 chap. theis be his vordes. Many
things hold me most iustlie vithin the bosome

N

of the church, the consent of pepill and nations
the authorite begun vith miracles, nurissit vith
hoip, augmented by charitie, confirmit by antiquitie and successiue preisthood continuing vnto this present bischop of Rome from Sāct Peter the Apostle vnto vhom our lord after his resurrection recommendit his scheip to be fed.

In the begin- and agane vnto the Donatistis Numer (sayis he)
ning of his 7. our preists from Sanct Peter and considder in
Tom. epist. 16 yat succession of fathers vho hes succedit vnto
agans the Do- vther. Yat seat is the roque vhilk the proud
nat. ports of hell can not preuaill vpon &c. and mo-
Optat. 2. book rouer in his epistle to Generosus he doth num-
Agans the ber all the bischops of Rome from S. Peter vn-
Donatists. to Anastasius then Pope. as Optatus in yat same age did inlykmaneir vritting agans Parme-
nian⁹ in this sort saying that the Episcopall seat
ves first geuin to Sanct Peter (to peter sayis he)
the head or cheif of the Apostles and tharfor
ves callit Cephas being head, as thai be callit schis-
matiques vho go about to erect ane vther chair
aganis this capitall chair. tharfor (sayis he) in yat
singular chair (vhilk is the first or principall) peter first satt vnto vhom linus did succeid (albeit
Clement vas nominat befor Linus) and so nu-
mering all the Romane Popes from Linus vnto
Syricius vho then occupyit the place at lenth he
brusted out in theis spechis. Scheu (sayis he) the
origin of your church, you vho vsurp the name
of the holy church. and ancient Irenæus did vse
the lyik enumeratiō of Romane bischops, vhilk
enumeratiō Eusebius did register in his 5. book

6.chap.of the Ecclesiastique History.

Then seing theis holy ancient and lernit Doctors, Irenæus, Tertullian, Cyprian, Hierom, Angustin, Optatus &c. be vniform defendars of this Apostolique succession I am bold to côprehend the same vnder this epithet or mark of Apostolique vhatsoeuer the enemis of the Romane church obiect to the conttarie. demanding of thame vith Tertullian and Optatus by vhat authoritie, thai do vsurp any authoritie, vissing tham to exhibit the origin of thair churchis, to expone the ordor or lineall descent of thair bischops, to name vhilk Apostle or Apostolique person hes bene thair first predecessor frô vhom thair preisthood or Episcopat hes succesfiuly and incessantly continuit vnto thair self. bot thai be not habill to scheu any such seruice or retour and tharfor thai must be estemit violent possessoris meriting to be eiected for thair Laules intrusion.

It ver too tedius particularlie to repeat all parteis and passages vhilk proue the church to be euidentlie knouin by this Apostolique successiô euer esteming the same succession as necessarlie to be côiunit vith treu doctrin as the print or armes of à Prince be vnto his money or as subscriptions and sealis be vnto attentik euidents.

If so be: then remouing all partialitie let vs à littil perpend and confidder vhilk church this day contending to merit the name of the treu church may exhibit clear testimoneis of Apostolique succession ioynit vith thair doctrin ex-

cept onlie the church Romane, vhilk by à continuall course or continuation of 236. bischops li-
neally succeeding one to ane vther from Sanct
Peter vnto this present most Clement Clemét
the.8.câ qualitie hir beginning, progres and present estat by testimoneis extractit out of the at-
thentik protocolls of famus historians and Doctors. and if none bot sche câ produce such euident arguments and indenyabill instruments,
suirly thai be too effronted and schamles that
deny hir to be Apostolique lyk as sche is alredy
prouin to be holy, Catholique and vniform and
tharfor the vndouted treu church militant. For
this cause separating our self from hir, impugning, moking or douting of hir authoritie ve becum parttakers and subiect vnto the punitions
of him yat vncouerit âd irridit his fathers schâ,
of tham yat did resist vnto Moyses, of tham yat
scornit to inter vithin the ark and of such as in
the desert douting of Gods promisis ver neuer
permitted to intre vithin the land of promissió,
and to be schort albeit it nether becummit me
nor vill I pronúce any hard sentence agans thâ
yat be separated in maneir forsaid villingly or
vnuillingly fró the glorî societie of this church,
because I do agknouleg the merceis of God not
only to be hid from vs as is his Iustice bot also
his merceis to be so infinit as thai exceid all his
vorks: Yit the ancients hes not sparit to compair
such persons to à canall or strâd cut of from his
fontane, to ane brench sned of his tree, to à mé-
bre cutt of his body âd to theis yat ver vithout

the ark during the deluge vnto vhom as thair
ves no fautie ſo doth the ſaid Doctors much
dout of the ſaluation of the vther pronuncing
yat in heauin thai ſall not haue God to be thair
father vho in the erth doth diſdane to admit
the treu church to be thair mother.

Bot heir I muſt ſaill à ſea of innumerabill cō-
tum elies th enemis of the Romane church all
crying and conteſting yat hir biſchop is ante-
chryſt and ſche the ſynagog of Sathan. Vharunto I vill auſuer vith greter modeſtie nor the ſalt-
nes of ſuch ſkandalus imputations doth merit
intending by Goodis grace to proue yat as the
infallibill marques deſingning the treu church
be only proper to the Romane church and hir
adherēts,ſo the propre marques in Scriptur deſingning the Antichriſt and Synagog of Satan
can not vithout manifeſt impudence and partialitie be attribut vnto hir ād hir holy biſchop.
in treating vharof I vill alleg no friuoll or ambiguus places vhilk eury party at thair pleſor doth
throu as à noſe of vax,as yat of the Apocalyps
ſpeking of the number of the beſt (vhilk as it is
applyit to the vord λατινος euin ſo the name of
Martinus Luterus vrittin in Hebreu lettres gro-
uit to the ſame number of 666.)and ſuch vther
Prophetique and profound paſſages ill vnder
ſtand to the perdition of the peruertars. I vill allanerly produce thre or four placesvhilk boyth
ſpek moſt clearly and vhilk the aduerſaris vſe
moſt ordinarly in this matter.

The firſt place is in the Epiſt.to the Theſſal.

That the po-
pa is not the
Anticryſt nor
Rome the ſy-
nagog of Sa-
tan.

Apoc.13.cha)

chap.2. vhar it is faid.Yat the Antecryſt ſall be the man of ſin ,the ſone of perdition and ſall extoll him ſelf aboue all yat is callit God or yat is vorſchippit ,in ſo much as he ſall ſitt in the tempill of God oſtenting him ſelf as if he ver God. The ſecond paſſage is in 1.of Io.2.chap.vhar it is faid:Vho is à lyar bot he yat denyit Ieſus to be Cryſt or the anoynted,and thus is the Antecryſt.The thrid paſſage is out of the xi.of Daniel vhar the Prophet ſayit ſpeking of the Antecryſt.Yat he ſall not agknouleg the God of his fathers and yat he ſall contem all goddis or godhead becaus he ſall exalt him ſelf aboue all.Vpon vhilk paſſages all the anciēts do agre yat the ſaid Antecryſt ſall proclam him ſelf to be the Meſſias and yat he ſall go about to tread vnder foot all Chriſtian doctrin that is to ſay preching of the vord, miniſtration of the Sacraments,yea the hoill ſcriptur.

Nou let vs try if any of theis monſtruus marques may be iuſtly applyit vnto the church Romane and Paſtors tharof, vho haue not only bene cheif propugnators of Cryſt and his ſcripturs from his aſcenſion vnto this hour,bot alſo of popes or Romane biſchops more nor à thretty haue ſealled vith thair hart blood the loue ād loyalty thai did bear vnto Cryſt Ieſus our bleſſed ſauior.Agane in the year of one lord 327. vho did conuocat the famus counſall of Nice for condemning the hereſie of Arrius affirming yat Cryſt Ieſus ves not cōſubſtantiall vyth God the father?Vas it not Pope Silueſter?vho did cōuocat in the year of our lord 383.the counſall of

Conftantinople to repres the Herefie of Mace-
doni⁹ denying the diuinitie and godhead of the
holy fpreit, vas it not Pope Damafus? Vho did
conuocat the counfall of Ephefus in the year
436. agás Neftori⁹ affirming thair vat tuo perfons
in Cryft, vas it notPope Celeftin⁹? vho did cōuo
cat thecoūfall of Chalcedō in the year 454. agás
Eutyches alleging yat our bleffed fauior after
his incarnatiō had ōly our humane nature, vas it
not PopeLeo the firft? vho did cōfirmvyth thair
Apoftolique authoritie all vther cōfalles affem-
bled for extinguifing of Herefeis as in Cartage
and Mileuetum agans the Pelagiens denying
the neceffitie of the grace of God for affifting vs
in fulfilling his commandements, and in many
vther places agans the Donatifts, Manicheans,
Luciferians, Angelites, Anthropomorphites, A-
pollinarifts, agás Cerynthus, Bafilid, Carpocrates, Hermogenes, Valens and the reft vnto this
day? Var not all theis Herefeis and Heretiques
fuppreffit by the Popes ād pouer of the church
Lomane? for none bot thai had vith à laufull
authoritie ane ernift yeall and competent pouer conioynit to refift fo many mychty Emprors
and fubtill Schifmatiques. if fo be he muft be à
ftráge Antecryft yat hes fo ftoutly defendit the
doctrin of Cryft (yea fum tyme vith effufion of
his auin blood)and fche muft be à ftrange Syna-
nage of Satā yat can not fuffer perfons or fpreit-
tis Satanicall or Hereticall remane vithin hir
fanctuary.

Let tham aufuer heirunto vith confideration

and not vith contention vith mondeſtie and no
malice:may thai luſtlie ſay yat the Popes bypaſt
or the preſent Pope (if he be thocht more intollerabill not the former)that he hes exalted him
ſelf aboue all yat is callit God or yat is adorit as
God? Seing he doth humill him ſelf as the meaneſt ſeruad of God to veſch, to veep,to kiſs the
feet of verey miſerable perſons (vharunto I
vas à ſeing vitnes in the laſt year of Iubilee
1600.) miniſtring alſo vnto thame all neceſſars
for food and rayment as thai had bene his do-
meſtiques or proper childring : in ſo much as
the almeſs vhilk his holines did euery day be-
ſtou vpó pilgrims ād poor ós vas'à matter incredibill : for in Trinitie hoſpitall at Rome(beſyid
à gret many of vther houſes ād hoſpitalles vhilk
var all repleniſſit) I did ſee more thonſands logit all at one tyme tharin nor can be veill truſtet
by tham yat knou not the place. This vas all the
ambitió yat indifferent beholdars culd perſaue
in him to vit to be à faythfull diſpenſator and
diſtributar of Sanct Peters patrimony ſpirituall
and temporall vhilk is in effect to be ſeruand of
ſeruands yat is to ſay yat poſſeſſing all he poſſeſ-
ſit no thing,and being greteſt and higheſt of all
he notuythſtanding rendrit him ſelf to be the
humilleſt and meaneſt of all:in the former follouing the aduyis of the Apoſtle in the laſt the
counſall of Cryſt Ieſus.

Agane hes his predeceſſors or he denyit Ies?ₜto
be the anoynted? The marteriſed blood of ſum
Popes paſt and the holy lyf of him yat is preſent

fent, yea heuin and erth vith all fuch as fetting partialitie apart vill behold his laudabill actiõs be fo many vitneffis to the cõtrary euidétly declaring yat as his faid predeceffors fparit nethet lyf nor liuelod to mak Iefus be knouin the anoynted: So he follouing thair footfteps doth fpair no coft nor panês agans allHeretiques and infidelles to th'end yat thai may boyth deuly vnderftand Cryft to haue bene crucifeit for thim and to lern for his faik agane to crucifie all thair concupifcence contradictions and curiofiteis.

Can any man be fo impudent as to fay yat ether thai or he haue cõtemnit the God of thair fathers feing yat boyth in and out of feafon thai haue perfuadit and he prefently doth pray, perfuad and importun not to tranfgres the limites or marks of Chriftian Religion inftitut by God and obferued by our fathers. His increbibill cair throuch allChriftendome to reduce all Heretiques to this Chriftian confideration, his diligence to vnit all Chriftian Catholique Princes (as he hes of lait vnited the moft Chriftian and Catholique kings) his extraordinar and fumpteus charges to preferue Chriftian dominiõs (namly in pannony and vther places from the violéce of the Turk the Archiinfidell and capitall conténer of God) togidder vith his almefs deadis daylie beftouit for goddis caufs vpon more nor ten thonfand indigents, his irreptchenfibill lyif and Good exempill in all his actions boyth publict and priuat fpecially vhenas he celebra-

ted or affifted vnto diuyn feruice his humiliatiõ
thairin being accúpaneit vyth fuch burning ar
deur, contufions and tears as veill expres the fupernaturall fontane and furnace of the holy
fpreit (cõparit vnto fyir and vatter) to poffes his
hart: otheruayis hou culd it be by naturall operation yat at one tyme fuch cõrrarius effectis of
floods and flams fuld glans and goufch out by
the canalls and conduir of his ardent and allbe
grouttin eyis: all theis arguments proue yat he is
no contemner of God, and yat he can not be
callit Antechrift bot by fum antiches nor the
church of Rome the fynagoge of Satan bot e-

Of the hoor ther by fum Ironie, arrogance or ignorance.
of Babylon. The fourt paffage is extracted out of the 17.
Apocal. Vhar Sanct Io. defcryuit the feat of
the Antechrift in this fort, faying. I *did fee à vomã*
fitt vpon à beaft of coccin or cramfin colour hauing fe-
uin heads and ten hornes replenißit vith names of
blafphemy, and in the forhead tharof vas vrittin à
myfterie, gret Babylon, *mother of fornications and ab-*
hominatiõs of the erth, and I *did fee the voman drõk*
vith the blood of sainéts. and à littill after. *The fe-*
uin heads be feuin montans vpon vhilk the voman
doth fitt and at th' end of the fame chaptor, *the*
voman vhom you did fee is the gret citie vhik regnit
ahoue all the kings of the erth, By this paffage v-
henas I had not fo much as remouit one ftone of the Romane church more nor rabfake
did of the church of Ierufalem for all his rail-
ling, I did nothuithftanding once think yat lyk
ane other Iofue agans Ierico by the only found

of this fentéce I had maid hir baftions and bul-
uerks equall vnto the groũd,lyk as all enemis
of the faidRomane church cõtinu ftill in the felf
fame ignorance and induration : for thai alleg
faft and firm yat all this prophefie ves forfpo-
kin of Rome vhilk hauing feuin hills hes alfo
had the empyir aboue all vther kings,yɔa aboue
the hoill vorld:as alfo yat fche is dronk vyth the
blood of Sainɕts as of theValdenfes,Albigenfes,
Huffits,Viklefits,Lutherians,&c.that fche is the
mother of many abominations be refon of the
multitud of fins reigning in hir : That in vther
places of fcriptur fche is callit Babylon as in
the firft epift.of Sanɕt Peter laft chap.Vhilk is
confirmit by authoritie of the fathers. firft by
Tertulliã in his book agãs the Ieuis and. 3. book
agans Marcion.Saying yat Babylon mentionat
in Sanɕt Io. is the figur of Rome.Nixt by Sanɕt
Ierom vritting vpon the 47.chap.of Ifayas and
in his 2.book agãs Iouinian about the latter end
tharof, and in his epiftle to Marcellin vhar he
callit Rome the porpre or fkarlat hoor,Thridly
by Sanɕt Auguftin in his 18. book of the citie of
God chap. 22.Vhar he callit hir ane vther Baby- *Orof.lib.2.*
bylon.and Laft of all by Orofius vho by many
argumёts goeth about to perfuad yat fche,ɩgreit
vyth Babylon in many refpeɕts.For vhilk caufes hir aduetfars conclud hir to be the feat of
the Antɩcryft and hir bifchop to be the only antecryft. *Matth.10.*

Vharunto I anfuer yat the forfaid paffages of
holy fcriptur and anciёts proue nɔ́moir the Po -

O ij

pe and church Romane to be Anticryſt and the
Antichriſts ſeat nor yat of th'Euangell vhar it
is ſaid I came not to bring peace bot the ſuord
doth proue Cryiſt to be the author of diſcord
and not of concord. For thai vho comprehendit
Rome vnder the name of Babylon thai did
tak Rome for the Citie and empire of Rome
not for the church Romane. and yat Rome
vhilk in thair opinion vas Babylon, the pur-
purit harlot and the gret citie dyit in the
blood of the Sainćts, vas Rome Ethnique not
Rome Chriſtian, the empyir of Rome and not
the Romane church. to be ſchort yat Rome
vhilk is deſignit vnder the name of the hoor of
Babylon is not Linus, Cletus Clemens and thair
faythfull ſucceſſors, bot Nero, Domiti⁹, Diccle-
ſian: Yat is to ſay not Rome ſuffring patiét, Apoſtolique: bot Rome perſequutor, infidell Anti-
apoſtolique.

In this ſort Tertulliã in the forſaid place doth
expone him ſelf ſaying: Babylon is à figure of
the citie of Rome not of the church Romane.
I do notuythſtanding confes the citie of Rome
to haue ſurpaſſed boyth Babylon of Egypt and
Chaldæa for pryid and perſequution of the ſer-
uants of God: for as the Chaldæan and Ægyptiã
kings did afflićt the Hebreu church, ſo did the
Romane emprors much more perſequut the
poor Chriſtian church : For by thair meanes
boyth Cryſt him ſelf and Peter and Paul the
principalls of the Apoſtles vith many Romane
biſchops and ane infinit multitud of vther con-

stant Chriſtians var martyred partly at Rome
partly at Ieruſalē partly at vther places ſubiect
to thair dominions. and for this cauſe Sanct
Hierom after he had callit Rome à Babylō and
purpurd hoor &c. For the multitud of ſins vhilk
regnit in hir(as vſually thai do in all gret citeis) *Hierom epi-*
he addit notuythſtanding theis vords, ſaying *ſtle to Mar-*
thair is in hir ane holy church,à treu profeſſion *cellin chap. 7.*
of Cryſt and the trophees or enſeinges of many *book agans*
bleſſed Martyrs and morouer by this confeſſiō *Iouinian.*
of Cryſt(ſayis he)the blaſphemy or myſterie v-
rittin in the forhead of that citie, is effaced and
veapt auay.For theis be his vords in yat ſame
place ſpeking to Rome. Vnto the I vill ſpek o
potent citie commendit by the voyce of th' A-
poſtle vhilk by confeſſion of Cryſt hes veapt
auay the blaſphemy vrittin in thy forhead.

Rome then in reſpect of hir Ethnique Empyir and perſecurion of Cryſtians mycht veill
haue bene callit Babylon bot in reſpect of the
Chriſtian church yat euer hes bene in hir ſen
the dayis of th' Apoſtles ſche nether vas callit
nor vas Babylon. Morouer (if vee ſall ether giue credit to hiſtoreis or Doctors of the prim i-
ue church) it is certane yat vhen Nero tyranni-
ſed in Rome Sanct Peter dogmatiſet thair vnto
yat church vhilk in the laſt chap.of the firſt e-
piſtle of S.Peter is callit th' elect church vhilk is
in Babilō ād yat after S.Peter thair var many holy Romane biſchops martyriſed thair by infidell
ēprors boyth th' one ād vther remaning at one
tyme vithin the ſaid citie.Yea after the emprors

tharof becam Christians sche did ceas any more in any respect to be Babilonique, and vas callit Apostolique if vee may trust antiquitie.

Vharfor vhenas Sanct Augustin and Orosius
doth compare hir vnto Babylon all yat is in respect of ethnique infidell emprors not in respect of the Christian, faytfull pastors and treu
church. and this phrase of spech as it had bene
of auld so is it in this age vsit. For as the prophe-
seis yat var agans Ierusalem being yit Iebusæan
an Cananæan vas not meant of Ierusalein Hæ-
bræan or Iudæan, nor the threttinnings pronūcit agans Ioram, Achab, Zedechia directed agás
Iosias, Iosaphat ád Ezechia So in theis dayis the
acerbitie vhilk many protestant ministers vse
agans sindry Citeis, nations, and peapill is not
meant of thair auin felloubrethring remaning
in such citeis and nations bot of thair aduersars
as for exemple. Vhen thai call paris à den of idolatrie and à goufre of all vyce, tharin thai only
comprehend Catholiques Romane and not
thair auin confrerie duelling in Paris: Vhen at
Paules thai call london à Laque of Licherie and
at Sanct Geles, Edinbnrg à boucherie, à Bordell
and brybing house: by theis vords thai mean no
thing les nor of thair auin churchis in lódon ád
Edinburg, designing only tharby vhoormon-
gers, homicids ád corrupt Iuges duelling in the
one and vther place.

Bot I remember sum tyme to haue redà more probabill interpretation of this passage of S.
Iohn. collected out of Sáct Augustin and Sanct

Augusſt. vpö
61. Psal. and
of the Citie
of God 20.
book. 9. chap.
commentars
vpon the A-
poc. put out
vnder the na
me of Sanct
Ambrose ád
ane vther cō-
mentar amāg
the vorks of
S. Augustin.

Ambrose vho do not interprit theis seuin montans for theis seuin materiall hills of Rome (in
vhilk this day nether the Pope nor the Roma
ne peapill doth duell bot in yat place vhilk ves
callit campus Martius) Nor the purpurd harlot
ãd coccin beast, nor Babylõ ãd the seuin heads
and gret citie for Rome or any one particular
Empyre or citie, or societie of vickit men yat hes
molested the church of God sen the Ascension
of Cryst: bot thai tak the same in ane vther sens
more agreing vith the text, esteming the said seuin heads and seuin montans &c. to be seuin diuers kingdoms vhilk hes persequuted the
church of God boyth befor and after the incarnation of Cryst: yat is to say the Egyptiens
in Moyses dayis: the Cananæans after Iosue vas
dead: the Babyloniãs vnder Nabuchodonosor:
the Persians vnder Darius and Cyrus: the Grecs
vnder Allexander and his successors namly by
Antiochus Epiphanes: and theis be fyue kingdoms yat vexit the Hebreu church. the Saxt vas
the Romane Empyir and the seuint sall be the
gret Antecryst vhilk destroying the said Romane Empyir sall go about also to destroy the
church of Cryst. and theis be the seuin heads or
hills of vhillk (as the same Sanct Io. doth
say) fyue var past and gone befor his dayis that
is to say the empyirs preceding the Romane
vhilk did torment the Hebreu church. and one
nou is(sayt S. Iohne) yat is to say the Romane
Empyir vhilk in S Iohns dayis did domin, and
the other or the last (sayis he) is not yit cum and

cúming it behouit him to left bot à schort space, and this is the Antecryst, vhilk sall not be the
hoill beast, or hills, or heads bot one or the last
of the said hills, heads or kings. Vharby it is euident yat the Romane Empvre must be endit ād
gone befor the Antecryst begin and yat the said
Antecryst sall bot left à à schort tyme if vee vill
credit this same text of Sanct Io. allegit: Bot the
Romane Empyr yit doth left in the hous of Au-
strisch and the Popes haue continuit nou neir
by 2600. year: tharfor thai can not be vyth reson
estemit the Antecryst nor Rome the Synagoge
of Satan: It apperit rather yat the Antecryst sall
sit in Ierusalem nor in Rome if vee sall ether beleif Sanct Paul or the said Sāct Io. th' one saying
yat he sall sit in the tempill of God, th' other in
the 11. of th' Apocalyp. saying yat the beast or
Antecryst. Sall kill the tuo vitnessis in the gret
citie vhilk is spiritually callit Sodom and Egypt
vhar thair lord vas crucifeit: vhilk must apperātly be meanit of Ierusalem vhar the tempill of
God vas and vhar Cryst vas crucifeit and not in
Rome.

Bot all this can not content the contentius
vho still insist saying yat albeit the Romane
church hes resisted vnto Heretiques and maid
much in scheu of the text of scriptur, yit thai ha
ue so corrupted the sens tharof, infected the sacraments and forged such errors as sche is altogidder intollerabill. Vhirunto I ansuer vith in-
terrogation demanding if the scripturs haue bene puirly interprit vithout Heresie or infection
or the

or the Sacraments deuly adminiſtrat at any tyme à 1300.year ago?if thai ſall grãt(as thai muſt
neads orells condem many vhoſe ſcho lachets
thai be not vorthy to looſs)thē do I as the treuth
is affirm yat boyth the doctrin and decent ordor Eccleſiaſtique vſit in the primityue antiquitie forſaid Yea at yat ſame tyme vhen the Chriſtian fayth vas firſt planted in Scotland (vhilk
vas about à 1400.year ago)is vſit preſently and
obſeruit in the Romane church. For probation
tharof nedit no more bot to reid the confeſſiõs
Auguſtinian prented in places vnſuſpect and
fathfully collected out of S. Auguſtin vho flo-
riſſit about à 1200.years ago:vith the Hierarchy
ãd Apoſtolique inſtitutiõs of Dioniſ the Areo-
pagit and of Clemens Romanus vho var auditors of the Apoſtles.

For all this,the inſatiabill vill not yit be ſati-
feit ſtill replying yat the names of tranſſubſtan-
tiatiõ,purgatory,meſs &c.var not hird of à lõg
tyme after the Aſcéſion of Cryſt Ieſus.I anſueir
Yat no more ver the ſacred names of trinitie ãd
conſubſtantiall vſit or hard of till more nor à
300.years after the Aſcéſion:and the reſon is for
yat neu errors producing neu erronius vords to
obſcuir or corrupt the veritie gaue occaſion to
the ancients for illuſtration of the ſaid veritie to
inuët and vſe neu religius names in matters cor-
rupted.Euin as if à fyne pretieux ſtone ſuld be
douted vpon and brocht in queſtion amangs
vnskilfull lapidars,and as if the auner the more
to ſcheu the bonte and beaute tharof ſuld poli-

P

se and inchaſs it in pure gold and tharefter call it not à pretieux ſtone bot à bage, à button or targat according to the neu form reſauit the ſtone aluay remaning in the auin nature notuithſtanding this neu nomination procurit by the ignorance of the lapider not by any craft or malice of the auner. Euin ſo the ancients partly to obuiat Heretiques, partly to inſtruct ignoráts haue found out many neceſſary vords for edification of the church (lyk vnto the forſaid) neuer peruerting the nature or ſubſtance of things ſignifeit tharby.

Agane thai can not auay vith coppes, cornerd cappes, mitres, ſurplices &c. eſteming all theis to be recent and ridiculus: bot thai forget yat roúd bonnetts, ſyid gounes and larg breikks, mules and skarpins ver not in vſe in th'Apoſtles dayis (vho vér for the moſt part bairfoottit and bairleggit) nether ſall vee fynd in ſcriptur or Eccleſiaſtique Hiſtory the names of companation brocht in by Martin Luther, of imputation brocht in by to Io. Caluin, of Proteſtants inuéted in Germany and of commiſſionars, moderators, modifiers vith many more inuented amags our ſelf. and the treuth is yat apparell and ceremoneis be bot things indifferent and mutable and ſuch as merit not of neceſſitie to be authoriſed by antiquitie: yit the moſt part of Romane ceremoneis ſall be foond in Sanct Deniſe and Sanct Clement vho var auditors of the Apoſtles as is afor ſaid. Morouer I haue obſeruit in Proteſtant churchis the ſelf ſame libertie in

changing of rites and rayments at the plesor of
thair minister and consistory. For in sum places
thai baptis befor, in sum places after sermon:
Sum resaue thair communion kneling, sum pas-
sing, sum sitting and in sum places the vemen
stand and the men sitt only at thair table: in sum
places men be commandit to communicat in
thair best, in vther places in their verst apparrell
and In sum places be vsit (for marques to inter
to thair table)billzetts of stapit paper or kardes,
others thinking such marks of kards sumvhat
prophan vill haue none bot of lead. heirby may
the indifferent readar considder if the Romane
church authorised vyth so many euident arguments of ancient possession and precedence be
much to blame in vsing neu names rites and ceremoneis in the policie of thair church seing
neu intrants laking all laufull authoritie ancient
or modern presum daylie to form and reform
neu vords, rites and ceremoneis after thair auin
appetit.

Morouer vhar thai say yat the Romane church
doth go about to discredit the authoritie of scripturs vsurping pouer aboue tham as things imperfyit and insufficient, calling tham à diuinitie
of ink ane nose of vox à reull of lead &c. to the
end thai may bring in thair traditiôs repugning
to scripturs. Tharunto I ansr yat if it be vsurpa-
tion of any authoritie aboue thame or contemning of tham to agknouleg not only the hoill
body tharof bot euin eury period or clause tharof to be most puir perfyit and sufficient in th:

The Romane church doth not vsurp any pouer aboue the scriptur.

P ij

self abeit yat in respect of our grosnes , imperfection and insufficiency thair nedit many things
to mak our dulnes comprehend tham (as the
treu interpretatiõ tharof, ministration of the sa-
crements by persons me it for yat function vith
many ceremoneis and supplements for celebration of diuyne seruice and support of our insufficiency): Vhilk suplements the nouators thair
self be forcit to vse vith no les confidence nor as
if all thair formes var expreslie contenit vithin
the compas of holy scriptur:if this I say be to discredit the scripturs the said nouators be socij
criminis yea more criminall nor Catholiques
vho haue the primityue church for thair author
in any traditiõ thai vse the said nouators hauing
no authoritie bot thair auin. Bot to mak this
matter euident by exemples.Canst you deny bot
yat thy Prince and his authoritie Royal in the
self is sufficient aneuch to gouern his realan?Yit
you seest yat the same Royall authoritie must di-
still as from à fontane by seuerall cãnalles thro-
chout all places and persons hauing nead tharof, as by his bailleis,steuartis , Schriffees Com-
missars,Courtes and sessions:vharby his dignitie
Royall is no thing diminissit by such as think
theis subaltern cõplements neadfull for the seruice of his realme.Bot to hold vs at matters of
the same nator vith that vharof ve treat.Behold
the passion of Cryst Iesus is sufficient in the self
to saue vs, yit befor the same can be applyit vnto vs many vther accessory matters and Christian exercises be necessar(as fayth,hoyp ,chari-

tie, prayers, penitence, and holy lyif &c.) and in
one vord. is any thing more sufficient nor he yat
is all sufficient? yit yat supreme sufficiency disdanit not bot hes determinit subaltern cooperators to concur vyth him boyth in actions naturall and spirituall, begetting vs by our parents,
nurissing vs by naturall food, defending vs by
Magistrats, instructing vs by his holy vord and
prechors tharof, finally he ordorit all things on
erth yat kepit any ordinar course by the ministry
of sum other things yat be not of his essence:
Yit the vsing of theis ministeriall cooperators
(taking aluay thair originall pouer from him)
doth not argue or convict his maiestie of any in-
sufficiencye: Euin so all imperfection or insufficiency yat is or can be obiected vnto the scripturs is bot in respect of vs: For thai be in thair
self as à sufficient quantitie of fyne and sufficiet
seed and ve be as ane feild yat long hes Lyin vn-
laborit vnfit and insufficient ether to resaue the
said seid or to bring out any fruit tharby except
Vve be pleuit, harrouit heggit or hirdit and vat-
tred from aboue. So if at any tyme the said scripturs vhilk in the selfbe as inflexibill and firm
as à vall of brass and more significatiue nor humane sens can comprehend, if notuystanding
tharof thai be callit à diuinitie of ink, à reull of
lead à nose of vax all yat is in respect of such as
vrest, throu ãd peruert thame to thair auin perdition as sayit Sanct Peter in one place, delyting
in yat vhilk the said Apostle in ane vther place
hes expreslie defendit to vit in priuat interpre-

P iij

Pet. 2 epist. 3.
chap.
Pet. 2. epist.
11. chap.

tations of prophefeis or fcripturs. of vhilk perfons thair hes euer bene Good ftoir throuchout
all ages fen the afcenfion fpecially fen Martin
Luther of vhom hes procedit more nor à 60. of
fchifms all throuing the faid fcripturs to thair
auin priuat fens as if thai had bene bot à reull of
lead, à nofe of vax or à diuinitie of paper and ink
and not à doctrin defcending from aboue. in
this fens S. Paul fayis yat albeit the treu fens of
fcriptur doth quikkin yᵗ the letter tharof doth
Kill. in this fens he not only callis him felf the
fauor of deth vnto fum albeit he vas the fauor of
lyf vnto Vthers bot alfo he callis Cryft Iefus the
only corner ftone to be à ftumbling ftone vnto
the reprobat.

Laft of all vharas the faid Nouators reiects as A-
pocryphe findry books ād fragmēts of holy feri
ptur vhilk the primitiue church hes refauit for
canonicall (to vitt the books, of Tobias, Iudith,
Efther, the Vifdome of Solomon, Ecclefiafticus,
Baruch, the fong of the 3. childring, the Hiftoreis
of Sufanna bell and the Dragon vith tuo books
of the Machabees follouing tharin the exempill
of ebiõ and his fellouis vho as fayis Tertulliã in
his prefcriptiõs tho thai euer appeall to fcripturs
yit vhen fcriptur is cited agans tham thai ether
deny tham to be attētik. or ells t hai expone tham
after thair auin fantafie.) all vhilk books ve fynd
rekkinnit for canonicall in findry counfalls nā-
ly in the 3. counfall of Carthage vhar Sanct Auguftin vas prefent. For probation vharof let his
cataloge be red vhilk ve fynd in his 2. book 8.

chap. de Doctrina Chriftiana and yat vhilk he
vrittit in particular of the prophefie of Baruch
in his 17.book 33.chap.de Ciuitate Dei.

Nou let any indifferent perfon Iuge betuix
Catholiques and Proteftants vhilk of the tuo
doth moft difcredit the fcripturs, vhidder thai
yat folloving thair auin priuat opinions agans
the opinions of the primitiue church vill cutt of
fuch books of fcriptur as fpek agãs thair errors
ãd vill haue all vther fcriptur(vhilk plefis tham
to admit)to be interpretit after thair fantafie:or
thai vho hes captiuat and renúcit thair auin opinions grounding thair felf vpon the pillar of
veritie obferuing after the counfall of the Apoftle 2.Theffall.2 chap.all traditions refauit ether
by vord or vrit from the Apoftles and thair vndouted fucceffors vho vith the chartor of thair
doctrin can alfo produce attétik fealls of lineall
defcent from the faid Apoftles.

And as to theis paffages fo impertinently allegit by fum fpeking of this matter,albeit fuch
friuolus allegations merit no anfsr as proceding
from men yat rether haue in poft run ouer nor
red the faid paffages or at left beleue yat other
men haue not red thame at all:Yit I vill in one
or tuo vords for the benifit of fumpill ons aufsr
tharunto. Thair firft paffage is out of the 4.of
Deuteron. Vhar it faid by Moyfes you fall nether eik nor pair to the vord yat I fpeK,&c the
fecond is in the Euangell of Sanct Io.vhar it is   *Ioan.20.*
faid.theis things be vrittin yat you may haue e-
ternell lyfe in his name. the thrid is in Sanct

Paul 1.Corinth, 4.chap.Vhar th' Apoſtle ſayis,
let no man beleif aboue yat vhilk is vrittin, and
the laſt is in the laſt chaptor of the Apocalyps.
Vhar the Euangeliſt Io. ſayit vho eikkit vnto
this, God ſall eik vnto him the plages vrittin in
this book,and vho diminiſſis from the vords of
the Propheſy of this book God ſall diminiſs his
portion out of the book of lyfe and holy citie.
as to the firſt paſſage if no thing ſuld be eikkit
nor no thing diminiſſit vnto yat vhilk Moyſes
hes ſpokin in his Pentateuch then as all the ſa-
crifices and ceremoniall lau muſt yit be kepit
ſo all books of the Prophetes and all the reſt of
the auld and neu teſtamét muſt be cut auay and
aboliſit.to yat of Sanct Iohns Euangell. Vpon
theis vords,theis things be vrittin yat you may
beleif and haue ſaluation:to conclud heir vpon
yat no thing more neadit vnto ſaluation then
that vhilk is vrittin in the ſaid Euangell:by yat
vyiſs argument you ſall cut of all the reſt of the
auld and neu teſtament in vhik be many things
vrittin yat is not to be red in the Euangell of S.
Io.To yat of Sanct Paul ſaying.let no man beleif aboue yat vhilk is vrittin, I anſsr yat beleuing vnurittin traditions I beleif no thing aboue yat vhilk by vrit I am commandit to do yea
and vthers befor me haue bene commendit for
doing the ſame.behold in 1.Corint.11.chap. the
ſame Apoſtle commendis the ſaid Corinthians
yat thai kepit his traditions and agane in the 2.
to the Theſſalonicen.2.chap.ve be commandit
to ſtand and keap the traditiós vhilk he had ge-
tiin ether

uin ether by his fermon or epiftle, vhilk is to fay
by vord or writt, vnurittin or vrittin and for the
malediction contenit in the Apocal. Vpon the
augmentars and diminiffars of the vords of the
prophefie of yat book let any equall man luge
vho meritis moft the faid malediction vhidder thai yat prefum not at all to interprit the
fame contenting thair felf in yat point (as many holy and lernit men haue done) rather in
ane reuerent ignorance nor in ane arrogant
fcience, or if thai interprit or apply any part
tharof thai aluay conform thair interpretations
vnto th' antients of the primityue church : or
thai vho vith the Gnoftiques and Anabaptiftes
prefuming to much of priuat infpirations tak in
hand to expone the miftereis of yat profond reuelation as ordinarly and confidenlie as if no
matter var tharin contenit bot fuch as var altogidder clear and Hiftoricall: Vhilk temeritie can
not be vithout dangerus diftorfion and alteration of the fens of the faid Euangelift and
tharfor can not be denyit to be ane euident and
impudet eikking and paring vhenas thai be not
afrayit to mak fcornfull mytologeis of theis facred miftereis finding the Pope and Romane
Prelatts in many paffages tharof as partially ād
Iniuftly as Achab did imput the trubiliing of If-
raëll vnto Elias and Sedecia the fone of Chanaana the fpreit of fals Prophetie vnto Micheas.

Bot of all exclamations the foreft is agans the
vitieux lyf of the Romane Clergie or church

Q

The vitiaux lyf of church men suld not mak vs abãdõ the church

men : Vharin (as Basilius Magnus in his 69. Epistle doth cõplene) vho vas most apt to blaspheme vas estemit the best prechor: Euin so is it in this miserabill age : For the enemis of the Romane church not knouing by vhat raison thai may confound hir doctrin and dignitie agans all raison thai do inuent and obiect infinit criminations agans the person of the Doctors of the said church. Vhilk kynd of vniust crimination S. Augustin also complenit to haue bene in his age the authors tharof going about by such partiall imputations and rhetoricall motions to excitat and inflam the myndes of the ignorants vhilk be euer inclynit to auarice and lnuy , and intending by this meanes no thing bot priuat commoditie and preferment thai pretend notuithstanding boyth republict and religiõ , vhilk be the tuo fals pretexts yat all factius persons haue vsit heirtofor. So did Theobutes , Simon Magus , Valentin , Marcion, Arrius,and the rest abandon and impung the virgin church incorrupted at yat tyme vith fals doctrin as sayit Eusebius in his 4.book of his Ecclesiast. Histo.all becaus thai var debarrit from the profit and preferrement vhilk thai expected vithin the said church. and heirof vee haue à most manifest exẽple in Martin Luther(of vhõ nottheles I sall be loth to alleg any thing yat can not be qualifeit by.Io.Sleydan his freind and fauteur.) For vhat caus I pray you did the saidMartin mak defection from the Romane church?bot for yat the publication of pardons or Indulgence cal-

lit of the croiſſad (and ſo namit becaus the Prechors tharof ver aſtricted to bear à croſs vpon
thair vpper garment) var granted in germany
to Frere Io.Tetzed Iacobin and not to the ſaid
Martin nor to any of his confrery of Auguſtin
Heremitts vho of à long tyme befor var prouydit to publiſs ſuch Pardons.In the mean tyme
he kneu full veill yat this Indulgence ves pro-
mulgat by Pope Leo the 10 For fiinſſing the ſta-
tly church of Sact Peter, and for gathering ſum
treſor to reſiſt Solyman vho at yat tyme by Hu-
gary had Enterit to far vithin Chriſtiendom:
notuythſtanding vharof the ſaid Martin prefer-
ring the priuat vtilitie of his particular ſocietie
to the generall vtilitie of all Chriſtiandome, of
à mok he became à malitius Enemie and of ane
Hermit ane Heretique preching agas the prodi-
galitie and pryid (tho vith greter pryid) of Pre-
laltis eury vhar crying and conteſting yat it ves
more Iuſt and neceſſary to reſiſt the Pope nor
the infidell pagan.

Bot granting vnto theis men yat Popes and
Prelatts oft haue declinit and daylie declyne
from the tenour of thair vocation polluting
thair ſelf vyth infinit vyces, is it tharfor reſo-
nabill yat the ſeat Catholique vyth the fayth
and vndouted Chriſtian doctrin vhilk thai tech
and cauſis be techit ſuld be contemnit and caſt
auay?ſeing à holy lyf tho it be à gret ornament
to ſound doctrin yit it is not the principall cauſe quhy vee ſuld follou or flee the doctor. For it
is moſt pertinently demandit by Terullian in

For the vyce of officiars offices ſuld not be biſpyſit.

Q ij

his prefcriptiõs fpeking of this purpos, fuld vee
(fayis he) approue perfons by thair fayth or the
fayth by perfons: that is to fay yat fo long as the
Pope, Paftors or Prelats do tech treu fayth and
caufe it to be techit vithin thair iurifdictiõs (lyk
as thai do if the Symboll of the Apoftles be the
treu fayth) vhat doth it belong or apertene vnto me vhat lyif thai lead? Agane vhar am I yat I
fuld luge ane vthers feruand fitting in the chair
of Sanct Peter, feing he fallit or ftandit vnto his
lord and is only to rendre compt vnto him of
his lyf and function. For vhen vee fall compeir
befor the tribunal feat of God it fail not be askit
at vs hou our cheif Pontif or Paftor hes leaued,
bot vee muft giue à rekkinning of our auin lyf
not of his, and vee muft fuffer in our auin perfons according as vee haue done (as fayit the A-
poftle): tharfor the hoill flok much les one tuo or
fum feu particular fcheip fuld not prefum to cé-
fur and put ordor vnto thair Paftor vho is apó-
ted to ordor and gouern tham: nether fuld thai
think yat it can much impefch thair belth houfoeuer he liue prouyding he conuoy and keip
tham in holfum paftures.

Bot vhat nead I by fimilitudes to explane this
matter feing Cryft him felf hes expreffit his
auin vill in this behalf faying in the 23. of Sanct
Math. the Scrybes and Pharifeis fitt in the feat
of Moyfes: do as thai bid not as thai do. For thai
fay and do not. Vhilk is to be vnderftud yat thai
command Good out of the chair off Moyfes,
bot do euill out of the chair of malice, thai fay

yat vhilk is of God bot do yat vhilk is of thair
self. then the obedience deu vnto the Good office is not to be reiected for the ill officiers nor
the vnitie of the flok to be diffolunt for the diffo-
lut lyf of the Paftor. For as fayit S. Augustin agâs
the lettres of Petiliã. firft book 2.chap. refpect
of perfons ãd not of places is the mother of all
errors:in vhilk place the faid S Aug.doth affirm
yat the fayth may be frutfully prechit euin of
perfides yat is to fay of diffoyall trators.Vee read
alfo yat our lord vouch fit once to fpek by ane *Numeri 22*
a s: Vhat thẽ can empefch his Majeftie to fpek sũ
tyme by men fubiect vnto beaftly lubriciteis?
Vee knou yat the fpreit of our lord doth breth
and bruft out vhar and in vhat fort he vill , fum-
tyms contrar the mynd and intention of tham
that hes refauit the fame.Lo Balaam being corrupted and hyred to curfs the peapill of God
vent forduart to haue done fo:bot contrar his
deliberation hou fone he did fee the pepill of
God he vas forcit to blefs tham. king Saul vent
out of fett purpofs to haue killit Dauid,bot cum- *1.Kings 19.*
ming to Nayothramatha (vhar Dauid vith v-
ther Prophetis did fing and Prophefy) the fpreit
of God did fo ouerreull him yat he did entre in
amang tham and remouing all vrath and vindication did ftrip of his clothis finging and pro-
phefeing all nakit vith the reft of yat fanctefeit
focietie. Vho knouit not the vickitnes of the
preifts in the dayis of Herod,yit thai being inquirit vhar Cryft fuld be born thai ceaffit not for

Q iij

all thair vickitnes to aufuer euin prophetically
yat he fuld be born in Bethleẽ of Iuda. Vho culd
be more curfit nor Cayphas? (For obtening his
Pontificat iniuftly he did vfe and exerce the fame more iniuftly) yit vhen as he faid yat it vas
expedient yat one fuld die for the pepill to th' end the
hoill nation fuld not perifß, he fpaK not yat of him felf
(*as fayis* S.Io.) *bot being the hie preift for*) *at year he
did* Prophefy.

Io.11.

Sanct Hierom exponing yat place of the 10
of S. Math. vho refauis à Prophet vnder the name
of à Prophet fall refaue the reuard of ane Prophet,
and vritting alfo vpõ theis vords: Vho refauis you
refauis me. The faythfull (fayis he) mycht haue
heirby taKin occafion to think yat thai var cõmãdit to refaue Iudas the trator or any fals Prophet cumming vnder the name of à Prophet:
bot (fayis he) Cryft be vay of preoccupation
doth anfuer heirũto vhenas he fayis yat the name of ane Prophet and not the perfon of à Prophet fuld be refauit and yat the refauers be vorthy of reuard albeit thai be for thair persõs vn-
uorthy yat be refauit.

Then Cryft vill not haue the perfons of Paftors to be refpected bot thair names: vhilk is to
fay yat he vill not haue vs too folift or curi9 vpõ
the lyif, merit or maners of him vhois miniftry
God vfit in gouerment of his church , vhidder
he be Iudas or Peter: bot yat vee fuld be content to knou yat he doth fit in the laufull chair
laufully, yat he is ane Apoftle, yat he is Cryft Iefus Vicelegat, à preift or bifchop ordorly auoyn-

ted out of vhofe mouth vee be commandit to
heir the vord of God.tharfor tho he be Iudas fo
long as he is ane Apoftle and exercefit the lega-
tion of Cryft our mafter let it not moue the to
contépt ãd cõtradictiõ tho he be à theif bot do
as he cõmãdit not as he doit not hauing refpect
(as fayit)S.Aug.)ũto him bot ũto hʉ lord vhoʉ legatiõ
he bearit,for vho refauit him not refauit not Cryft, in
fo far as it vas generally faid to Iudas,peter and Iohne
and to all the reft of the Apoftles vho reiected you reiected me,bot if it be y at Peter and Iohne fall vfe the
fame legatiõ you fuld ftudy boyth to obey thair vords
and to imitat thair vorks,thʉ much Sanct Auguftin.
To be fchort tho our Paftours be lyik the carpentars yat beildit the ark of noah vorking by
the vill and apontment of God the vork of our
faluation neglecting thair auin:tho thai be lyik
the candill yat clearit vs confuming the felf: tho
thai be as Mercurs ot figns fet vp in vilfum vayis
to direct vs in the rycht pathe thai thair felf ftill
remaning vithin the defolat defertsvhar thai be
fixit,vee fuld not difpyis the Good benefites of
God offrit by thame for thair leud behauior,No
more nor Noah difpyfit the ark notuythftan-
ding the vncleã beafts yat var thairin logit vith
him,nor Cryft Iefus the focietie of finuars and
Publicans.Var it not à foolifch thing in à patiét
to contem his potion becaus the Apotacary is
fubiect to feiknes? and var it not à gret fimpli-
citie to think yat the beames of the fone can be
defylit tho thai fchyne in vilanus and filthy pla-
ces:as foolifch is it for the vyces of men to abã-

2.Book agans
the epift. of
parmen.ij.
chap.

don the church vhilk is the pillar of all veritie,
or to think yat the verteu of the vord and facra-
ments can be diminiſſit by the impuritie of the
preiſt. For this cauſe in the dayis of Sanct Auguſtin the Donatiſts and in the dayis of Sanct
Bernard ſum calling tham ſelf Apoſtliquis var
boyth pronuncit Heretiques becaus that denyit
the Apoſtolique church to be any vhar bot vhar
thair vas à lyf comparable vyth yat of th' Apoſtles meſuring aluay the vtilitie of the vord and
Sacraméts by the verteu and dignitie of the miniſtres tharof.

Yat laufull By this diſcours it is euident yat the vocation
Princes and and not the lyf of Paſtors is to be reſpected, and
Paſtors hes yat à iaufall vnction or vocation h:s euer con-
euer had à comitance of th: holy ghoſt in vhatſoeuer per-
ſecret conco- ſones preferrit to b: ch:if Princes or Paſtors, as
mitance of by th: exemples of Balaam, Saul, Cayphas and
the holyſpreit others euin debauſch:r and reprobat Princes ād
houſoeuer Paſtors heirtofor reherſit is manifeſt.
t'ai ver in
lyf verteus or Yea it is alſo to be conſid:rit yat it is not vi-
vitius. thout gret reſon vhy God hes ſuffrit his darreſt
ſeruands and elect vaſchels vhom h: fand euin
to be mé agreing vith his auin hart (as vas king
Dauid) to fall moſt dangeruſl,, to th' end ve ſuld
not giue vnto men the praiſs and honor vhilk is
deu to thair office ly'c as vndoutedly ve vold
do if the ſinceritie of mé var in all points equall
vnto the dignitie of thair office. For this canſs
albeit Sanct Peter vas verey vea'c in his fayth
and theruithall moſt vnuorth:ly denyit his
lord and maſter, yit yat did not impeſch out
                                        lord al-

lord after his refurrection to cõmit his flok vnto him faying Peter fead my fcheip:nether did
the damnabill trefon of Iudas caufe the reft of
th' Apoftles to abhor his place bot mouit tham
the moir to plant ane vther tharin.by whilk tuo
exemples ve be clearlye admonifit to hold fuch
for laufull Paftors as this day fitt in the feat of
the faid Apoftles and yat be laufully authorifed
vitth thair doctrin and lineall defcent vhatfoeuer perfonall imperfection thai haue fo long as
thai poffes the faid place:as alfo the faid Paftors
falling to be difplaiffit(as vas Iudas) yit for all yat
the dignitie of the place fuld not be difdanit bot
aluay reuerenfit and the faid place rendrit vn
to fum vther more Idoneus, in Somuch as vho
vold go about to bring in any vther form in lyk
cafes thay imitat not Cryft Iefus and his Apoftles bot the turbulent ten trybes vho for the folie of à Yonug Prince did fchaik of all oblifit o-
bedience chufing à feditius Ieroboam for thair
fouerane lord and erecting in Dan and Bethell
conftitill calues contrar the tempill of Ierufalé:
Vheras thai be bound to bear vith the imperfe-
ctiõs of thair Paftors(cheiflie of fuch as be cor-
rigibill as vas S.Peter)and if any of the faid Paftors cum to be difplaiffit for high offenfes (as
vas Iudas) then fuld the confiftory of Apoftolique fucceffors elect fum vther vnto the vacant
place euin as the faid Apoftles did inftitut Mat-
thias:ve not going about at our auin hãd to ab-
rogat the dignitie for the defaltes of the Doctor
more nor ve vold vifs the minifteriall eftat to

be aboliſſit for the capitall crymes ẏat many
Miniſtres haue cõmitted: Vhilk crymes as thai
ſuld not (in our opinion)preiug nether the place nor perſons of other miniſters ẏat be innocent: no More ſuld the allegit offenſes of libe-
rius, Marcellin, Sylueſter the 2.Iohn.the 22. (in
caiſs all var treu ẏat is obiected agans tham)
animat vs agãs Innocent Popes and Prelats and
thair Apoſtolique function.

Bot to adher vnto our purpos tuiching Paſtors
I vill vpon this ſubiect for auoyding prolixitie
only alleg one exemple vrittin in ancient Anna-
les of vigilius 61.Pope in number.This Vigilius
interit to his Pontificat by vnlaufull meanis, for
by inſtigation of Auguſta the Empriſſe he procurit the baniſment and eiection of, S. Siluerius
(afteruart marteriſed for the Chriſtiã fayth)the
ſaid Auguſta being highly offendit vith the ſaid
Siluerius becaus he vold not reſtore hir freind
Authemius to his Epiſcopat of Conſtantinopill
from vhilk he vas Iuſtly eiected (as one métey-
ning the Hereſie of Eutyches) by Agapetus predeceſſor vnto the ſaid holy Siluerius. Nou Vigilius to obtene the Pontificat did promiſs vnto
the ſaid Auguſta to reeſtabliſs hir ſaid freind
and by this meanis he is maid Pope and holẏ
Siluerius caſt out. Bot the ſaid Vigilius vas not ſo
ſone inſtallit and ſet doun in the chair of Sanct
Peter vhen thair chanſit vnto him ane accident
boyth admirable and laudable. For as king Saul
going out fulfillit vith the ſpreit of malice and
of deliberat mynd to haue killit Dauid vas not

nithstanding surprised by the spreit of mansuetud far by his expectation: so Pope Vigilius Intring in to his suprem dignitie of set purpos to haue fulfillit his vnlaufull promis vas posselfit vith the holy spreit by verteu vharof (as Sanct Paul going to be à persequutar vas turnit in à Pastor) he chusit rather all reproch, ignominy and punition nor to bloit the Pontificall place of his glorius antecessors by fulfilling à filthy iniquitie promisit allanerlie vpon auarice and ambition. So after he had most Christianly and constantly indurit imprisomment famin and many vther torments by means of the said Augusta he did vith gret patience confes yat most iustly he had merit such torments and more for his iniust dealing agaus holy Siluerius. So this Vigilius at his first entree vas not vnlyik Cayphas: yit the secreit blessing of God still accnmpaneing the place and function vhilk he did posses preseruit him from accopliffing his peruersit promis.

Bot in ansring this vay to eury particular matter yat the curi⁹ and capti⁹ tak exception agas or to refut point by point eury head cótenit in the negatyue cófessió of fayth vsit vith in scotland(vhilk in effect is no thing bot à denyall of the fayth and form yat vas vsit in the churche euer till the dayis of Martin Luther or rather of Io. Caluin) it is nether my meaning nor vold I viss yat any man suld so deall vyth tham for if ve fall go and disput vpon all ceremoneis from the holy vatter vnto the hie altar ve fall bet vrágill one vith ane vther vithout edification.that for to knou if all rites and cuſtoms vithin the Romane church be laufull or not me thınk no belter mean is nor euer to reduce the aduerſrs to yat point yat thay may be cōtent to try if ſche be the laufull and treu church or not,for in trying onlyyat one point(vhilk may be done vith as litill or les pane nor to try the meaneſt of all the reſt) as on th'one part tharbyyou may in gros iuſtly declyn and deteſt all hir ceremonies trying hir not to be the treu church:ſo on th'other part being found to be the treu church (as vndoutedly ſche is)then you muſt be eſtemit too to arrogant and impudent diſpyſing hir ordonnāces houſoeuer thai ſeam conttarius to your priuat ſens For exempill vharof Behold if à ſeditieus fellou ſall ſtart vn in Scotland and find falt vith many things authoriſed by the kings laues: as ſuch à oneſuld be iuſtlic eſtemit ſeditius ſo he he var no les ſimpill yat vold auſsr'vnto him any vther vay bot yat ſuch laues proceding from à Prince hauing à laufull pouer vith incomparabill prudēce ſuld not be put in queſtiō reducing the partie aluay to yat point if he had reſon to impung the Princes authoritie.For in particulat to diſqut vith ſuch à mad headit fellou vpon the particular reſons mouing the Prince in his taxations,donations,reuocations,forfaltors, reſtitutions,pardons and punitions, &c. var à matter boyth endles and ſuch as none bot the Prince him ſelf culd veill reņder reſon for : ſeing the harts of Princes be only detected and directed

vnto and by God. Agane I fynd à lord in poſſeſſion of à fair ſeigneurie, I inter vithin the ſame,
I mark all his palices and plantations, his tryne
and tenents. I fynd ſum of his houſes to my có-
fait ſo ill ſituat ſo ill proportionat, his familie ád
fermes ſo out of ordor yat I muſt not only reprehend bot I muſt alſo put to my hand at my auin
hand and reform, and not only reform bot poſſes my ſelf vithin the ſaid lordſchip becaus I cá
reuil it better nor the heritor tharof hauing no
patience firſt to try if the ſaid lord be iuſt pro-
prietar or not. Euin ſo vhen ve ſall indifferent-
lie ponder the procedur and actions of tham yat
be moſt greuit vith the Romane church ve ſall
fynd tham no more formall nor better foundit
and tharfor thai muſt aluay be forcit to cum to
the fundamentall queſtion to try if the church
Catholique Romane be the treu church vhilk
being tryit to be ſuch ⟨as no dout it is⟩ then hir
ordónances ſuld be vithout cótradiction obeyit
and the reprehenſions, reformations, poſſeſſiós
of hir aduerſars eſtemit bot ſa mony iniuſt imputations, deformations and violent vſurpatiós,
and finially all incorrigibilly refuſing to hear hir
voyce ſuld be according to yat in the 18. of Sanct
Math. reputed for Ethniques and Publicans.

Then to conclud this ſection ſupponing yat
all var treu vhilk thai obiect agans the Romane
church vhat remeid I pray you var moſt conuenient and Chriſtian to reduce all theis turbulét
tempeſts afflicting the church vnto à quietnes
according to the vniform ancient eſtat yat ſche

vas once into, to the glory of God ãd vniuerſall
quietnes of the ſaid church. Suitly after I had
much meditat vpon this matter vith ſuch indif-
ferẽcy as my meannes culd aford I culd find no
middis more agreable or æquall to all parteis
contending then theis yat foullou.

Vhat ſeamit
the beſt re-
mead to paci-
fie all ſchiſmes
perturbing
the church.

Furſt as is aforſaid yat diſtinguiſing betuix
the name and perſons of Paſtors vee reſpect
not ſo much the vyce as the office, the Doctors
as the dignitie, the perſon as the place: Vhilk if
vee ſuld do vee ſuld neuer abãdõ or leif the ſeat
of Rome vhilk hes ſo euidẽt argumẽts of Apoſtolique ſucceſſion, albeit all var treu yat is obiected agans hir. vharunto Sanct Auguſtin expres vords did exhort the curius and contentius
of his age in his 2. book. 5. chap. agans the lettres
of Petil. Saying : *Vhat hes the chair of the Romane
church done vnto the in vhilk chair Peter once did
ſitt and nou ſittit Anaſtaſius ?* and immediatly tharefter. *Vhy callis you the Apoſtolicall chair the chair
of peſtilence? if it be becauſe men ſitting tharupon ſpek
the lau of God and do it not, did our lord Ieſus Chriſt
for the Phariſeis of vhom he ſayit (thai ſay and do
not) do any iniury vnto thair chair? no bot he reprehendit thã rẽdring aluay deu honor vnto thair chair)
ſaying in this ſort: thai ſitt on the chair of Moyſes, vhat
thai ſay do, bot do not as thai do, for thai ſay and do
not. If you ſuld follou this exempill* ſayis the holy father then ſuld you not for mẽ vhom you defame, blaſphem the Apoſtolique chair vith vhilk you vill not
communicat.

Nixt let vs vithout partialitie conſidder trou-

chout all the 1600. centureis or aages fen the natiuitie of Cryft Iefus vhat moft famus confalls
and Doctors haue bene in eury aage and lett vs
ferch out decifions of matters controuerted in
traditions or interpretations of fcriptur from
thame refauing as it ver licht at fuch as did liue
in aages narreft Cryft Iefus ād his Apoftles vho
var the licht of the vorld:for(as fayit Sanct Auguftin in his 2. Book agans Iulian the Pelagian
and in the epilog tharof, theis blafing ftarrs and
illuftre lamps of the church ar to be eftemit vn-
fufpect Iuges in yat thai neuer kneu any of the
parteis contending and fo thai be vndoutedly
voyid of all fead or fauor and irreprefenfibill
for any fufpition of partialitie. Then if I can euidently proue by Ecclefiaftique annalles and ancient Doctors yat in every age (yat is to fay
eury hundreth, year) fen the natiuitie of Cryft
our mafter the principall Doctors and counfalls
haue bene of the felf fame opinion in matters
this day controuerted yat the Catholiques Romane be of prefently, and yat thai vho haue a-
bandonnit or renuncit the faid Romane church
of Vhatfoeuer fect thai be fall neuer be-habill
to produce any one counfall or Doctor no not
any one man of Good lyif and lerning trou-
thout all ages preceding yat in all points of doctrin hes faid as thai nou fay:For befor Io. Hufs
vas neuer one in all points of his opinion:
befor Luther noue abfolutly à Lutheran:Befor
I Ieffufius, Melāchton and interimmifts vas neuer one altogidder vbiquitar or femilutheran as

Biſchop Lindamus callis tham, and befor Zuing-
glius, Æcolampadius and Io. Caluin vas neuer
one in all reſpects Æcolampadian, Zuinglian,
or Caluiniſt: ād motouer if I can proue the modern nouators to haue no vther authors and e-
xempills of thair erronius opinions ibot ſuch as
haue bene trouchout all ages condemnit Here-
retiques, it muſt be à matter indeniabill yat Catholiqus Romane be better foundit nor the ſaid
nouators. For probation heirof.

Vee fynd in the firſt age the firſt vrittars vz.
the Euangeliſts and Apoſtles, to confirm the
cheif point controuerted to vit of the reall preſence. as by Sāct Luc 22. Sanct Marc 14. ſaying
this is my body. and by Sāct Io 6. ſaying *except you
eat the fleſch of the ſone of man and drink his blood
you ſall not haue lyif* and by Sanct Paul 1. Cor. 11.
ſaying in expres vordes yat thay vho eat of this
bread and drink of this coop vnuortely thai be
gilty not of bread or vyne bot of the body and
blood of Cryiſt Ieſus: Vharby is moſt euidently
ſignifeit à drinking and eatig not of the materiall elements bot of the myſticall aliment of
Chryſts body and blood.

Lyk as vther vrittars of the ſame age hes left
vs the Liturgie or hoill ſeruice of the meſs, viſh
the ſelfſame ceremoneis and traditions yat the
Romane church doth this day vſe confirming
alſo vnto vs the conſecration and dedication of
tempills, voluntar pouertie, voues of chaſtitie,
aponting of certane tyme for faſting and penitence, the vſe of the croſs and ſigne tharof, mar-
tyrdom

tyrdom to be of Gret merit vith the primacy of
Sanct Peter. All vhilk doctrin partly in Ignatius
Linus, Polycarpus, Philo Iudæus, partly in Cle-,
mens Romanus and in Dyonisius Areopagita
auditors of the said Apostles is extant and euident. and in this goldin age feu Hereseis being
yit sprüg vp ād the Apostles being more ttublit
vith Ieuis and infidels nor vith Heretiques ve
reid of no counsall bot of yat originall counsall
haldin at Ierusalem vharin the Iudaism vas cōdemnit: Yit in the same counsall vho vill indifferently considder it he sall persaue the same
form of counsall this day obseruit in the Romane church toggider viih the primacy of Sanct
Peter manifestly confirmit in yat the said S. Peter as Chancelor and President of yat synod did
first ryis vp and brek the matter vnto the rest
schauing hou God had chosin or thocht Good
yat by his mouth the Gentils suld hear and beleif th' Euangell. And Albeit (as sayit Egesippus)
the church at yat tyme vas as one indefylit virgin yit thair did ryis vp in the flour of hir virgini-
sit desbauchit men going about to deflor hir ād
theis var the first Hereriques to vit Theobutes,
Simon Magus, Menander, allexander ærarius
and Hymeneus, vhose first heresie vas à defectiō
or à schismaticall separation from the Apostles:
and vnto such schismaticall thai must neadis be
successors vho in this age separat tham self from
the societie of yat church vhilk allone of all v-
ther can produce attentik euident of Apostolique succession.

S

In the second age cheif Ecclesiastique vrittars var Iustinus Martyr, Irenæus, Egesippus,
Tertullianus, Victor Papa, Aquila Pōticus, Dyonisius Corinthius: and theis douted no thing of
freeuill, of transsubstantiation, prayers for the
dead, purgatory, the crism and vther ceremoneis
of baptism, differēce of meatts, of lent ād of the
sacrifice of the mess. Lyik as rhe fyue celebre co-
vnsalls of yat age assemblit agans the tessaresde-
cades or quatuordecimās and vther Heretiques
did confirm the same doctrin preceding, euin as
the Romane church dois this day. bot hir enemis, the Trinitars, Anaptists, &c. denying yat
Cryst is Deus de Deo & ex substantia Patris sed
de Patre and Scorning yat part of the Symboll
of Athanasius calling it à battalogy or à superfluus idill repetition vhar it is said Deus de Deo
lumen de lumine, Deus verus de Deo vero, so
doing thai haue lernit yat lesson at the scooll of
Valentinus, and the Caluinists taking vpon thā
speciall knouleg and reuelation of rhe veritie
hid from ages preceding tham thai follou Basilides and Carpocrates, and disputing by Philo-
sophique and naturall reson in matters of fayth
as thay do in the matter of trāssubantiatiō thai
be successors to Marcion and Heracleus and to
thair colleges cōdemnit Heretiques in the said
second age.

Speking of
Origenes and
Tertull. I rek-
kin thā amāg
famus vrit-
In the thrid age or hundreth year partly the
13. celebre counsalls partly the famus vrittars as
Clemens Allexandrinus, Origenes, Gregorius
Neocesariensis, Tryphon, Dyonisius and Euse-

bius Alexandrinus, Cyrillus Antiochenus, Ar-
nobius the Master of Lactantius. Theis heir and
thair deseryue the mess to be à sacrifice and to
contene the treu body of Cryst, baptism to confer grace repeting the vnction and ceremoneis
tharof: thai affirm Purgatory, thai call côfirma-
tion and matrimony Sacraments, thai allou the
primacy of Sanct Peter, Images, lent, freeuill,
difference of meatts, merit of Good vorks, prayer
to Sancts and Apostolique indulgence, euin as
the Roman church this day doit: bot the Noua-
thors of this age pretending à particular inspi-
ratiô of the holy spreit repugning to the church
thay Imitat the Nouatians vho vanly ostéting
thair self of aneimaginar puritie ver callit cathari
euin as sû this day be callit puritás. In displacing
ordinary prelats and Pastors out of thair places
and vsurping the same by violence thai follou
Paulus Samosetanus vho by the mycht of quene Zenobæa did expell Demetrius laufull bischop of Antioch and did intrus him self tharin:
In bragging yat yat the treu church is vyth tham
and not vhar the euident Apostolique successiô
is sene to be thai be lyik vnto the Donatists vho
gesting at Apostolique succession did alleg the
treu church only to be vith tham in Afrique:In
denying freeuill and all pouer to do any thing
tharby, as if ve ver stôs and stoks and no liuing
men, and gloring in peculiar illuminations and
pretending ane assurance of à licht and leading
of the holy spreit more nor any church had be
for tham thai becum Manicheás vho defending

ars so far as
thai consent
vith other
doctors not
vher as thai
follou thair
ouin priuat
opinions.

S ij

the self same opinions ver conuict of damnabill
Heresie.

Of the fourt age the counsalls and notabill
vriitars to vir Sanct Ambros, Athanasius, Lacta-
tius, Epiphanius, Damasus, Gregorius Nazianze-
nus, Basilius, Eusebius Cesariesis, Hieronymus,
Hilarius, Palladius and Optatus : all theis heir
and thair do yit more clearly confirm the points
preceding as the Roman church nou doit bot
the nouators dissenting from hir and disposses-
sing hir of hir digniteis thai becum lyk the My-
letians in Ægypt vho scorning to follou the
church planted thair by th'Apostle Sanct Marc
vold neads intruse thair self vithout all laufull
vocatió) and lyik vnto lucius yat thrust him self
in the chair of Alexandria obiecting many ska-
dalus imputations agans the ordinary Pastor of
yat place, euin as did all the Arrians of yat age.
Finally thai becum lyk Eunomius vith his sect
callit anomi (Vhilk is to say laules) in yat thai
contem ancient ordinary calling pretending à
iustification by fayth only and à peculiar knouleg of God ād of his veritie more nor any vther
of à long tyme hes had or presently hes : and in
dispysing Ecclesiastique ceremoncis and ornaments in veschels, vestiments and suchlyik com-
mendabill decoration of diuyn seruice thai be-
cú vnuars lyk Iulian, Heron, Felix, Elpidius and
vther Apostats of yat age.

In the fyst age the 32. famus counsalls tharof
and notable vriitars to vit Theodoritus, Orosi⁹,
Gelasius, Prosper, Socrates, Sozomenus, Seduli⁹.

Hilarilius Arelatenſis, Petrus Chryſologus bot
ſpecially S. Auguſtin and Chryſoſtom be moſt
ſtrong propugnators of all traditions this day
vſit in the Romane church, and the enemis tharof conforting and ſuſtening Schiſmatiques be
lyk the opulent Lucilla of Aphrique vho by hir
ſubſtance bair out the ſchiſm of Donatus: thai
reſemble the Pelagiens of yat age and the Peter-
bruiians and Henricians of ages follouing vho
denyit baptiſm to confer any grace ſpecially
vnto childring laking fayth: Thai follou Fauſt⁹
and Xenaias vith ſuch Eutycheans contemning
beautifull temples, altars, incens, lycht torches
and church ornaments. Finally thay be cóform
to the enthyſiaſtes vho affirmit that ver ſo in-
inflámit and fulfillit vyth the holiy ſpreit as only
thair interpretations and deciſions in Religion
vas to be embracit and ro vther.

In the Saxt age the 41 famus counſalls tharof
vyth the holy vrittars to vit, Fulgétius, Symma-
chus Pótifex, Euodius, Gregorius Magnus Euagrius, Victor Vticenſis, Nicephorus in expreſs
vords defend all yat is condemnit ſo partially in
the Romane church: and the ſaid counſalls and
Doctors condemning the Enthouſiaſm of the
Eutycheans, Manicheans, Montaniſtis, Mono-
thelites and agnoits vith ſindry vthers do in effect condem the reuelations and ſecreit inſpi-
ration yat men ſeparating tham ſelf from the
churchpreſum this day to haue. In the ſeuint
age ád all vthers ſucceeding úto this age all coú-
ſalls and Doctors of the church in eury one of

tham thai do so particulary debat the sentéce of
the church Romane and defait the contrary yat
hir enemis think thame all partiall and suspect.
and if at any tyme thay cite or alleg passages out
of the said Doctors and counsalls for côfirming
thair errors it is not to be thocht strange: For so
thai do cite passages of holy scriptur as all Heretiques haue done from the beginning bot thair
citations be ether manqne and mutilat orells
throuin and vitiat. and vho vold exem if heirin I haue treuly allegit the names and authorite of Doctors and counsalls let him reid theis
goldin centureis of the most Illustre Cardinall
Baronnius the ornamét of this age, or if perhaps
theis seam to tedius let him peruse that of Gene-
brardus callit notæ Chronicæ, or if all theis be
suspect be reson the authors tharof be Catholique Romane, I am content to be censurit by
thair auin centuries cailit centurriæ Magdebur-
géses euin theis yat be prented at Hedelberg or
Basse.

Bot if nether the distinctió betuix person ãd
places, nor the authoritie of counsalls and Doctors can content vs let vs yit be content vith
experience the scoollmaster of foolles: by vhilk
experience vee sall fynd yat all controuerseis
vhilk hes from the Apostles dayis fallin out tuiching Religion haue bene decydit by the authorite of the Romane church. For in the secôd age
the question of the celebration of easter vas de-
fynit by Pope Victor. In the thrid age the dete-
stable Heresie of Nouatus vas condemnit by au-

thoritie of Pope Cornelius. In the fonrt age Pope Syluester did condem Arrius and in yat same age Pope Damasus condemnit the Macedoniãs In the 5. and. 6. age vho bot the Romane bischops did extinguis the Hereseis of Nestorians, Eutychæans, Pelagians and Sindry others, and vnto theis dayis from the Apostles no vther church hes presumit to conuocat any Oicumenique counsall for citing, examing or condéning any Heresie or Heretique: if so be vby suld ve so obstinatly oppone our self vnto such laudabill consuetud confirmit by all Ecclesiastique historians and Doctors boyth Grec and Latin. specially in yat the Romane Emprors haue remittit all controuerseis in religion to the determination of the Roman church: Vharin if any man sall dout let him reid Euseb. 7. book chap. 26. Gratian th' Empror in his Epistle to the bischop of Aquileia in Italy, Theodos: the younger in his epistle to the Synod of Ephes. Athanasius in his Epistle to tham yat leadit à solitar lyif: Basilius in his 31. Epistle. Tertullian in his book of prescriptions. Sanct Ambrose 32. Epistle, Sanct Ierosm in his Epistle to Damasus Sanct Augustin agans cresconius Donatist chap. 33. Bot Ireneus as most ancient so spekit he most euidently of this matter in his 3. book 3. chap. saying.

Vee conuict and condem all such as for lak of vnderstanding, for curiosite, for malice, for vane gloir or greid gather or conioyn thair self agãs the gretest and most ancient church constitut at Rome knouin vnto eury man tohaue bene foundit by the tuo most glo-

rius Apostles Peter and Paul:For vnto hir be reason
of hir principall pouer it is *neceʃʃar* yat all vther
church ʃuld conuene or obey and S.*Cyprian* in his firʃt
book 3. *chap.* vritting vnto Pope *Cornelius* ʃayit in
thus ʃort.Suirly Hereʃeis and ʃchiʃmes haue not procedit elʒuhar bot for yat men did not obey the preiʃt of
God ãd for yat ve vill not admit vthin the church of
God à Preiʃt or Sacrificator to be Iuge as Cryʃtis vi-
cegerent or Lieutenant, vnto vhom if ve ʃuld as ve
be commandit yeild and obtemper no man ʃuld moue
or attemp any matter agans the college of Preiʃts or
prelats.

Bot Inuane do I allege the exéples and autho-
riteis of Catholique Orthodox in this matter
(ʃeing thair hes bene none of thã Sen the Apo-
ʃtles dayis yat hes not refertit matters in religiõ
controuerted vnto the determination of the
Romane church:)becaus not only thai bot euin
the verey Heretiques haue ʃo done if ve ʃall treʃt
credibill hiʃtoreis.For vee reid yat Euʃebius biʃchop of Conʃtantinople tho he vas ane Arrian
he did notuythʃtãding ʃend to Iulius biʃchop of
Rome requiring the ʃaid Iuli⁹ to be Iuge betuix
him and Athanaʃius:and not only theʃaid Euʃebius bot alʃo the hoill Synod of Arrian biʃchops
aʃʃemblit vyth him at Anthioche deʃyrit thair
Actes and decrees to be ratifeit by the ʃaid Pope Iulius.Sanct Cyprian alʃo makit mention yat
Fortunatus ane biʃchop eʃtabliʃʃit by Heretiques and Baʃilides ane Heretique did boyth
notuithʃtanding appeil vnto the ʃeat of Rome,
and Peter habailardus for all his hereʃie did the
ʃame

same in the dayis of Sanct Bernard:Sanct Augustin also in his 2.book of originall sin chap. 7.doth affirm yat the Archi Heretique Celestiⁱ durst not disobey the lettres or citatiõs of Pope Innocentius.and Berengarius archidean of Angiers did submit him self to Pope Victor the 2. and vnto Stephanus the 9. and so did Martin Luther once vnto Pope Leo the 10. Vnto vhom the said Luther did submissiuly vrit theis vords. Most blessed Pope Leo,I do offer my self prostrat befor thy feat vith all yat I am and haue: quicken or kill:call or reuok:approue or disapproue as plesit you:I sall hencefurth agknouleg thy voyce to be the voyce of Cryst presiding and speking in the albeit this humiliation of the said Martin lested no Longer nor that of celestius forsaid.

Bot heir if you sall say yat the ancients as veill heretiques as Orthodox had Good reson to rédre such honor ãd prefermēt(as holines and verteu did veill deserue)vnto the anciēt bischops of ro me preceding the fourt age bot tharefter the bischops succeding only to the dignitie and not to the doctrin, to the place and not to the precedēt pietie,thair cã be no resõ to agknouleg thame as thair predecessors did veill mereit to be agknou legit.Heirunto I ansr yat the same doctrin is yit techit in the Romane church yat vas techit in the primityue church if ve vouchaf to call the articles of fayth and tuo Testaments the self same doctrin.Vharin tho thai seã to vs(yat be bot à feu membres) to peruert the said doctrin by

T

cıking or parīg, or interpreting the same sinister
ly, or yat thair maners be dissolut ād damnabill,
vhat reson haue ve being bot à feu to condem
the hoill the cause yit depending and the que-
stiō yit vndecydit? Suld vee dispyis our Prince at
all tymes vhen vee think yat he either denyis, de-
layis, or peruertys Iustice? or suld vee abādō our
Pastors hou sone thair doctrin and lyif apperit
vnto vs reprehensibilia? suirlie if this be permittit
boyth pietie and policie may tak thair leif. Such
inutill animositie suld be aluay auoydit and such
curius branes suld be vsit and gouernit lyk febri-
citāts: For as thai yat haue the ague vhenas thair
hart is brint vp vyth the extraordinar flam of
the feure and thair branes oppressed by the vehe
mentnes thairof, thair taist and all thair senses
lossit incontinent thair rycht operation all meat
and Medicin seaming vnto tham bittir and di-
sagreable housoeuer thai be sueit or salutar of
thair auin natur: For vhilk cause the gard or ke-
pars of such febricitants doth minister vnto thame not after the Idill consait of the seik persons
bot after the prudēt aduys of the Phisitian; Euin
so heady hoit felouis hauing thair hart and har-
nes inflammit vyth the fyir ether of vanegloir,
malice, curiositie, auarice, (yea sum tyme hauing
boyth hart ād head oppressed vyth no other di-
seasse bot vith mere folie and ignorance) thai cā
think, spek, nor pronunce no thing bot Idill in-
uectyue vords full of the flams of contumely ād
sklander: Bot hou sone this burning ague of heresie sall leif thame and yat thair malice sall be

turnit in the modeſtie of the anciét fathers then
ſall thai begin to think and ſpek of the Pope ád
Prelats of this age euin as the ſaid anciéts did of
vther Pops heirtofor:yat is to ſay vh nas thai ſall
be inſpyrit vyth the Good ſpreit yat did gouern
S. Auguſt. S. Bernard, S. Hieró vho did ſo much
honor Anaſtaſius, Honorius and Damaſus: then
ſall thai not be aſchamit to réder the lyk honor
to his holinesyat ſittet this dayin the ſame place
(for pietie and Iuſtice comparabill if not preferabill to any of his predeceſſors:) Bot ſo long as
thair Eyis be obſcurit vyth Schiſmaticall blyndnes no maruell tho thai nether ſee the lycht nor
the Schyning lamps of God:For vhat the Ee is
vickit all the body is dark. In one thing notvithſtanding boyth the Pope and Prelats may reioys
yat in ſuffering ſuch reprochis thai ſuffer vyth
th' Apoſtles vheras thair aduerſars ſall fynd no
exempill of thair inſolent inuectiós bot in Iannes ád Iambres yat did blaſphem Moyſes:in feſt⁹ vho allegit Sanct Paul to be mad:in theisyat
ſaid th' Apoſtles ver dronk vith neu vynes and
in theis yat diſdanfully callit Cryſt Ieſus à carpétar and à carpentars ſome.

Thridly if the laudabill practique and cóſuetud of the church ratifeit by attétik teſtimoneis
of Hiſtoriás, Doctors, Emprors, cá not moue vs
to à mediocritie nor to vſe ane remeid approuit
by ſo famus vitnes. Let vs yit patiently conſidder vhat the holy Prophets of God did in the
lyik caiſs vhenas thai perſauit the impietie and
inſoléce of the Hebreu preiſts boyth in doctrin

ãd maners. did the said prophreits difpyife the
holy preifthoid for the vnholines of the preifts
or the Mofaicall dignitie and offices diuyne for
the deteftabill vyces of the Doctors? did thai a-
bandon the tempill of God for the vngodlines
of men aponted to gouern the fame? did thai
intrufe thair felf in the poffeffions and places of
the preiftes? did thai feditiufly drau the ignorant
peapill in fectes, fchifmes, monopols and factiõs
erecting à Samaria agans à Ierufalem and alter
agãs alter? No No: thai did Prophefy vithin the
tempill affixing thair Prophefeis vpon the portes tharof: thai vat contentit to liue poorly and
frugally vpon thair auin not brigging or ambi-
tiufly afpyring to the places and poffeffions of
the parteis vhom thai reprehendit : yea thai ab-
horrit fo much all factions as thai chufit rather
vithin the tempill amang the preifts and Princes of Iudæa to fuffer all torments nor amang
the fchimaticall and factius vithout the tempill
to liue at thair plefure delyuerit of all danger.
Vhilk conftant patience and exemplar moderation vee reid to haue bene in Amos vho vas killed by Amafias hie preift: in Efaia vho vas fauin
in tuo by Manaffe king of Iuda : in Ieremia vho
by the Iudaique peapill vas ftonit to deth: in E-
zechiell vho in Babylon amang the Ieuis vas
murtherit: in Michæas vho by Ioram in Iudæa
vas throuin headlong ouer ane precipice and in
Zacharia vho vas murtherit befyd the altar vithin the tempill.

Laft of all if vee vill nether follou the exẽple of the Prophets nor no laudabill confuetud preceding let vs at left marque veill that allegoricall nauigation of the Apostles being imbarquit vith Cryst Iesus at that tyme vhē the storm and tēpeſt did ſo toſt and tormēt thair bark ād it may be perhaps yat thair beauior in yat materiall nauigation in à materiall barque may mollifie our ſtif hartis and moue vs to lern by thame hou to behaue our ſelfes in this miſticall nauigation vithin the miſticall barque of the church.

The ſaid Apoſtles being imbarquit in Maneir forſaid ſeing the fearfull image of deth in the extraordinar tēpeſt thai var ouertakin vith extraordinar fear: Yit ſo long as thair apperitvnto tham any hoip of ſautie thai kepit ſilence and vold not preſum to auaik thair lord and maſter much les to tak on and trubill him or the ordinary Pilolts or Marinells: bot finding at lenth the ſchip all moſt ſittin doum and ſonk then thai came to auaik him not diſdanfully bot deutifullie, not rigoruſlie bot reuetētlie ſaying Lord or Maſter ſaue vs, vee peris. Vho vold be callit follouars of the Apoſtles hou can thai refuſe to follou thair exemple in this nauigation. ar thai inbarquit vithin the ſchip of the church? find thai hir toſted to and fro by impetuus vaues and vynds of vyces boyth in doctrin and maners? ſee thai hir ready to peris by rigor of the ſaid tēpeſt and Cryſt Iesus à ſleap in his Vicars or Vicegerents vho ſuelling in ſenſualiteis and lying dead dronk vith all delicatnes can not auaik call, cry and pull as you liſt: In ſuch diſaſtre or danger

thai fuld not tak on and truble the hoill eſtat of
the church:thai fuld not vith veapins ād by maneir of vindication go and ſteir vp perſons imbarquit vyth tham by ciuill varris and ſchiſmes
attempting to diſcredit and degraid the ſaid vi-
cepilotts:bot in all humilitie folluing the forſaid exemple thai ſuld rin vnto Cryſt the cheif
pilot and ſteirſman for his ſaik reſpecting ſuch
as he hes reſpected and honorit vith his Lieute-
nantry and vnto him yat hes no les pouer vithin
the miſticall bark of the church nor he had in
the materiall forſaid thai ſuld vith all reſpect ād
reuerence pour out thair complants ſaying
lord ſaue vs vee peris: Auaik lord in theis vnto
vhom you haue committed your deputation in
gouerning the diſtreſſit barK of your church:
Let the ſueit found of your breth blau away frō
thair ſlummering eyis this deadly Laſines to th'
end that thai being once valkinnit thay may cō-
mand the vynds and vauis of all concupiſcen-
ce,ſklander and ill exemple boyth in thair ſelf
and vthers to ceaſs vharby after ſo deſperat dā-
gers men ſeing à deſyrit tranquillitie may maruell,and magnifie God and ſay : Vho is this vnto vhoſe miniſteriall membres boyth vynd and
ſea doth obey.Suirly for my mean opinion this
var the only mean to quiet the church : for
experience may tech vs yat all vther turbullent
courſes vhilk factius men daylie vſe by vritting,
declaming ād inuading one ane vther by ſlycht
and mycht be bot ſo many belliſſes making this
fyir of diſcord burn the more furinſlie.

Be côːétit thé my dearty belouit kins folk ãd cú-
trey men vith the Prophets and Apostles to Remane vithin the tépill ãd barque of the church
notuythstanding any naughtines yat can be in
preists or pilotts, Lest yat feparatíg our felf yar-
fra as did Chore, Dathan, and Abiron, Simon
Magus, Theobutus, Allexander the copper
fmyth and Hymenæus vyth findry vthers you
boyth merit and incur the infamy and vnhappy
end vhilk fell vnto tham.

And heir the laudabill exemple of Conftan-
tin the gret fall not be impertinent to be remé-
britːvnto vhom vhenas fum mutinars did prefent infamus libelles agans thair ordinary bifchops hə not only caufit burn the faid sklande-
rus libelles bot alfo anfuerit in this fort to the
prefentars faying yat in fpirituall things he vas
to obey his Paftors and not to be obeyit and yat
he thocht it fo vnfeaming in him or in any of
the flok to fpy out curiufly the lyif of thair Paftor as if he fuld chanfe to fee any of tham commit any foull offens yat he vold couer the fame
vyth his Clok left the eyis of vthers fuld be offendit tharuith.

Vold God yat this Chriftian modeftie of Cô-
ftantin the Gret var this day obferuit: vold to
God at left yat Innocents allone fuld prefum to
throu the firft ftone agans malefactors. if fo var
vndoutedly fuch as be moft prompt to pique ãd
fpek agans vhers fuld abftene from thair ordinary inuectiós knouing firft thair felf not to be
altogidder irreprehenfibill and fyne yat in the

church yair had euer bene chaf vyth the corn,
dregs vyth the vyne and much refuse and of-
skourings about mettels yat be moft fyne. Vas
thair not in the familie of Abraham ane Ifmael?
in the familie of Ifaac ane Efau'in the familie of
Dauid ane Abfolon? vith Moyfes Miriam and
vith Elizee ane Gehazi?Vas not one of the tuelf
Apoftles à Iudas? and vhen thair vas bot eight
perfons in the church vas not one of tham à
Cham? and vhen fche had bot four childring
vas not one of tham à Cain?and confifting bot
of tuo perfons in Paradis,did not the one tempt
the vther to incredulitie and difobedience?Vhat
Maruell then if amangs 236. Popes and amang
millios of Prelattes and profeffed religius men
thair be found à Iudas, à Cain, à Cham, à Ifmael &c. For vhofe preuarication or peruer-
fitnes if vee fuld abandon the Romane church,
vhy fuld vee not by the lyik reafon abandõ and
abiure the churchis impugning hir in vhilk
thair be alfo for all thair finall number à great
deall of tairres, goats, fcabbit fcheip and de-
baufchit childring vhilk daylie for licht faltes
be fynit and forcit to fitt on the ftuill of repen-
tance,and for greter crymes be cenfurit by thair
fpirituall fuord of excommunication yea fum-
tyme vyth the temporall fuord of the Iuge criminall . bot heir I both pitie and fpair tham by
my felf of all men moft fragill knouing humane fragilitie, viffing nottheles yat fering to be
Iugit after the counfall of the Euangell ve fuld
not rafchly Iuge and yat vee fuld firft tak the
beam

beam out of our auin Ee befor vee perſaue à
moit in our nychtbors vnderſtanding yat thai
be moſt redy to raill and reprehéd vho be moſt
reprehenſibill:Vharof vee haue manifeſt exemples in Achab agans Eliah,in the fals Iuges agás
Suſanna,in Sedechia the ſone of Chanaana agás
Micheas and in the vyf of Putiphar agans Ioſeph.

Bot to th'end this Paræneſe exceid not the
number of ſum feu ſcheittes of paper (as I did
determin)for concluſion I ſubmit my ſelf to the
indifferent readar to conſidder vhat groundes I
haue had to rendre,or rether vhat grounds heir
be ſett doun to perſuad him to rendre and captiuat his auin priuat ſens vnto the obedience of
the Catholique , Apoſtolique church Romane
not becaus ſche is Romane bot becaus of all
Chriſtian churchis contéding for the glorius name of the treu church ſche allome may vyth
Good reſon gloir in the treu marques tharof as
heirtofor I beleue be ſufficientlie prouin. And
yit to be callit Romane is no ſmail preferment
ſeing yat epithet allone doth contene boyth v-
niuerſalitie , antiquitie , vnitie and puritie Apoſtolique. For in yat th'Apoſtle vritting to the
Romás doth extoll tham ſaying thair fayth vas
annunciat or prechit throuchout the hoill vorld
he doth firſt by theis vords ſignifie the antiquitie and origin of thair church to haue bene in his
da yis à 1602 Years ago: nixt by theis vords the
vniuerſalire tharof is manifeſted in yat he ſayit
thair fayth vas preſchit eury vhar:Laſt is deſcry-

uit the vnitie tharof and puritie Apostolique in
yat by à certane emphase or exaltation he vou-
chasit to call the vniuersall fayth to be thair
fayth. For thus caus sayis S. Augustin in his 162. epistle
yat it vas not vithout Good reasö vhy such prerogatiue hes euer bene geuin to the romane church more nor
to any vther laking the dignitie of the cheif Apostolique chair. For sayis he the churchis plätted by all vther
Apostles haue maid defection, only this Rome holy ãd
Apostolique, mother ãd nource vnto all vther churchis
by supernaturall grace of God did neuer declyn from
the puritie Apostolique nor defyill hir self vyth Hereticall nouelteis bot did constantlie obserue the self same reull vhilk sche at the beginning resauit of the tuo
principall Apostles Peter and Paull. Lo (sayis he) the
church of Ierusalem var Sanct Iames, the church of
Achaia vhar Sanct Andro, the church of Asie vhar
Sanct Iohne, the church of Persis vhar Sanct Iud brother to Iames, the church of India vhar Sanct Thomas, the church of Æthiopia vhar Sanct Matheu, the
church of Phrygia vhar Sanct Philip the church of
Grecia vhar Sanct Paul did prech, haue all declynit:
only the Romane church is yat church (as also sayit
Sanct Cyprian. lib. 1.3. Epictle) vhilk neuer maid defection and in vhilk no persidie nor infidelitie culd haue place: vharunto agreit veill yat of Sanct Hierom
saying in this sort. be assurit (sayis he) the Romane
church being so highlie commendit by the Apostle S.
Paul can resaue no neu illusions albeit ane Angell suld
annunce the same: For vhat sche hes found sche hes
follouit, vhat sche learnit sche hes taught, vhat sche
hes resauit from hir fathers sche hes faythfullie ren-

prit vnto hir childring.

O Ancient Citie! ô Citie ſo much commendit by the voyce of the Apoſtle and by commun
elogies of all Apoſtolique mē! ô Citie throuch
thy force ſumtyme lady ouer all other Citeis and
Seignoureis, nou throuch thy fayth far ſurmon-
ting the praiſe yat any mans pen can giue vnto
the!ſuld I be aſchamit (I the ofſcuring, of my
fathers hous, the horrour of my auld acqnen-
tance, the vofull huſband and father of ane
hartbrokin vyf and familie: Finally the ludibry
or lauching ſtok of fortoun)ſuld I(I ſay) ſo vn-
uorthy à vorm be aſchamit to intre vithin the
Azil of thy bleſſed ſanctuary¡? Suld I diſdane to
lik vp the crommes yat fallit from thy tabill (I
ane forlorn child, à publican, à harlott yat hes
not had the honor to inter vythin thy vyneyard
befor the aleuit hour)No NoI vill not be aſchamit bot I vill go ād labor tho I haue oft and ob-
ſtinatly refuſit lyk him mentionat in the 21.of
Math.Euangell: I vill no more vreſſill agans the
Good Angell of God ſeing my loyin is alredy
out of ioyint.I vill no more preſum vith Cham
to vncouer the ſchame of my father: I vill not
hyid my ſelf any more vith Adam from the
voyce of the lord,I vill not any more vith Ionas
flee vnto tharſis from his preſence.Finally I vill
not any more ſeik Cryſt in corners bot in his
church ſituat vpon the top of à montane kna-
uing yat as he is the corner ſtone of all veritie ſo ſche is the piller of the ſame veritie
vhilk louit the lycht and can not·abyid to be

schoot vp in corners seing such only hait the lycht as by doing ill fear to haue the veritie pronuncit. So the treu church vharsoeuer sche be, is estemit not only to be in the lycht bot to be as à clear lantern geuing lycht to vthers becaus sche neuer ferit tryall bot the more sche be exemd the more sche is eminent: vheras hereticall churchis be aluay in darknes housoeuer thai seå galland or glorius becaufe thai dar not abyid lycht and tryall of the treuth. Inioying this lycht I had rether be à doorkeaper vithin hir courts nor to reign vythin the tabernacle of hir enemis.

Tharfor I vill nou return vnto my fathers hous to eat of his falt calf lamenting vyth my hart yat I haue so long and so vnthrifsely vaisted my fathers subftance in ane vncouth laid vhar I culd fynd no food bot suaddes: I vill nou licht my candill, sueip my hous and seik the penny that I haue sleuthfully loft to the end yat finding the same agane I may reioifs vyth my freinds and nychbors. Yea I sall be glaid to selk all yat I haue to inioy this pretieux ftone ád inestimable feild vharin lyit hid the trefor of my saluation. Follouing hir I can not Erre or go aftray and if I sall erre I sall not at left erre folloung my auin voyce or the voyce of any strager bot I sall erre vith the moft lernit, moft holy, moft ancient fathers, vyth the Patriarks Prophets, and Apoftles yea vith Cryft Iesus him self vho is voyid of all error.

Then (My dearlybeleuit) be not afchamit vith me rather tymuffie nor to lait to chang

theis your altars of contradiction vith this ark
of benediction and your insolid partialitie fer
this solid pillar of veritie: For you knou not at
vhat vach the bryid grome sall cum, Nor vhen
you sall be inuyted to the vedding, nor vhen the
theif sall inuad your cottage of clay vhilk you
so pett and pamper: You haue then (and vee all
haue) gret nead not only to vach and vard bot
to be veill armit vith the spirituall armure of
this church mentionat in Sanct Paull: vee had
nead in tyme to licht our lamps at hir lycht and
to intreat hir as our dear mother for a vedding
garment : lest being surprised and vnprouydit
vec be ether hold or put out at the dreadfull cū-
ming of the gret bryidgrome vhenas heuin and
erth sall be mouet and the vorld lugit vith fyir.

O my dearly belouit if you vold deuly considder the danger you stand into in Cossing the
clear fontans of this holy church for trubled
puttes of your auin priuat Imaginations vhilk
nether can hold nor keip sueit vatter. vharin lyk
Adā you Lofs Edé for ane apill : Lyik Esau you
Lofs your birthrycht for a meas of pottage and
in one vord you lofs Lycht for darknes and the
piller of veritie for a puddill of vanitie. O if you
vold vyth patiéce and reson ansuer and declair
ūto me vharfor you haue so vnkyndlie separated your self from a societie so much extollit by
the Apostle ād all venerable ātiquitie: yea such ā
societie as euidētlye is markit vith all the signes
of the treu church. In doing vharof do you not
persaue hou you condem as infidells and repro-

bats all yat hes precedit you, sib jand fremd,
freind and fo, lernit and vnlernit, holy and prophane Good and bad: For if your fayth and profeſſion be Good and the only vay to ſaluation:
then all yat befor your age be dead muſt be in
danger of damnation becaus thai deit in à contrary profeſſion.

Agane if I ſuld let it pas yat you had iuſt caus
to abandon the Romane church, yıt vold I
at leſt vnderſtand of the vharfor you ait mouit rather to follou more one of the ſectes
abandoning hir nor ane vther? in reſpect all ſectes impugning hir be thai Lutherans, Semilutherans, Antilutherans, thai all pretend equall
aſſurance of the holy ſpreit and produce var-
rands out of the vord of God eury one of tham
conteſting yat ſche is the treu church. Heirunto
if thou ſall ſay yat thou lyıkit beſt ſum one or
vther of the ſectes deſcending from Bernardus
Rotmannus father of th'Anabaptiſts vhilk be
in number 13. or yat thou lyıkit more ſum fra-
ternitie of the Homologiſtes or Proteſtants deſcending from Melanchton vhilk be in number
32 or yat thy mynd be moſt of all vpon ſum
ſocietie of the Sacramentars deſcending from
Caroloſtadius, Zuinglius and I o. Caluin vhilk
be in number 8. all of one ſurce or ſead to vit
of Martin Luther, and all vnknouin to the
vorld bot ſo much as thai haue bene ſene ſen
the year of our lord 1517. if I ſay thou vill alleg
and affirm yat thou hes choſin ſum one or vther
of theis ſectes as yat vhilk in thy opinion or iug-

ment seamit vnto the most agreable and consonant vnto the veritie: then mark I pray the
thy dangerus presumption in establishing thy
priuat opinion to be the reull of thy fayth, vsurping vnto thy self vhilk you vill not giue nether
vnto Doctor, cousall, nor hoill church becaus in
thy opinion thay may all err and as if you culdst
not erre at all and this folloving thy priuat fan-
tasy vithout resipiscence, you fallis in the damnabill error of ancient heretiques.

Bot if I suld grant vnto the yat it is lesum to
follov in matters of fayth such as se amit to the
most consonant vnto the veritie: yit let me once demand if you canst produce vnto me any
one man of all ages preceding yat in all points
did follou and affirm yat sam form of veritie
vhilk thou dois affirm and follou? Heir thou
must haue recours only vnto thy coryphé or author of thy sect for befor him such noueltéis all
in one person var not hard of.if so be, vhat arrogance, vhat ignoráce, vhat impudéce to quyit
and condem the vniuersall ancient doctrin of
the hoill body of the church euer sen the ascension of our lord and master vnto this day for a
particular recent doctrin of sum feu infected
membres tharof start vp allanerly sen the defection of Martin Luther: Darst you affirm yat so
many Chast Virgins preceding the, so many co-
stant confessors, so many famus Doctors, so many glorius Martyrs vho haue by thair incredibill
holines, vóderfull miracles, and precieus blood
pláted, vatterit and propagat the church of God,

darſt you (I ſay) affirm tham all to haue bene
bot ignorant idolators hauing no greter reſon
for the bot becaus you ād the author of thy ſect
vnderſtādit better the ſens of ſcriptur nor euer
any of tham did: as if thy ſpreit(vhilк you ima-
ginis to be the ſpreit of God and tharfor vill not
ſubmit it to any mans ſpreit preceding the)vat
to be preferrit vnto our ſpreit vho diffyding in
our auin кnouleg knouit vith Fear after the
counſall of the Apoſtle and doth captiuat out
ſpreitts and opinion vnto ſuch ancients as vn-
deutely had the ſpreit of God in more abondan
ce nor thou canſt be thocht to haue it till by thy
vorks thou ſall declair the lyik pouer of the
ſpreit to be in the yat vas in tham. O Chriſtian
Socrates vhois cheif knouleg vas to knou no
thing! ô Ethnique Chriſtians vho pretend to
knou all things mote nor any preſent or preceding thame. Ve knou notuithſtanding yat our
foliſs predeceſſor ſerching only to knou more
nor did apertene vnto him vas depryuit of his
originall innocence and knouleg: vee knou yat
ſeditiuſe mariam bragging to much yat ſche
had knouleg and the ſpreit of God as much as
Moyſes had hir body vas ſtrikin vith leprocy to
mak hir vnderſtand yat ſuch mad apprehenſiõs
of knouleg var bot leproſeis of the mynd. Ve
knou vat one of the anciéts hes ſaid yat кnouleg vith ſobrietie is ſuir knouleg:Ve кnou yat in
one place of ſcriptur it is ſaid knou or vnderſtand vith fear,and in ane vther vho preſumit.
to much of his knouleg knouit no thing at all,
and in

and in the thrid yat thair is better hoip of à verey fooll nor of one yat estemit him self to knou
much.

Vold thou then knou the incertenty of thy
speculatyue knouleg, thou must go à litill out
frō it. For as thai yat valk in à mist do not see it
so veill as thai yat stand vpon à hill vyid from it:
So fareth it in discerning of our oune knouleg
vhose propertie is to blīd thā that trust to much
tharin, vharby thai can not see the miserie of
thair aun estat: For this loftie opinion of knouleg euin as à Rauen first of all pikit out the poor
scheips eyis to 'h' end sche may not see the vay
to escaip his tyrānie: So it bereuit the of thy spirituall sicht in such sort as you can not rychtly
iuge betuix vanitie and veritie: It bindit the in
sueit bondes, rokkit the in à creddill of curio-
sitie making the sleap in cairles securitie: it settit   *Matth.* 4.
the vpon the pinnacle of ambitiō scheuing vn-
to the many digniteis ād making the tkink you
art capable of vhatsoeuer thy hart can consait. it
presented vnto the many fair and pretieux Clo-
thes bot in no case may thou look vithin the
peices or cary thā to be discernit vyth the licht:
it had 400 fals Prophets to flatter the as Achab   *3. King* 22.
had and to keap the from the hearing of Mi-
cheas cousail (yat is from the church vhilk vold
tell the the treuth) it had à 1000. cūning fischars
to giue the fair bait bot all furnisit vith dāgerus
hookes. It hes infinit strūpets to offer the drink   *Apoc.* 17.
in goldin cooppes bot all replenissit vith dead-
ly poyson. it lakit not at all occasions sum allu-

X

ring Iaëll to tempt the vith the milk of à glorius mynd, bot all haue hammers and nailles in thair hāds to murther the vhen you fallit à sleepe: it had in eury corner à flattring Ioab and fals Iudas to kiſſe, to kill and to betray the.

Finally it hes all arguments and allurments to caus the glorifie thy ſelf and contem vthers: vold you then perfyitlie ſee thy auin infirmitie in this behalf. Then aſcend vp into ſum mohtane vhar you may behald the foggy miſt vhilk hes repleniſſit theis corners and dennes vharin you hes ſo long duelt. Bot you vill ask vnto vhat montane I viſs the to aſcend: not vnto the mōtane of thy auin imaginatiō vharin Satā Goeth about to mak the bou vnto him, vhilk in effect you doth vhenas thou extollit thy ſelf to much: bot I viſs the aſcend vnto the montane vhar Cryſt is transfigurat or tranſſubſtantiat yat is to ſay to the montane of the church Catholique Apoſtolique Romane ſett vpon the top of à montane vhar you hes Moyſes and Helias, Peter, Iames and Iohne in thair laufull ſucceſſors to talk and confer with the: cōferring vith tham thou ſalt lern knouleg of laulines not of loftines, of ſubmiſſion not of preſumption, of confirmitie not of any faction or contradiction.

O yat you vold vith vnfenzit hart indelaitly aſcend this montane and mak all the Sancts of heauin reioyſit at thy happy conuerſion! o yat you vold not greif the ſpreit of God øffring vnto the this fair occaſiō! o that you vold lyik ane vther Sanct Auguſtin or ane vther Sanct Paul change fchifm and fectes for the focietie and feloufchip vharin all thy moft nobill Princes of moft vorthy memory, all thy dear anteceffors, finally all men and vemen of thy nation young and auld poor and rich did liue and die frō the year of our lord 203. vnto the year 1559. O yat you vold fett forduart in this courfe ād fay vyth yat ould champion of Cryft Iefus Sanct Hierofm: if my father ftood veping on his knees befor me and my mother hanging on my nek behind me, and all my brethring, fifters, childring and kinsfolk houling round about to retene or hinder me from this happy refolution, I fuld fling of my mother to the ground, difpyife all my kinred, rin ouer my father and tread him vnder my feet tharby to run vnto Cryft vhen he callit on me. Béuar, beuat my dearlybelouit te giue Cryft Iefus occafion to fay vnto you as once he faid vnto Ierufalem. Ierufalem Ierufalem hou oft vold I haue collected thy childring as the hē doth hir chickins vnder hir vings bot you vold not, tharfor thy hous fall be left defolat. Beuar lyk the hoggish Gerafens to prefer your fuyne yat is to fay your fluggish and lafie opiniōs vnto Cryft Iefus and his treu church: beuar to excufe your felf lyik theifs mentionat in the 14. of Luc. faying you haue bocht à ferm and yok of oxin or mareit à vyf as if any erdly refpect fuld ferue for excufe being thus fo freindly and effectually Inuyted. So for conclufion I befech vith vnfenzit hart the lord of lords in vhofe hāds be

the hartes of all men yat theiss my Homlie In-
deuores may be red vith pitie and cōpaffion in
refpect of my veaknes, refauit vith gratfulnes in
refpect of my gooduill, ād yat thai may produce
effects agreable vnto the finceritie and fingilnes
of my mynd to the glory of God almychty and
your eternall faluation.   Amen.

Soli Deo honor *&* gloria.

NOs subsignati diligenter legimus hunc tractatum lingua Scotica conscriptum nuncupatum, à Pa rænese or admonition of M. Iohn. Coluille, &c. *Et nihil in eo reperimus Catholicæ fidei aut bonis moribus contrarium : imo multa quæ utilitatem non vulgarem, afferre poterunt legentibus. 2. Augusti. 1601.*

Ita testor G. Bishope, Doctor Sorbonicus.

Et ego Ioánes Boseuile Bacchalaureus Parisiensis facultatis Theologicæ.

Et ego Ioannes Fraserius Sacrę Theologiæ Bacchalaureus.

Iacobus Cheyneius Ecclesię Cathedralis Tornacen. Canonicus & Pęnitentiarius.

ERRATA.

PAg.2.fonrty, for fourty. pag.5. ſcuh, for ſuch. lerming, for lerning. pag.10.chunch, for church. pag.
27. nooght,for nocht. pag. 33. oſtend, for oſtent. pag.
36. all, for at all. pag.46.ont, for out. pag. 50. chauſit,
for chanſit. pag.51.ad,for and ibidem.ſnch,for ſuch ibi-
dem.thain,for thai. pag.67. vnto the note in the mar-
gin. pag.69. eik theiſs vords. (imputing alſo iniuſtly
many things,vhilk in effect thai not the Catholiꝗues
do vſe. ſcotlad, for ſcotlhand. pag. 71. this is body,
for this is my bod .pag.90.in the laſt lyne of the 96. p.
for 250. 318. and after the vord biſchops ad. of conſtantinopill vhatin did aſſiſt 150. biſchops).

ROBERT SOUTHWELL

*An Humble Supplication
to Her Maiestie*

1595

AN
HVMBLE
SVPPLICATION
TO HER MA-
IESTIE.

✠

printed at Dowaye or
some other place
in the low countrys.

Printed, Anno Do. 1595.

AN HVM-
BLE SVPPLICA-
TION TO HER
MAIESTIE.

MOST MIGHTIE and moſt mercifull, moſt feared, and beſt beloued
Princes, they are at the bottome of a help-
leſſe miſerie, whome both a condemned e-
ſtate maketh common obiects of abuſe, and
an vnpittied oppreſsion barreth from diſ-
couering their griefes to thoſe, that onelie
are able to afford them remedy. Euery one
trampleth vpon theyr ruine, whom a Princes diſgrace hath once ouerthrowne. Soueraigne fauours being the beſt foundations
of Subiects fortunes, and theyr diſlikes the
ſteepeſt downe-falles to all vnhappineſſe.
Yet a Prince ſupplying the roome, and re-
ſembling the perſon of Almightie GOD,
ſhould be ſo indifferent an arbitrator in all
cauſes, that neyther any greatneſſe ſhould

A 2 beare

beare downe Iustice, nor any meanes be
excluded from mercie; and therefore an
humble confidence in your Maiestes good
nesse, (perfect in all Princely duties, & the
only shot anker of our iust hopes) induced
vs to lay open our manifold extremities,
which heretofore (as it seemeth) hath bin
scarcelie heard, lesse beleeued, and nothing
regarded. And though our condition be
so desolate, that wee can neyther be freed
from outward miserie, but by becomming
inwardly more miserable, nor complaine of
our troubles, but our very complaints are
punished: yet an infamed life, being to free
mindes more irkesome then an innocent
death, we had rather put our vttermost ha-
zards to your highnes clemencie, thē seeme
with our silence to giue credit to our ob-
liques: to which if wee doe not, it may be i-
magined we cannot answere.

There hath beene of late published to
our vndeserued reproch, so straunge a proclamation, that it hath made your most af-
fied Subiects doubtfull vvhat to beleeue:
sith they see so apparent and vncurable
truthes, countenanced with so Reuerende
authoritie, & warranted with the most Sacred sight of theyr most honored Queene:
the

the due respect that euery one carrieth to
your gratious perfon, acquiteth you in their
knowledge, frō any meaning to haue falſe-
hood masked vnder the veile of your Maieſtie : yet when they ſee your Soueraigne
ſtile ſo abaſed, to the authorizing of fiſti-
ons, that the Magiſtrates of the vvhole
realme, moſt generally ſooth thinges ſo directly diſproued by common ſcence, and
contrarie to their own, and all mens knowledge, it cannot be but a torment to theyr
Chriſtian mindes : yea, and it muſt make
them of force iuſtlie to ſcorne that anie
Subieϛ ſhould dare in ſo high a degree, to
blemmiſh both his Princes, and her officers
credits, as to draw them to auerre his plaine
and inexcuſable leſings : for what can they
thinke, but this to be either a racking of
publike authoritie to priuate puſpoſes, who
being yet ripe to reueale their owne dan-
gerous grounds, are forced to borrow theſe
deluding ſhadowes, or an open condemnation of your Maieſties actions, as though
they bare themſelues vppon ſo vniuſt and
lawles motiues as could not able them for
righteous, but by begging releeſe of theſe
counterfet illuſions.

    Wee verily preſume that none of your

Maiefties Honorable Councell, would eyther fhew fo little accquaintance with the
Princes ftile, as to deliuer in your name a
difcourfe fo full farced with contumelious
tearmes, as better futed a declamorous
tongue, then your highnes penne, or be fo
lightly affected to the regard of your Honor, as to defile it with the touch of fo many falfe affertions: yet all men iuftly mar-
ueile that any Inditor durft aduenture to
difgorge their priuate ill will, rather then
to obferue decencie in fo publike a thing:
yea they lament their own cafe, when thefe
abufes make vncertaine what to credit in
ferious points, importing their Countrie, &
their owne fafeties, when they fee in this
(which feemeth to be but a Prologue to
future Tragedies) the ftrongeft foundati-
on to humane beleefe, applyed in all mens
mindes to fupport meere improbabilites.
And though the iniurie offered to your
Maieftie, and meerely concerning your
Realme, might in equitie challenge al mens
pennes to warne you of fo perilous courfes:
yet fith Prieftes and Catholikes, are the
markes chiefflie fhot at, wee aske humblie
leaue of your Maieftie and Councell, to
fhew how chollericke the humor was towardes

wardes vs, that cared not though the arrow
hit your Highnes Honour in the way, so
the head therof might enter into our harts.
It is an easie thing to be a true Prophet, in
foreseeing how this necessarie clearing will
be aggrauated to your Maiestie with hei-
nous words, sith those that would dislodge
vs out of all good opinions, will doubtlesse
endeuour to fulfil any such Prophecie: but
now we humble our Petitions to your care
of innocencie, that it may arme your eares
against such partiall appeachers, and incline
you to measure your censure with equitie.

To make therefore our entrie vvith the
vnfauorable tearmes, wherein we are often
and generally called vnnaturall Subiectes,
wee desire to haue it decided by your Maiesties owne arbitrement, whether we haue
iustly deserued to weare so base a liuerie: if
wee liue at home as Catholikes professing
our name, and refusing to professe a contrarie Religion, we can neyther keepe our places in the Innes of Court, but wee are im-
prisoned for Recusancie, impouerished,
troubled, & defamed. And yet if we leaue
all and seeke free vse of our conscience, depart the Realme taking such helpes as the
Charity of other countries affordeth vs, we

A 4   are

are ſtrait rekoned for vnnaturall Subiects.

It is rather an vnnaturall thing to diſobey the author of nature for any creature,
in forſaking the faith by which wee hope
only to be ſaued, and yet we muſt doe this
to the wilfull murdering of our ſoules : or
if we refuſe it, be we at home or abroad, by
theſe hard cenſures we are proclaimed vn-
natural. All bonds both of nature & grace
inuite vs to loue God, and our Countrie
more then our liues, and our neighbours as
our ſelues: which if we obſerue in the higheſt degree, we hope what other title ſoeuer
we deſerue, we ſhall at the leaſt be deemed
not to ſwarue from the rules of Natiue
curteſie: we are in ſo mightie & warranta-
ble proofes aſſured by all Antiquitie, that
our Catholike Faith is the onely truth, (to
which all that haue bin, or ſhall be ſaued,
muſt owe their fidelitie) that we thinke it
a worthy purchaſe, for the perſeuerance in
the ſame to forfet our beſt fortunes, & en-
gage our liues to the great cruelties, thē by
reuolting from it, to enter league with error, & to make our ſoules the price of in-
fernal paine, if thē we eſteeme it at a higher
rate then our liues, beleeuing that out of it,
neyther God can be truelie ſerued, nor any
ſoule

foule faued : fo if wee feeke with our dee-
peft perrills to plant it in our Realme, and
to winne foules from misbeleefe vnto it,
we thinke that we owe a moft fincere, and
naturall loue to our Countrie : for euen by
Chrifts owne teftimonie, no mans Charitie
reacheth to any higher point, then to yeeld
his life for the benefit of his friend. And if
others that fo deepely touch vs for vnnatu-
ral creatures, would with as much diligence
haue fearched out the truth by an indifferent triall, betweene the learned on both
fides, as they haue with violence martyred,
and oppreffed vs, they vvould happilie
thinke themfelues more vnnaturall, for hauing miffedde infinite foules into endleffe
perdition, then vs that with the fweat of our
deareft blood, feeke to gleane a few fcat-
tered eares, the fillie reliques of their infor-
tunate harueft. And if our due care of our
Countrie be fuch, that to reare the leaft fal-
len foule amongft your Maiefties Subiects
from a fatall lapfe, we are contented to pay
our liues for the ranfome, how much better
fhould wee thinke them beftowed, if fo
high a penny-worth as your GRACIOVS
SELFE, or the whole Realme might be the
gaynes of our deareft purchafe.

But

But though they that hunt this fault in vs, might beſt be their owne pray (faith being the ſtrongeſt of true and naturall fidelitie: yet muſt we be accounted vnnaturall, being ballanced in their affections, that draw all cauſes of compaſsion to motiues of crueltie, and make theyr condemning reports, the contraries of our dutiful meanings with the like ſpirit, ſtill breathing more ill will, then truth: He tearmeth the Right Honorable the Lord Cardinall Archbiſhop *Allen*, and Father *Parſons* (both learned & reuerent men) two ſeditious heads, looking happily through ſuch eyes, as iudge all men by theyr owne colours, & what cauſe haue they giuen to this ſlaunderer, vnleſſe it be counted ſedition to gather the ruins of Gods afflicted Church, and to haue prouided Sanctuaries, for perſecuted & ſuccourleſſe ſoules: which forced at home, either to liue with a goared conſcience, or to lie open to continuall vexations, rather chooſe to leaue theyr countrie then their Catholike Religion. It was no ſedition for many in Queene Maries time, to be harboured in Geneua, maintained the by thoſe that now enuie againſt vs. It is no ſedition to admit ſuch multitudes of ſtraungers, as for theyr faith

faith swarme into England, out of all countries. It is thought Charity to aid the Stats
of Flaunders in the behalfe of Religion. It
is extolled in your Maieftie as an Honorable fauour to protect the Portingall, and S.
Horatio Palanifinc: but if wee (whofe cafe at
home) in refpect of our faith is more mife-
rable then any Proteftantes in any other
Countries, haue chofen two venerable men
to procure vs fome refuge, from our dome-
fticall fcourges, where wee may follow our
ftudies, and exercife Pietie, ftrait your Maieftie (though induced to practife the fame
curtefie to others) is informed againft them
as feditious heades. So true it is , the fame
thing is not it felfe in diuers perfons, & yet
as God almightie and the world is our witneffe, nothing in thofe Seminaries, is either
intended, or practifed, but the releefe and
good education of fuch forfaken men, as
from the ftorme of our Englifh fhoare, flie
thether for a calme roade , that perficed in
the courfe of learning & vertue, they may
returne to offer theyr blood for the reco-
uerie of foules: As for the bafenes of theyr
birthes, which among other like pointes, is
interlaced vvith as impertinent, as fcorne-
full a parenthefis , as a fitter noate for the
                                        penners,

penners, than for your maiesties obseruatiõ.

I meane not to dwel long vpon it, for the thing neither importeth any offence to God, not crime against your Maiefty, nor greatly abaseth them, whom excellent vertue, the onely true measure of worthinesse hath ennobled. Yet this without disparagement to any may truely be auoided, that the *Cardinalls* grace, is of as good & ancient a house, & euery way as worshipfully allied as some of the highest Counselours were in their meaner fortunes, till your Maiesties fauors, and their rare abilities, made them steppes to clime into their present honours. And whether he might of likelihood haue carried as high a sail if the time had equally fecunded him with fauorable gales, I leaue to their iudgementes who are priuy to his present estate, greater than England can afford to any cleargy man. For your Maiefty being as able to know, & we lesse willing to vfe the excellēcy of your subiects, thã other Princes, it may be iustly presumed, that he might as well haue entred into credite at home, if his Faith had not drawen his foote from the first step, as with strangers in a forraine country, wher nether familiarity with the Peers, nor acquaintãce with the Prince but the only fame of his worthines, sent an admiration & loue of him into thir harts, & whosoeuer confidereth the manner of his

aduancement, being created *Cardinal* alone,
out of the ordinary times , (a prerogatiue
seldom yeelded but to speciall persons, who
marketh his wisdome to haue bin in such re
uerence, that in *Pope Greg.* the 14. his sicke-
nes, he was thought sitest among the *Cardi-
nals*, to be vizgerent in spirituall causes: who
is ignorāt of the smal cause of our country,
by laws, libels, & other meanes, seeeking to
vndermine the *Popes Sea* (hath giuen him to
reward her subiects, with so high promoti-
ons: who finally weyeth the aduentures of
our Councel, to hinder his preferment, and
darken his vertues with hard information,
shal easly beleeue the mā to be of rare per-
fectiōs, that hauing no other wings to beare
his credite, but learning and vertue, could
reach to so high points of fauour, notwith-
stādiug so mighty lets: As for Father *Parsons*
he hauing placed the vttermost of his ambi
tion, in cōtempt of honor, & the highest of
his wealth in voluntary pouerty: will easlie
acknowledge his birth to haue bin of more
honest thē great parents: yet were they not
so meane, but that they were able to afford
him such education , as might haue made
his good parts a way to no small prefermēt.
And albeit his credit be great with the K.
of *Spaine* , yet did hee neuer Vsurpe the
Title of the KINGES CONFESSOVR, as

as this inditor would perſwade your Maieſtie, though ſome of the ſimple ſort of our Engliſh ſouldiers, in the Gallies, vpon error and ignorance, muttered ſome ſuch ſpeeches amongſt them-ſelues. As for other Prieſtes how many of them are Knights & Eſquires ſonnes, as otherwiſe both to worſhipfull and noble houſes alleyed, & heires to faire reuenewes, let their owne friendes and Parents diſperſed through the whole Realme beare witneſſe. This onely vvee may ſay in anſwere of our obiected baſeneſſe, that in the ſmall number of the Catholike Prieſtes of our Nation, (vvhich reacheth not to the tenth of the Proteſtant Miniſtrie) there are very neare as many, yea happily more Gentlemen, then in all the other Cleargie of the whole Realme.

Now whereas we are moſt vncourteouſlie called a multitude of diſolute youngmen, wee deſire no other euidence to diſproue this accuſation, then an indifferent cenſure: For firſt before our departure out of the Realme, we muſt reſolue to abandon our Countrie friendes, and all ſuch comforts, as naturally all men ſeeke and finde in theyr natiue Countrie. Wee muſt relinquiſh all poſſibilities of fauour, riches, and credit.

credit. We muſt limite our mindes to the reſtrained and ſeuere courſe of the S o c i- e t y o f I e s v s, or the Seminaries, where the place is in exile, the rules ſtrickt, the go- uernement auſtere, our willes broken, the leaſt fault chaſtiſed, & a moſt abſolute ver- tue exacted. And who can imagine thoſe to be ſo deſolute humors, who this deter- mine to abridge themſelues of all actions, of diſolutenes, and to impriſon their affec- tions within the preſinct of a reguler and ſtraight order, and leſt happily it may be imagined that wee ſay more then in proofe we finde, it is knowne to thouſandes, and daylie ſeene, and witneſſed by trauellers, that we are there tide to ſo preziſe tearmes in diet, apparell, exerciſe, & all other things, that wee are much more ſhortned of our ſcope, then in any Colledge of our Engliſh Vniuerſities. I omit the prayer, faſting, haire- cloth, and other chaſtiſements of the body, vvhich being voluntary, yet vſuall; are to any if not more then partiall Iudges, inuincible groundes againſt this ſlaunder, of being diſſolute: but let our intertainmēt at our returne, be a finall ouerthrow of this falſe impoſition : for who can thinke them diſſolute, that being by the L a wes, by ex-
amples,

amples by commō experience taught, with
what bloody conflictes they are heere to
encounter, & howe many feares, daingers,
and agonies, both in life; and death, they
vndoubtedly expect, (are notwithstanding
contented) for reclaiming of soules vnto
Gods folde, willing to yeelde their bodies
to the hasard ot al those miseries foreseene,
and foreknowne, and aduisedly chosen before all worldly contentments.

But it may be that some, vnaquainted
with our states, will measure our mindes,
by our apparell, (beeing as we confesse)
more agreeable oftentimes, to the com-
monfashion, than to the graue attire that
seemeth our calling, neither is our habit, or
behauiour so ruffian-like, or disordered,
(as this inditor, euer forgetting trueth,
when he remembreth vs, would willingly
haue it imagined) but in this we must yeeld
our reason, (sith we cannot reforme the in-
conuenience) till your Maiesty thinke it
good to licence vs without daunger, to ex-
ercise our functions, much-more mighty is
the saluation of our soules, than the externall decency of our apparell, which though
it be necessary in time and place, yet is it
not so essentiall a point, as for the care
there-

thereof, to neglect the charge of Gods
flocke,& the safetie of our owne liues: *Dauid* vpon iust cause fained him mad, but his
madnes was an effect of perfect wisedome,
and reason the guide of his seeming follie.
Iudith laying aside her hairecloth,and wid-
dowes weed, disguised her selfe in such ornaments, as were fitter to allure laciuious
eies, thē to beare witnes of her sober mind.
And if God added grace & beautie to her
youthful dresses,to further her iust reuenge
vpō her enimies, much more may we hope
he will allow a lesse disguisage in vs, to reuiue the soules of our dearest friends. It is
no sure argument of inward beautie, to be
vaine in shew,seeing a modest and an humble minde, may be shadowed vnder the
glorious & courtly robes of a vertuous *He-
ster.* And if angels for the benefit of bodyes
haue suted their shapes, to the requestes of
their Ministers: now appearing like souldiers,as to *Iosua:* now like trauailers, as to *To-
bie:* now like gratious youths,as to *Lot*: yea
if Christ as the occasion required, seemed
to the two Disciples a Pilgrime, & to Saint
Marie Magdalene a Gardiner, why may
not we for the winning of soules, (which as
God is our witnes is the onely cause of our

B				com-

comming)frame our behauiour and attyre,
to the necesfity of our daies, as we read the
auncient bifhops did, in the perfecurion of
the *V andalls*, this therfore cãnot be eftemed
a iuft prefumption of a diffolute minde in
vs, whom not any will to fuch finenesse, but
a defire of safety enforceth vs to weare the
liueries of the time.

Nowe whereas the heauy aduerfaries of
our good names, hath abufed your Maiefties eares with a truethlesse furmise, that
we fhoulde auoide the Realme for lacke of
liuing, we humbly refigne his folly, to the
correction of your Highnesse wifedome,
for to whom can it feeme probable, that we
flie for lacke of liuing. of whom many haue
vowed all, willingly excepted a voluntary
pouerty, leauing that we had, without either hope, or care of getting more, our
wealth beeing nowe in well-doing, and our
passions, our beft possessions, is it like that
for wante of liuing any woulde enter into
a courfe, wherin without possibility of preferment they were in apparant hazarde to
loofe their liues: are anie fledde for fuch
pouerty, that at the leaft they coulde not
haue liued in feruice, with more eafe and
lesse labour, than they tie themselues vn-

to, in a moſt ſtreight life, where they doe
more by a willing obedience than they
ſhould haue beene put vnto in a hired ſubiection, or are they of ſuch qualitie, and
of ſo manie pleaſing partes, that they can
in theſe ſeuere times winne men with pe-
rill of their Liues, Landes, and Poſterities, to entertaine and comforte them, and
could they not haue found without plung-
ing themſelues in the Sea of daungers, ſome
more eaſie meanes for a competent main-
tenance, then to beg it out of ſo manie ex-
egints, and to wring it through ſo grieuous
oppreſsions, and why ſhould theſe feares of
wantes pinch them more then infinite o-
thers, whom they left behind them? They
are men of as pregnant wittes, as deliuered
tongues, as mature iudgements, as moſt of
the Innes of Court, or Vniuerſities where
they liued: yea, they were already ſtepped
ſo far into promotion, that they needed not
to haue doubted, nothing leſſe then lacke
of liuing, diuers of them hauing bin Proc-
tors of Vniuerſity, Fellowes & Officers of
Colledges, and likely to haue riſen to anie
higher preheminencie. To remitte thoſe
that haue Reuennewes, and Annuities
of they owne, beſides the allowance and

kinred

kinred, vvith rich & moſt wealthy families.
It pleaſeth further this vnfriendly informer
(who ſeemeth beſt pleaſed with diſpleaſing
vs) to deriue our departure from a conſcience guilty, of crimes committed, being ſtil
himſelfe in the likeneſſe of his ſpeeches, as
voide of veritie, as full of ill will: for if
Prieſtes at theyr arraignement, be in manner charged with Originall ſinne, many of
them hauing bin ſcarcely borne, at the ri-
ſing in the North, which is alwaies a common place to declaime againſt them. If all
the notorious faults, that may any way cō-
cerne Catholikes, are made ordinarie in-
ditements, to condemne thoſe that neuer
heard of them, till they come to the barre:
how much would any fault of their own be
obiected, yea and multiplied in the vrging,
if any ſuch could haue bin found: but yet
none was euer touched for any thing committed before his departure, as all teſtimo-
nies may depoſe, and the verie recordes te-
ſtifie in our behalfe, and to preuent any inſt
groundes of this oblique, the ſuperiours
(not ignorant how many eyes are buſied
in watching for the leaſt aduantage againſt
vs) make diligent ſcrutenie, for the perfect
notice of theyr vertue, whome they admit

to

to Priesthood, who being for the most part among many of theyr owne houses, or standing in the Vniuersities, could not cloake any great enormitie from notice: yea the very age of the greater part (they going euer very young) is a warrant to quite them from any such offence, as should force them to flie their Countrie. And as for the rest, which are of riper yeares, they haue bin so notified for theyr morrall life, that they haue made common report theyr harbinger, to take vp their due roomes, in euerie mans good opinion. In some this being an approued accusation, deliuered by one that in the same discourse, hath empanalled an enquest of vntruths, to finde out him in this also guilty of falsehood, it needeth no other answere, but a wise censure of the Reader: But now most mercifull Princesse licence our too much wronged innocencie, to relate the sharpest doubt of this vnkinde aduersarie, ioyned vvith those three odious tearmes of fugitiues, rebels, and traytours, & dipped as deep in the bitternes of gaule, as hee would haue it enter into our dearest blood: And first wee craue most humblie but the right of Christians beleefe of our oath, which is the only Certificat to make

our

our thoughtes vndoubted; vppon hope
whereof we oppose our guiltlesse hartes a-
gainst these titles, as our best armour of
proofe, protesting vpon our soules and saluation, and calling Almightie God and his
Angels to witnesse, that as we hope to haue
any benefit by the most precious woundes,
and death of our Lord IESVS CHRIST:
the whole and onely intent of our comming into this Realme, is no other; but to
labour for the saluation of soules, and in
peaceable and quiet sort, to confirme them
in the ancient Catholike faith, in the which
theyr forefathers liued & died, these thou-
sand foure hundred yeares, out of which we
vndoubtedly beleeue it is impossible that
any soule should be saued.

This from the sincerest of our thoughts,
before the throne of God, wee must truelie
professe, intending if no other remedie may
be had, to let your Maiestie seale it vvith
the best blood that our faithfull, & faultles
harts can afford. And if any be so hardened
in a set incredulitie, as rather to condemne
vs to periurie, thē to cleare vs vpon so deep
an oath, we will make reason his guide into
our intentions, by which if he think vs not
as much perished in our wittes, as he suppo-
                                        seth

feth vs to be in our fidelitie, he shall easilie
see the truth of our protestation : for first,
treason being an offence that carrieth with
it selfe a staine of infamie, as can neuer be
taken out, and maketh them that commit
it dead,& vnpardonable persons. Who cā
imagine any so foolish, desperate, as to in-
curre so reprochfull a crime full of certaine
perils hauing no other possible marke for
his hope, but the vttermost of worldlie e-
uils. And if any one should chaunce to be
so farre distracted from his sence, and to
throw himselfe into so bottomles a destruction: Yet that so many, and so learned,& so
graue men, as dayly suffer for their cōming
in Priestes, would cast away their labours,
liues and credittes, for nothing but a cruell and eternall reproch ; our bitterest enimie would neuer deeme it likelie, and what
other inticement shuld allure vs to be traitors, not any perswation that our selues can
compasse so great an exploit, (there being
scarce 300. Catholik priests of our nation in
the whole world; a sillie armie to subdue so
great a Monarchie) not any confidence in
Catholik assistance, whō none is so mad to
think able to doe such an enterprise, being
few in nūber, dispuruied of munitō, narowly

B 4 　　watched

watched by Officers, restrained in their liberties, impouirished in their goods, & disabled in all prouisions. Not the imagination to be aduiunced by forraine power: for then we would rather expect the conquest, till the time and oppertunitie were ripe, for vs to enter vpon our hopes, then so venterously to presse vpon the swordes of our enimies, and hazard not only our future expectations, but our present safeties, wee would rather liue abroad, though it vvere with as hard shifts, as those that now possesse honorable romes did once at *Ceneua*: then ieopard our welfare, to so many so knowne and vneuitable harmes, which we are more likely soone to feele, then so long to eschue. And if wee were to come as rebels into the Realme, our education in Colledges should be aunswerable to the qualities, we should be trained in martiall exercises, busied in publike and ciuell affaires, hardened to the field, & made to the weapō: whereas 1000. eares and eyes are witnesses, that our studies are nothing els but Philosophie & diuinity, our teachers religious men, acquainted with no other knowledge but learning and vertue, all our warlike preparations, the wresting for our wils, the mortifying of our

bodies,

bodies, and a continuall warfare with Nature,to get the victorie ouer our selues:and
for other schoolepoints of sedition, wherein this our hard friend findeth vs to be instructed, Almighty God is our witnes,that
wee neyther learne nor teach any, hauing
only had in our studies, the common end
that all men shot at, namely to attaine such
knowledge, that might be an ornament to
our functions, a help to our conuersations,
& a benefit to our countrie. But if by these
Schoolepoints of sedition be meant that religion which there we are taught: and here
wee professe this meaning aunswereth it
selfe: For this cannot be any way treasonable to your Maiesties estate,vnles that it be
esteemed offensiue, which was the faith of
all your royal auncestors,these 1400 yeres,
is the faith of the greatest part of Christendome, and for the defence whereof your
Maiesties most worthy father, attained the
glorious title of defender of the Faith. But
vvhatsoeuer this informer meant by his
schoolepoints of seditiō, we hope that your
Highnes censure,wil free vs from the thing
it selfe, sith neyther likelihood to effectu-
ate any hope at home, nor any likenesse of
our education abroad, can in your vvise-
                                        dome

wisdome seeme to argue vs guiltie of anie rebellious intentions. Let this further be an assured proofe to the contrary, that sith we are so religiously addicted to the end of our comming, that for the atchiuing thereof, we recount our torments, triumphes, & our deathes a glorie: If this end were the ouerthrow of your Maiestie: or if your displeasing had bin the point, that with so many bleeding woundes, wee haue witnessed to be so deare vnto vs, wee would with the losse of fewer liues, haue perfitted our purposes, and long ere this haue brought the cards to an vnfortunate shufling: for whosoeuer hath contented his own life, is Maister of anothers: and he that is resolute to spend his blood, will rather seeke to sell it for the intended price, then with a fruitles affection cast it away for nothing.

No no, most Gratious SOVERAIGNE, Heauen and Earth shall vvitnesse vvith vs in the dreadfull day of doome, that our breastes neuer harboured such horrible treasons, and that the end of our comming is the saluation of soules, not the murthering of bodies, wee beeing rather willing to die, then to contribute the least haire of our head to the latter, and not so wil-

ling

ling to liue, as to fhed the beft blood in our bodies: for the firft, giue then (O moft gratious Queene) wife men leaue to fee, that they fhew themfelues no leffe difloyall to your Maieftie, thē enuious to vs: that durft diuulge thefe Fables vnder the name of your Highnes, making their Prince the patroneffe of theyr fayned, and deuifed falfehood.

Now with what fhadow or likelie-hood, can it fincke into any found beleefe? that we come with ample authority, to perfwade your Maiefties Subiects to renounce theyr duties, and to bind them with othes & Sacraments, to forfweare their naturall allegence to their Princes highnes, & to yeeld all their powers to the Spanifh Princes forces: for to fay we doe it vppon hope, to be inriched with thofe poffeffions that others now enioy, hath but fmal femblance of probabilities, confidering how much likelier wee are to inherite your RACKES, and poffeffe your place of EXECVTION, then to furuiue the prefent incombences of fpirituall liuinges, or to liue to fee any dignities at the KING of SPAINE his difpofition, and fith both the daylie Martyrdomes of manie before our eyes, and

our

our own euident and hourely daungers, can
not but kill in vs all such aspiring fantasies,
if any minde were so muddie, as to sell his
soule at so base a rate.

Let it be scanned with equitie, how little
seeming of truth it carrieth, that so manie
should vpon so improbable and vncertaine
expectations, offer their liues to most probable and certaine shipwracks. And can a-
ny imagine vs to be so simple, that we cannot see how impossible it is for Catholikes
to do the king any good, though they were
as much bent that vvay as their accusers
would haue it thought: doe we not see that
they are scattered one among thousandes,
and at all such accurrants so well watched,
and so ill prouided: that to vvish them to
stirre in the Kinges behalfe, were to traine
them to their vndoing, & to expose them
to a generall massacer by domesticall furie,
and what better aduocate can plead for vs
in this case, then your Maiesties own experience, who in the last attempt of the king,
found none more forward to doe all duties,
and liberally to stretch theyr abilities, then
Catholikes were in your highnes defence,
and though they were ceassed for men
and money, farre aboue their reuennewes,
                                                    and

and fo fleeced of theyr armour and weapons, that they were lett vnfurnifhed, for
their owne fauegards : yet were they fo far
from mutining,or touch of difloyaltie, that
they willingly yeelded more, then any
other of their qualitie, vvhich doubtleffe if
Priefts had fworne them with othes, or
bound them with Sacraments, to the contrarie they would neuer haue done : fith
they venture both liues and liberties, for o-
ther charitable works of farre leffe weight,
then the auoyding of the damnable finnes,
of periurie and facriledge. It is alfo vvell
knowne euen vnto the Coyners of thefe
vntrue furmifes, that if the King fhould
come fo flenderly prouided, as to need the
handfull of Catholikes helps,(who neyther
haue conntenance,charge,nor authoritie in
the common wealth) your Maieftie neede
not greatly feare, fith it were impoffible he
fhould be ftrong, to whome fo weake, and
bootles a fuccour fhould be neceffarie. And
to what effect fhould wee then perfwade
Catholikes to leaue theyr obédience to
your Highnes, fith it can neyther benefit
vs, nor auaile them: but rather draw vpon
vs, both a manifeft fubuerfion : yea did we
not rather ftrengthen them in their duties,
                                        and

and so confirme them in patience, that with conscience and religious feare they restrained nature. It were imposible for fleshe & blood to disgest the vnmercifull vsage that they suffer by such persons, whose basenes dubleth the iniury of their abuse: for who, if it were not more than the feare of man that hath helde them, could not rather die vpon the enimies that sought their blood, (as for men of ill mind it were no hard matter) than to liue to continuall death, & to leaue the authors of their euills behinde them, to triumph ouer their ruines, and to send after them more of their deerest friendes. What gentleman coulde indure the peremtory & insolent imperiousnes of a company of gredy & manerlesse mates, which still are praying vpon Catholickes, as if they were common booties, & ransack them day & night, brauing them vnder their own roofes, with such surlinesse, as if euery cast-away were allowed to be vnto thē an absolute Prince. But happily because we desire to recouer the lapsed, & confirme the standing in the ancient faith of their forefathers, it may be presumed that this is a with-drawing from your Maiesties obedience. But if indifferēcy may be one of the Iury, disloialty shal

                                             neuer

neuer be found the fequell of any article of
our Religion, which more than any other,
tyeth vs to a moft exact fubmiffion to your
Temporall authority, and to all pointes of
alleageance, that either now in Catholicks
Countries, or euer before in Catholickes
times were acknowledged to be due to any
Chriftian Prince: doe not nowe Catholicks
gouerned by the Principales of their faith,
yeelde in refpecte thereof with a knowen
mildnefle, their goods, liberties, landes, &
liues, and doe they not with a moft refo-
lute patience obay a fcourging, and afflicting hande.

Then howe much more woulde they
bee willing to double their duties and in-
creafe their feruiceable affections to your
Highneffe, if they founde but the like clemencie that other fubiectes enioye, and
were not made (as nowe they are) common ftooles for euerie mercileffe and flint-
harted, to ftrike out vpon them the fparkes
of their fury.

It is a point of the Catholike faith, (defē-
ded by vs againft Sectaries of thefe daies)
like fubiects are bounde in confcience vnder paine of forfeting their right, in Heauen, and in incurring the guilte of eternall
                                        tor-

torments, to obay the iuſt Lawes of their
Princes, which both the Proteſtantes and
Puritanes deny, with their father and maſter *Caluin*. And therefore if we were not
preſſed to that, which by the generall ver-
dit of allegeance, was iudged breach of the
Lawe of God: we ſhou!de neuer giue your
Maieſty the leaſt cauſe of diſpleaſure, for
(excepting theſe points) which if vnpartial
audience were allowed, we coulde proue to
imploy the endleſſe miſery & damnation
of our ſoules, in all other ciuill and temporall reſpeſtes, we are ſo ſubmitted and pli-
able, as any of your Maieſties beſt beloued
ſubieſtes. If then your highneſſe woulde
vouchſafe to behold our caſe, with an vn-
fained eie, and not to viewe vs in the mir-
ror of a miſſe-informed minde, we woulde
not doubte, but that your excellent wiſe-
dome woulde finde more groundes euen in
pollicy, and in the due care of your ſafetie,
to incline your gratious fauour towards vs,
ſtil inthralled in our preſent vnhappineſſe.
But it may be, that ſome more willing to
rip vp olde faults, than to admit any clearing of them, when in their hearts they haue
already condemned vs to all puniſhments,
will heere bring in *Ballards* , and *Babingtons*,
traitors

matters against vs, as a *Golias* to ouerthrowe
all other proofes of our good meanings. To
this first we aunswere, that it were a harde
course to reproue all *Prophets* for one *Saule*,
all *Protestantes* for one *Wyat*, all *Priestes* and
Catholickes for one *Ballard* and *Babington*.

Your Maiesties sister reigned not the sixt
part of your time, & yet sundrie rebellions
were attempted by the Protestant faction
against her, in that short space, as euerie
Chronicle can witnes: whereas in this your
Maiesties prosperouse raigne of 35. yeares
in all England, the Catholikes neuer rose
but once in open field to haue wonne the
freedome of conscience, which the Protestants in those few yeares laboured vvith so
many mutinies: for as for *Parrie*, hee neuer
professed in life, nor action to be a Catholike: yea, and he tooke it offenciuely vvith
signification of his minde, in hoat wordes,
that some vpon surmise, had so named him,
and therefore howsoeuer hee might by aspiring thoughts, or mercinarie mutinies, be
by any forraine enimie vsed to euill practi-
fes, it cannot iustly be layed against vs, who
neyther priuitie nor consent to his intentions, can any way touch: and as for the action of *Babington*, that was rather a snare to

                    C   intrap

intrap them,then any deuise of their owne,
sith it was both plotted,furthered,and fini-
shed, by S. *Frauncis Walsingham*,& his other
complices,who laied & hatched al the par-
ticulers thereof, as they thought it would
best fall out to the discredit of Catholiks,&
cutting of the Queene of Scots: for first it
is to be known to all,that *Poolie* being Sir *F.
Walsinghams* man, and throughly seasoned
to his Maisters tooth,was the chiefe instru-
ment to contriue and prosecute the matter,
to draw into the net such greene wittes, as
(fearing the generall oppression,and partly
angled with golden hookes) might easilie
be ouer wrought by M.Secr. subtile & sift-
ing wit: for *Poolie* masking his secret intentions vnder the face of Religion, and abusing with irreligious Hypocrisie all Rites &
Sacraments, to borrow the false opinion of
a Catholike, still feeding the poore gentlemen with his masters baits, and he holding
the line in his hand,suffered them like silly
fishes to play themselues vppon the hooke,
till they were throughly fastned, that then
he might strike at his own pleasure, and be
sure to drawe thē to a certaine destruction.
And though none were so deepe in the very bottome of that conspiracy as *Poolie* him-
                                         selfe,

felfe, yet was hee not fo much as indited of
any crime, but after a little large imprifon-
ment (more for pollicy thē for any punifhment) fet at liberty, & in more credit then
euer he was before: for it being a fet match,
& he hauing fo well performed his euil part
(though to pleafe *Babel.*) A ftroke was giuē
to beat him, yet doubtleffe he was largely
fed in priute pay, as fo Chriftian pollicy did
beft deferue. It is alfo known by *Phillips* the
deciphers letters to his party pradifioner,
G.Gifford, in whofe cheft and chamber they
were taken at *Parris*, & by *G. Giffords* owne
examination, that thefe Gentlemen were
bought and fold, being drawen blindfolde,
to be workers of their ouerthrow, and carrie with filly *Ifaac* the fire, in which they thē
felues were to be facrificed. And fure it is,
that all the letters that fed them with forraine hopes, all the deuifes that wrought
them into home-bred imaginations, fprung
all out of the Fountaine of Sir FRAVNCIS
WALSINGHAMS fine head : for GIL-
BERT GIFFORD hauing fome yeares before beene Maifter Secretaries intelligen-
cer, (as the date of *Phillippes* Letter vnto
him difcouered) when the matter was once
on foote in England, was made the meane

to followe it in Fraunce among certaine
of the Scottish Queenes friendes, more apt
to enter, then able to go through great dif-
fignements, where he knowing of the letters, and the courſe how they were conuey-
ed, difcouered all to M. Secretarie, to whō
alſo he brought diuers of the like tennor,
written partly to the Queene, partly to *Babington*, at his owne comming into England:
wheras more thē 3. months before, the coū-
cell would ſeeme to know theſe intentions:
and whereby often reſort, to Sir *Frauncis
Walſinghams* houſe, in priuate ſort hee had
taken of him priue directions, to make his
courſe the more plauſible for his proceedings in Fraunce, he practiſed here with the
French Embaſſadours *Mounſieur Catanenſe*,
whom then he knew to be verie well affected both to the Scottiſh Queene, & to the
Duke of Guyes, & though he were a man
of more then ordinarie diſcourſe: yet with
ſo forſworne an hipocriſie, and ſo deep periuries, did *Gifford* ouer reach him, that when
the traine was diſcouered, ſome of the
Gentlemen inraged with ſo great impietie,
ſaid that though it were a great part of the
Goſpel that an Engliſh man would be true,
they ſhould hardly beleeue it, for that Diuell

vell *Giffordes* fake , as in their pafsion they
tearmed him: But fo it was that *Gilberts* wit
farre too good for fo bad an owner,& new-
ly refined by M. Secretaries forge, wonne
fo much credit, that he being commended
and beleeued, as his defire was, he went o-
uer to intreate by meanes with the Duke
of Guyfe, and fuch others as were thought
fit to be taken in , as ftales to countenance
the matter , and to put the Gentlemen in
vaine expectations , till the thred were
fpunne to the intended length . And fo far
was this vnfortunate wretch giuen ouer to
defperate malice , that firft to poffeffe him
more of M. Secretaries good opinion, and
to fhew his aptneffe to be vfed in fuch ex-
ploits, he dedicated to him, a booke of hys
owne compiling, breathing fuch Infamies,
and Atheifmes, as beft became the fpirit of
fo periured an Apoftata : and on the other
fide, to fhun the fufpition of being M. Secretaries bad inftrument in this vnchriftian
pollicie, he was himfelfe confeffed, purpofely Graduated , and as it is thought made
Prieft: fo impious were the meanes to wreft
the poore Gentlemen from their duties, to
theyr confufion. *Phillips* alfo, who was M.
Secretaries right hand, held correfpondent

with

with *Gilbert Gifford*, ſtil keeping the ice from
breaking, till they were all vpon it, whome
they meant to drowne in the ſame deſtruction. And to draw the Queene of Scottes
into the better opinion of this deſignemēt,
vvhome experience had taught to ſuſpect
ſo daungerous motions. The matter vvas
with continuall and ſecret meetinges verie
ſeriouſlie vrged with her agents in *Fraunce*,
in whome it is feared they relyed too much
affiance : but vvhether for loue to theyr
Maiſter, they were apt to entertaine anie
hope of her deliuerie, or for league vvith
M. Secretary, too ready to build vpon his
foundations, they induced the Queene to
like of their good will, that were willing to
aduenture their ſtates and liues to doe her
ſeruice, and as things were by theſe inuentions, ripening in *Fraunce* : ſo *Poolie* no leſſe
diligently plied the matter at home, continually conuerſing with *Ballard*, & the gentlemen, & laboring to draw more conies in
to the hey. It is ſtrange to marke with what
cunning, the graue and wiſer ſort of Catholikes, were ſounded a far off, not by reuealing any direct intention: but ſo nicely glā-
cing at generall pointes, with iffes & andes,
that they neuer vnderſtood the language,

till

till effects did consture these roauing speaches: yet when so much of their disposition was known, by their vnwillingnes to heare, & peremtorines in cutting off the Officers of such discourses, there was no lesse care vsed to conceale these purposes from them, then there had bin cuning to serch out how they would deeme of thē: for it was feared, their wisedome would haue found out the fraud, & vntimely haue launced an vnripe impostume. It is further knowen that the coppie of that letter which *Babbington* sent to the Queene of Scots, was brought ready penned by *Poolie*, from M. Secretary: the answere whereof, was the principal grounds of the Queenes condemnation. There was also found in Sir *Frauncis Walsinghams* accountes after his decease, a note of 7000. pounds bestowed vpon *Nato* & *Curlie*, who being the Queenes Secretaries, framed such an answere as might best serue for a bloody time, & fit his intentiō that rewarded them with so liberall a fee. This made *Phillippes* so bold to aduise *Gifford* by his Letters, that if he came in any suspition of detecting the Queene, he should lay it eyther to *Nato*, or *Curlie*, whose shoulders being bolstred with so large bagges, he thought vvould be best

C 4　　　　　　　able

able to beare the burden away: **It is also**
certaine that *Barnard* (made M. Secretaries
vndoubted agent) went ouer into Fraunce
about this practise, there free passages being warranted with all securitie: when they
had beene there so long, that *Barnard* might
looke into these proceedings, that in those
Countries were actors in the matter, he re-
turned againe with *Ballard*, and hauing a
large Commission from Sir *Fraunces Walsingham*, to take what manner of horses hee
would, out of anie Gentlemans Parke, or
Pasture, and of other vnusuall liberties, he
went with *Ballard* into the North, there he
sought with what sleights he could, to haue
wonne diuers Gentlemen, making *Ballards*
credit his countenance, and drawing the
poore men vnwittingly to be the occasion
of his own and others ruine. In the end hauing cusoned another to get a Letter of
commendations to the Lord Prior of Scotland: he sifted out of him what he could, &
taking vvith him a Letter touching this
matter, hee brought it vvith all the intelli-
gence and successe of his malicious Pilgri-
mage, to the Councell. And though hee
were thus inward and conuersant with *Ballard*, carrying him to sundrie Gentlemen of
account,

account, to feele & tempt them about this
action, and to drawe them into the desired
compasse: yea though himselfe were a motion to some, to enter into it, pretending
that he had ouerreached M. Secretarie, in
getting that Commission: yet was hee neuer called to the barre, but hired to stay a
time in restraint, with such a recompence
for his seruice, as might be well perceaued
to be large, by his liberal spending, & plen-
ty in prison, hee being otherwise a hungrie
and needy marchant, without eyther trade
or liuing to maintaine such expences : and
how priuie S. *Fran.* was to the whole course
of the Gentlemens actions, and to the certaine period of the time, wherein all his in-
deuours would come to the full point, may
be gethered by this, that being by a Priest
that was to be banished sued vnto for 20.
dayes respite to dispatch his busines: first
repeating the number, and pausing a while
with him selfe. No saith he, you shall haue
but 14. for if I should grant you any more,
it would be to your hinderance, as you shal
heare hereafter : wherein he said true, for
much about that time, was publike notice
taken of *Babbingtons* matter, all waies vvere
watched, infinite houses searched, hewes &
cryes

cries raifed, frights bruted in the peoples
eares, and all mens eies filled with a fmoke,
as though the whole Kealme had beene on
fire, whereas in trueth, that was but the
hiffing of a fewe greene twigs, of their own
building, which they might without any
fuch vprore haue quenched with a handful
of water, but that made not fo much for
their purpofe as this buggifh terible fhows:
and thought they were fo well acquainted
with all the Gentlemens hearts, that they
might euery houre in the daye or night,
haue drawen them in the nette, like a couie
of partridges. Yet forfooth, muft fome of
them be fuffred purpofely to flee that they
might haue the better colour to make thofe
generall demonftrations of a needles feare.
Iohn Sauage likewife when he came to the
Courte, was fo wel knowen to be a chicken
of that feather, that two *Pentioners* were
charged to haue an eie vnto him, and to
watche fo long as he ftayed there, and yet
was he fuffered to goe vp and downe, and
vfually to haunt the prefence, till all irons
were hotte that were laide in the fire, to
feare the credite of poore Catholickes, and
to giue the *Qveene* of *Scottes* her deathes
wounde: it was alfo noted, that after *Bal-*
lard

lard was inchaunted with *Poolies* charmes,
he became a ftainger to all Iefuites and o-
ther Prieftes, beeing limited by the poli-
ticke rules of his promptor, to fuch company as Mafter Secretary knewe to be of diuine fights, to fee through fo many miftes,
as he by his inftrumentes had alreadie caft
before their eies, the Gentelmen were alfo throughlye charmed, to keepe their
councells from the wifer and mature fort
of Catholickes, whome there was no hope
to make them parties. Of which *Iohn Char-
nocke* at the barre faide the reafon to be becaufe the older, the colder, yet the true
grounde was a fpeciall promife of Mafter
Secretary to keepe the threede out of their
handes that woulde foone haue vnwounde
it to the bottome, for what man that had
but knowne the firft fillable of pollicye,
woulde thinke it a likelye courfe for them,
to alter the whole ftate of fo great a kingdome to quite contrarye Religion and go-
uernmente, that neither hadde power to
backe them, (as then there was none readie, nor helpes at home to fupport them)
being al but priuate gentelmen, (neither of
wealth, nor fufficient credit for fuch a matter) to carry with them any great numbers,
                              who

who would not haue pittied their indiscretion, that intending so great an alteration, thought it a fit way to goe pickeing here & there one, as if such plots in so many young tongues could lie hidden so long, as to giue them respite to gleane a sufficient army. And for men that pleadged their heades in so daungerous attempts, to be so credulous, as to rest their hopes vpon so fliting & faire promises of forraine helps, without the certainty of such preparation of shippes & mē, as might come in due time to followe their beginnings, was a most childishe sight. And therefore for any man of experience that had looked to it, there would haue offered it selfe a iust suspition, that the plotte was rather a traine to entrappe the actors in it, than a meane to effect that intended by it. For though they had cut off some of the Councell: yea, and dismantled the realme of your sacred maiesty, (which Gods goodnesse neither woulde, nor we hope wil permit) yet had their purpose beene farre from any semblance of their desired issue, for then they must haue proclaimed either the Queene of *Scotts*, or at least by some means haue sought her deliuery, & consequentlie haue notified to the worlde that for her rising

fing was your Maiesties going downe. And
what a tide of refiftance would this notice
haue done, none can be fo feely but he muft
needs fee. For firft by the oath of affociatiõ,
al the Nobility had bin bound, to perfift hir
todeath, which many without an oth would
otherwife haue beene apte enough to doe.
The crowne alfo beeing lefte without anie
declared owner, a faire goale for them that
runne firft at it, no doubte but diuerfe com-
petitors woulde haue hindered her courfe,
to haue made her hopes-way to fo faire
an aime. Then the aft of PARLIAMENT
excluding ftraingers from the Crowne, (as
fhe by diuerfe meanes was diuoulged to be)
woulde alfo haue added dainger to her
claime, efpecially confidering the auncient
& deepe rooted diflike, betweene the *Scot-
tifhe* and the *Englifhe*, no fmall motiue to a
popular mutiny: but moft of all her vehe-
mency in the Catholicke religion, (againft
which both the Nobility, Cleargy, & com-
mons were moft violently bent) woulde
haue made them ready in that refpecte, to
take heed of the leaft of thefe lettes, to ex-
clude her from the Crowne, and to tranf-
late the title to fome other more futeable,
to their beleefe. All which impedimentes
meeting

meeting so full with euery eie, that did but loke towards them, must needs haue made any in reason to conclude it an impossibility for these gentlemen to haue compassed their drifte, which also they might easily haue discerned, had they not bin bewitched with master secretaries fine deuises, & deluded with his spies, cosoning letters and messages from forraine partes, for the *Spanishe* fleete was not ready in two yeers after, and in *Fraunce*, (more than a fewe that in *Gascoine* were imploied against the *Hugonits*) there was no kinde of prouision by sea, nor lande, yea the king was then knowen to be so sure a friend to *England*, and so sharpe an enimy to the *Guisian* partie, in which the Queenes affiance was only fastned, that he woulde neuer haue suffered her hopes to haue had officer by any *French* assistants. And from *Scotland* they neuer looked for any aide, knowing that if they were not euery way blinde, howe the king was wholly carried a-way with an *Englsh* byas, and so setled in the possession of the Crowne, and in the bent of the contrary faith, that what soeuer he might haue attempted for himselfe, it was neuer likely he woulde haue followed their designement, of which the

princi-

principall fcope was the alteration of Religion. And he that in refpecte of his beleefe,
refufed with the *Infant* of *Spaine*, the prefent
poffeffiõ of the Lowe-Countries as fiftance
for the chalenging of his other titles, and
promifed to be proclamed heire, if the *Spa-
nifhe* king fhould faile, was doubtleffe much
better armed againft their flender perfwa-
tions which could neuer haue tempted him
with fuch glorious offers. Finally the weak-
neffe of their beginning was an apparant
proofe that it was conceaued and bred by
them that woulde be fure to bring it to an
abortion, and neuer fuffer it to preuaile to
any other purpofe, but to make vs more
hatefull, and to bereaue your Maiefty of
your more infamed than faulty Cofen.

Thus much Gratious Soueraigne, is your
Highnes drawen by thefe indirect courfes,
to vfe your vnwilling fword, againft your
leffe fauoured, then faithfull Subiects, and
put in vngrounded feares of theyr difloyaltie, who are of themfelues fo farre from
defiling theyr hartes with any treafonable
thoughts, that theyr heauie enimies had no
other wayes to difmount them from theyr
beft deferuing, but by violenting them too
euilly; by thefe finefter inuentions wee
knowe

know your Maiesties minde to be, from
yeelding your Royall assent to so vglie
shifts, you euer binding your desires to the
limits of vertue, and measuring your Rega-
litie, more by will to saue, then by power to
kill. Yet it cannot but afflict vs, to see your
Highnes eares so gaurded against our complaints, and possessed with theyr perswations, that most maligne vs, that we can haue
no other orators for your gratious fauours,
then the tongues that cannot afford vs any
fauourable word. It hath bin alwaies the
pollicie of our aduersaries, to keepe vs a-
loofe from reuealing our vniust oppressi-
ons, lest they should incline your mercie to
pitty vs, and they so arme your Highnesse
with so hard informations against vs, that
they make our very sute for leuity seeme
an offensiue motion: yet sith wee must eyther speake or dye, seeing so many slightes
are put in vre to burie vs quicke in all miseries, we hope God will make our petitions
weigh into your hart, and winne your clemency to consider our distresse. Notwithstanding the slaunders that are published
against vs: and if we may make our benefit of that which others haue vsed to our
greatest harmes, we thinke that very act of

Bab-

Babington, may infure your Highneſſe of the impoſſibility of Catholickes to bee drawen to rebellion, for when our oppreſſions were heauieſt, our deathes ordinary, and ſo fine wittes buſied to drawe vs into the foyle, yet was there not in all *England* in ſo long time founde out aboue one Prieſt, and he one of the meaneſt, and fewe more than a dozen Lay-men, that coulde be wonne to ſtoope to theſe odious lures. Let not therefore this more preiudice vs than ſo open threats, and direct menacings of the whole ſtate, haue endamaged others, ſith of our ſide, there followed no effecte, & our numbers were leſſe likely to hurt (not ariuing to a ſcoare) than theſe that dared your Maieſties Scepter with many thouſands, but becauſe we like God-Almighties fooles, (as ſome ſcornefully call vs) lay our ſhoulders vnder euery loade, and are contented to make patience the onely ſalue for all ſores: many that ſee, are willing to vſe the awe of conſcience, for the warrant to treade vs downe, whereas they preſume not to meddle with others, although more fatall to your Highneſſe eſtate, knowing that if ſhe ſhoulde make them partners, but of halfe our afflictions, they woulde ſeeme to be-

D   wray,

wray more impatient ftomackes, for if
the working of their fpirites bee fo vehe-
ment, as with fo little feare and fo much
folemnity to proclaime a newe Chrift and
king of the earth , adding the creaft of an
vfurped Mefsias to countenance, the cha-
lenge of humane foueraignty. If being fo
freely permitted to vfe their confciences
to themfelues, and to enioie their honours,
offices, and fauours in the common wealth,
without any tafte of your fcourges, they
notwithftanding fparkle not fuch tokens
of a concealed flame, it can-not choofe
but bee feene and knowne, howe much
more caufe there is, to loke into their actions, and to feare their attempts, than to
wreake fo much anger vpon vs, that were
neuer chargeable with fo huge enormities.
And yet the death of one man fhut vp in
a filent obliuion, that open offer of vprore,
& moft blafphemous impietie againft God
and your Maieftie, though it be generallie
knowne that there were more fauorers and
bearers of that part, than coulde be euer
charged with *Babingtons* offence.

We fpeake not this to incenfe your Maieftie againft others, being fo well acquainted with the fmarte of our owne punifhe-
mentes,

mentes, to wiſhe any Chriſtian to be per-
taker of our paines. Our onely intent is,
moſt humbly to intreat, that if ſo impatient a zeale, accompanied with ſeditious
wordes and actions, was ſo eaſilie finiſhed
and remitted in the chaſtiſement of one,
your Highneſſe in clemencye, woulde not
ſuffer ſo many innocent Prieſts & Catholikes, to be ſo cruelly and continually martyred, who neuer incurred ſo enormous
crimes. And ſith we daylie in our liues, &
alwaies at our executions vnfeinedly praie
for your Maieſty, ſith at our deathes wee
alwaies proteſt vpon our ſouls our clearnes
from treaſon, & our dutiful & loyal minds,
ſubſcribing our proteſtation, with our dea-
reſt blood. Let vs not moſt mercifull So-
ueraine) be thus daily plunged deeper into
newe diſgraces, and ſtill proclaimed and
murthered for traitours. Let vs not be ſo
eſteemed for Godleſſe and deſperate mon-
ſters, as to ſpende our laſt breath in boot-
leſſe periuries, or at our greateſt neede of
Gods fauour, to ſacrifice to the diuell our
finall vowes, what reaſon then can moue vs
ſo damnably to diſſemble, when our expi-
red date cutteth off all hopes, our deathe
the ende of euills, hath in this worlde no

D 2   after

after feares, and a resolute contempt of our
own liues, excludeth al thoughts of meaner
liues, yea if any hope, feare, or loue carry a-
ny swaye, (as doubtlesse there doth in all
Christian minds) it is a hope to be saued, a
feare to be damned, aloue to God, to his
trueth, & our endlesse wel-doing, al which
in that dreadfull moment, (whereupon de-
pendeth our whole eternity) can neuer be
motiues vnto vs, to sende our forsworne
soules headlong to hell-fire. But let vs pro-
ceede in our necessary defence, as the inditor doth in his false accusations, (we are
charged for the easiar alteration of vnnaturall people, weake of vnderstanding to
yeeld to our perswations) to haue brought
Bulles, & Indulgences pretending to pro-
mise Heauen, or cursing damnation to hel.
It was but a forraine supply for want of true
factes, to fasten vpon this fonde conclusi-
on being so farre from trueth, and so full of
incongruity, that euery nouice in our faith,
can reproue it for error. I omitte the reprochfull termes of vnnaturall and weake
vnderstanding, most iniuriously fathered
vppon such a Princes pen, whome a Royall minde hath taught, not to staine her paper, or blemishe her stile, with those and
                                        so

so many other bafe and reuiling wordes,
as are peftered together in this proclamation. I reporte all men to their eies, and
eares for aunfwere to thefe flaunders, whether (the foule-rightes excepted) in all
temporall duties, Catholikes be not as naturall to their Prince, as beneficial to their
neighbours, as reguler in themfelues, as a-
ny other fubieftes, yeelding the vttermoft
of all that is exacted in Subfidies, Perfons,
Men, and Munition, befides the patient
loffe of our Goods and Landes for their
Recufanfie.

Let it be read in letters of experience,
whether Catholikes be of fhallowe braine,
or of fo weake vnderftanding, that they
woulde be carried away with thefe imagi-
nary Bulles, promifing heauen, and threatning hell, of which Catholikes eares neuer
hearde before.

This worlde can witneffe, that in Diuinitie, Lawe, and Phificke, and all other
faculties and functions, either of Piety, or
pollicy, all *Englande*, I may fay all *Chriften-
dome*, fcarce knoweth any men more re-
noumed than our ENGLISHE Catho-
likes, (without vanity be it fpoken in a iuft
defence) but though they were not fuch

D 3   *Sallomons*

Sallomons for wifedome, as fome others take
themfelues to bee, yet they bee allowed
ordinary fence and intendment, which if
it be but fo much, as may ferue them to
tell ouer the Articles of their Creede, it is
enough to be knowen that no Bulle can
promife Heauen, or threaten Hell, but for
keeping or breaking Gods Commaunde-
mentes.

Iudge then, (moft Soueraigne L A D I E)
whether that it be not too great an indignation to fee the facred name of our Noble
Q v e e n e, which next to Gods worde
fhoulde be honoured among the moft im-
pregnable teftimonies of trueth, to be with
vndeferued abufe by any fubiecte fubfcri-
bed to thefe moft vaine, and fo impofsible
fictions.

Who likewife (but meaning to make his
P r i n c e s paine a fpring of vntruethes)
woulde againft the certaine knowledge of
fo many and fo infinite people, as well feers
as hearers, euen as from your M a i e s t y:
that no P r i e s t is Indited, Arreined, or
Executed for Religion: fith it is fo often,
and in euerie Sefsions feene, that vnleffe
we our felues fhoulde confeffe manifeftly
that wee were P r i e s t e s, no other.
treafon-

treasonable crime, coulde bee iustly proued against vs, and for this (howe farre it
is from deseruing this odious title) your
Maiesty may easilye gather, for that all
Christendome hath these fifteene hundred
yeeres honoured for Pastours and gouer-
nours of their soules, those that nowe are
more than vnfauourably termed Traytors,
yea if to be a Priest made by the authoritie
of the See of Rome, & present within your
highnesse dominions, be a iust title of treason. If they that harbour, reliue, or receiue
any such, be worthy to bee deemed fellons:
then all the glorious Saintes of this Lande
whose Doctrine and vertue God Almightie confirmed with many miracles, were
no better than traitours, and their a-bet-
tours fellons. Then D A M I A N V s and
F V G A T I V s, that first brought Christi-
anity in King L V C I V s his time, 1400.
yeers past: then Saint A V G V S T I N E & his
companions that conuerted our Realme in
Saint G R E G O R I E s time were, who
in the compasse of treason, sith theyr functions and ours were all one equally deui-
ded from the Sea of Rome, from whence
they were directly by the Popes *Elutherius*
and *Gregorie* sent into this kingdome being
D 4   Priests,

Priests, and Religious men, as all antiquity
doth witnes, yea all the Churches and places of pietie, (chiefe ornaments of this Noble Realme) all the Charters and Indow-
ments bestowed vpon Priests & Religious
persons, & yet registred in the ancient laws
are but monuments of felonie, & fauourers
of treason. And if it should please God to a-
lot the day of generall resurrection in your
Maiesties time, (a thing not impossible as
vncertaine) what would so many Millions
of Prelates, Pastours, and Religious people
thinke, that both honored and blessed this
kingdome with the holines of their life, and
excellencie of their learning: much vvould
they rest amazed, to see their Relikes bur-
ned, their memories defaced, and all theyr
Monasteries dedicated once to pietie, prai-
er, and chastitie: now either buried in their
ruines, or prophaned by vnfitting vses: but
more would they muse to find their Priesthood reckoned for treason, and the releefe
of Priests condemned for felonie; these being the two principall testimonies of deuo-
tion, that theyr ages were acquainted with:
yea, what would your Maiesties Predices-
sors, and Fathers, with the Peeres & people
of your Realme thinke , when they should
see

fee themfelues in tearmes of felonie by the
cenfure of your lawes, for erecting Bifhop-
rikes, and endowing Churches, founding
Colledges, and fome other like places, for
the honoring and maintaining of Priefts, &
Religious men: yea and for giuing theyr
Ghoftly Father in way of releefe, but a cup
of cold water, though it were at the verie
point of death when they needed fpirituall
comfort, being to abandon their mortall
bodies: and though the Priefts at that time
were not made fince the firft yeare of your
Maiefties raigne, which is the onely point
which excludeth them from the ftatute, yet
were.they all fuch Prieftes, or Abbetors of
them, as were confecrated by authority de-
riued from the Sea of Rome, (as al regifters
doe record) and prefent within your Maiefties realme, which are the only materiall
points, for which we haue bin, or can be cō-
demned: for the Sea of Rome remayning
in the felfe-fame ftate, ftill indued with the
fame authoritie, and neither the manner of
our creation, or Prieft-hood it felfe, is any
thing altered from that it was. Why fhould
it be more treafonable to be made Prieftes,
in the midfomer day of your firft yeare, the
the next day before, or the laft of Queene
Maries

Maries Reigne, for neyther doth the Pope,
nor any other Bishop by making vs Priefts
claime or get any more authority in our
Realme , then they of *Bafell* or *Geneua* , by
making Proteftants Minifters, nor wee by
receauing our orders frō him, acknowledge
in him a mite worthy of authoritie , more
then euery lay-mā doth through all Chri-
ftendome:& as for othes & promifes in receauing Holy Orders, we neyther take nor
plight any but one common to the Priefts
of all Nations , vvhich is a folemne vow of
perpetuall Chaftitie , a thing rather plea-
fing then offenfiue to a vertuous Queene,
who hath for her felfe made choife of a fin-
gle life . And who then can finde any cul-
lourable pretence to verifie this flaunder
more grieuous to vs then death it felfe, that
wee are not condemned and executed for
Religion, but for treafon : we being alwaies
arraigned & caft vpon this ftatute of comming into England, being fince the firft of
your Maiefties Raigne , made Priefts by
the authority of the Sea of Rome: for what
can be meant by Religion , if it be not a
point, yea and a chiefe point thereof to re-
ceaue a Sacrament of the CATHOLIKE
CHVRCH (as wee acknowledge Prieft-
hood

hood to be) of the chiefe P a s t o v r and
P r e l a t e thereof, from vvhence vvee
can proue all lawfull Prieſt-hood to haue
deſcended this fifteene hundred yeares, &
to auouch vs Traitors for comming into
England, or remayning here is an iniurie
without ground, ſith in this reſpe &t, the ſtatute could not touch vs (ſetting prieſthood
aſide) many comming and going at theyr
pleaſure, without ſuch ſuppoſall ot treaſon:
But it is our comming in as Prieſts, that is ſo
highly condemned, & therefore our Prieſt-
hood and nothing els puniſhed by this law:
And howbeit the chiefe deuiſers of this, &
all the like decrees (euer ſeeking to attayne
their drifts, againſt religion vnder ſome o-
ther pretence) exempted the Q v e e n e
M a r i e Prieſtes, from the compaſſe of
this Statute, by a limitation of time : yet
vvas that but a colour to inueagle ſuch
eies, as either through careleſneſſe woulde
not loke, or through weakeneſſe could not
reach to their finall intentions, and little regarded that a few old & feble men, whom
neither age, nor courſe of nature, nor they
by any other a &ts might ſone cut off, ſo the
ſeed might be extinguiſhed & a new ſupply
of poſterity preuented, which by this Lawe
(though

(though in vaine) they purposed to doe.
Be it therfore neuer so much mistitled with
the vndeserued name of treaso,the base reproch cannot couer the truth fro your Maiesties best deseruing insight, which by this
cannot but apparantly see, that it is,it vvas,
and euer will be religion,for which wee expose our blood to the hazard of these laws,
& for the benefit of souls, yeeld our bodies
to all extremities. It may be also easily ga-
thered by the weakest wits,what huge treasons they be, for which we be condemned,
sith at all our araignements and deaths, we
are offred,that once going to church,shuld
wipe away the heinousnes of this treason: a
curtesie neuer mētioned to true traitors, &
a sufficient proofe it was a religious faulte,
that is so easily clered by a religious action:
yet we must with iust complaint of most vn
iust proceeding acknowledge , that at the
bar many things, (whereof not so much as
our thoughts were euer guiltie) are besides
our Priesthood,partly by inditement,part-
ly by some in office laid to our charge, and
yet so naked of proofs,or of any likely con-
iectures, that we can neuer be condemned
of any thing , but our owne confession of
Priest hood : and hereof the last araigne-
ment

ment of three Prieſtes at *Weſtminſter*, euen
ſince the Proclamatiõ, gaue ſuch an ample
notice, as the Lord chiefe Iuſtice ſaid; that
though many thinges had bin vrged, yet
was hee to pronounce ſentence of death a-
gainſt them, only vpon the ſtatute of comming into England, being made Prieſts after the Romaine order, ſince the firſt of her
Maieſties raigne: yet it hath bin ſome time
obiected againſt Prieſtes, that they ſhould
pretend to kil your ſacred Maieſty: a thing
ſo contrary to their calling, ſo farfrom their
thoughts, ſo wide of all pollicy, that who-
ſoeuer will afford reaſon her right, cannot
with reaſon thinke them ſo fooliſh to wiſh,
muchleſſe to worke ſuch a thing, euery way
odious, no way beneficiall. Wee come to
ſhed our owne blood, and not to ſeeke the
effuſion of others blood. The weapons of
our warrefare are Spirituall not offenſiue,
and vvee carrie our deſires, ſo high lifted
aboue ſauage and brutiſh purpoſes, that we
rather hope to make our owne Martyr-
dome, ſteppes to a glorious eternitie, then
our deathes, our purchaſe of eternall diſ-
honour. And who but men vnwilling to
haue vs thought owners of our right wittes,
vvould abuſe your Maieſties authoritie,
to

to sooth vpp so great vnlikelie-hoodes, sith
none can be so ignorant, how pernicious it
vvere for PRIESTES & CATHOLIKS,
to loose the protection of your Maiesties
Highnesse, and to forgoe present suerties,
for vncertaine chaunges. For if any would
bequeath his blood to so brutish a fact: if
hee were not as much enimy to all men, as
to him-selfe, hee vvould at the least haue
some apparance of benefite, that might
be supposed to ensewe to those, for whose
good, hee vvould be thought to haue cast
away his life: but none that looketh but a
steppe before him, into future accidentes,
can thinke it any vvaie auaileable vnto vs,
to be bereaued of your Maiestie: sith that
our hopes are now bent, not vppon anie
vnspected happinesse, but onelie vppon a
more intollerable miserie. And although
our cause at this present be so hard, that it
is the next degree to extremetie: yet vvee
see thinges hang in so doubtsull tearmes,
that the death of your Maiestie vvould be
an alarumme to infinite vprores, and likelier to breed all men to a generall calami-
tie, then CATHOLIKES anie cause of
comfort: and therefore vs to seeke it, were
not onelie an impietie to our Countrie, but

a

a tyrranie to our felues, vvho of all others vvere fureft to finde the fierceft encounters of the popular peoplesfurie, & though vvee could, (as then no man pofsible can) finde a priuie or fecret harbour from the common ftormes:) yet whome fhould vve look vpō that may promife vs any hope or comfort of bettering our fortunes, fith the likelieft to fucceede, are furtherfrom our Religion, then your Maieftie euer vvas, and likelier to charge vs vvith a heauier hand, then to lighten the burthen, vvherevvith vvee are alreadie brufed, and both your Maiefties Sex inclined to pietie, and the mildeneffe of your owne difpofition, rather vvrefted by others, then prooue of it felfe, too angrie refolution, maketh vs more vvilling to languifh in this quartane of our lingring cumbers, then to hazarde our felues to thofe extreame fittes, that might happilie be caufed by the heate of men, more vvar-like and leffe pittying mindes: for nowe our difpairefull eftate is much like vnto a vveake and tender Caftell, befeeged vvith manie enimies, and continually battered and beaten with fhotte, in vvhich though the aboade be amongft manie accounted moft daungerous

gerous and diftreffeful, yet without it there
is nothing but certaine miferies, reft you
therefore affured (moft Gratious Soueraigne) fith we are deuoted to fo harde a
deftiny, that we neither dare hope for any
caufe of contentment, or ende of vnhappi-
neffe, we had rather truft to the foftneffe
of your mercifull hand, (and next to God)
to reft to the hight of your pofsibilities, in
your fauor and clemency, than by any vnnaturall violents againft Gods annointed
to feeke the ruine of your Realme, and
drawe vpon our felues the extreameft of
worldly harmes, in this only we craue ad-
mittance of our loweft requefts, that euill
informers rob not our wordes of due beleefe, nor drawe your wifedome to their
friuolous feares, wholly grounded in meere
fictions, and purpofely deuifed to our igno-
minie. Nowe whereas he impofeth on fome
to haue faide, that they woulde take part
with the Armie of the Pope, againft our
Realme, it is a moft vnlikely thing, vnleffe
it were proceeded out of fome fraile toung
by force of torture, that was rather willing
to fay what they feemed to require, than to
abide the hel of their intolerable torments,
for fuch is nowe our forlorne eftate, that we
                                        are

are not onely prisoners, at euery promoters
pleasure, and common steps for euerie one
to tread vpon : but mē so neglected by our
Superiours, and so left to the rage of pittɪ-
les persons , that contrary to the course of
all Christian lawes, wee are by extreamest
tormēts forced to reuile our very thoughts.
It is not enough to confesse that wee are
Priests: (for it is seldome denyed) but wee
must be vrged vpon the torture, with other
odious interogations, farre from our knowledge, much further from our action. We
are compelled to accuse those whome our
conscience assureth to be innocent, and to
cause their ouerthrow by our confessions,
to whose souls we are Pastors, and they the
fosterers of our bodies. And if we doe not,
because without vntruthes and iniuries we
cannot answere, we are so vnmercifuly tormented, that our deathes, (though as full of
pangs as hanging, drawing , and vnbowel-
ling vs quicke can make them) are vnto vs
rather remedies, thē further reuenges, more
releasing then increfing our miseries. Some
are hanged by the handes eight or nine
houres, yea twelue houres together, till not
only their wits , but euen their senses fayle
them, & when the soule (weary of so paine-

E   full

full an harbour, is ready to depart, then apply the cruell comforts & reuiue vs, only to
martyr vs with more deaths, for eft-soones
they hang vs in the same maner, trying our
eares with such questions, which either we
cannot, because we knowe not, or without
damning of our soules we may not suffice;
some are whipped naked so long, and with
such excesse, that our enimies vnwilling to
giue constancy the right name, said that no
man without the helpe of the diuell, coulde
with such vndauntednesse suffer so much.
Some besides their tormentes haue beene
forced to be continually bobed & clogged
many weekes together, pyned in their dy-
et, consumed with varmine, and almost sti-
feled with stench, and kept from sleepe,
till they were past the vse of reason, and
then examined vpon the aduantage, when
they coulde scarce giue an account of their
owne names. Some haue beene tortured
in those partes, that it is almost a torture to
Christian eares to heare it, let it then bee
iudged, what it was to Chaste and Modest
men to indure it, the shame beeing no lesse
offensiue to their minde, than the paine,
though most excessiue to their bodies; diuerse haue beene throwne into vnsauorie
                                    and

and darke dungeons, and brought so neere
starving, that some for famine haue licked
the verye moisture of the walles. Some
haue beene so farre consumed, that they
were hardly recouered of life. What vn-
sufferable agonies we haue beene put vnto vpon the Racke, it is not possible to ex-
presse, the feeling so farre exceedeth all
speech. Some with instruments haue beene
rouled vp together like a balle, and so cru-
shed that the blood sprouted out at diuerse
partes of their bodies.

To omitte diuerse other cruelties, better knowne by their particular names, to
the Racke-Miasters, and Executioners,
then to vs, though too wel acquainted with
the experience of their smartes. It is not
possible to keepe any reckoning of the ordinary punishments of B R I D E W E L L,
nowe made the common Purgatorye of
P R I E S T E S and C A T H O L I K E S,
as grinding in the Mille, beeing beaten like
slaues, and other outragious vsages: for to
these we are most cruelly enforced, at the
discreation of such, as beeing to all other
despised, vnderlings, take their onely feli-
citie in laying their greedye commaunde-
ments, & shewing their authority vpon vs,

E 2   to

to whome euery warder, Iaylor, and Por-
ter, is an vnrefifted Lord.

Thus(moft excellēt Princes)are we vfed,
yea thus are we vnhumanely abufed, for
being Prieftes, & of our forefathers faith,
and of purpofe to wring out of vs fome o-
dious fpeeches, which might ferue at our
arraignments for ftales to the people, to
make them imagine greater matters than
can be proued: whereas neither euill meaning, nor trueth, but torture onely was
guide to the toung that fpake them, within
fo hard conflictes of flefhe & bloode, with
fo bitter conuulfions, is apte to vtter anie
thing to abridge the fharpeneffe and feue-
rity of the paine. Such vndoubtedly were
the wordes alleaged of taking part with the
armie of the *Popes*, againft our Realme, if
they euer iffued out of Prieftes mouthes,
or elfe they were fpoken by fome vnskilfull
Lay-man, that knowing not howe to aunfwere fuch captious queftions, and for reuerence of the chiefe Paftour of GODS
Church, not daring to fay that he woulde
not take part againft him, had rather venture his life, by faying too much, than hazard his confcience in not aunfwering fufficient. But the ignorance of one muft not
                                    meafure

measure the meanings of all, whom knowledge of our deathes teaches aunswers far
different from his, and maketh vs ready to
defend our Realme, as the Catholike subiectes, of you Maiesties auncestours, or any
other Princes were, or euer shall bee. For
did we carry so traiterous mindes as our e-
nimies giue out, we coulde not possible bee
so cowardly or foolish, as to suffer these ty-
rannies for nothing, beeing otherwise re-
solued to dye, and knowing the heads and
handes from whence these cruelties pro-
ceede, without your Maiesties priuities.
But as with patience and mildenesse we hitherto haue, and hereafter meane to indure
our scourges, hauing no way deserued thē,
but by seeking the saluation of soules, and
praying for their good that torment vs, so
in aunswere of this point, do we assure your
Maiesty, that what armie soeuer shoulde
come against you, we will rather yeeld our
breastes to bee broached by our enimies
swordes, than vse our swordes to the effusion of our Country blood. But let vs now
come to the confusion of some that woulde
auouch Cardinall *Allen* to be *Pope*, and Father *Parsons* to the king of *Spaine*, to haue
shewed certaine scroles of the names of ca-

E 3   tholikes,

tholikes, and to haue tempted him to renue
the war, by promising many thousands that
shoulde be in England ready to aide them,
concerning which there needeth no more
to be said, but that the penitents that made
the confession, knew wel enough that they
were not with their right ghostly father, or
else they woulde neuer haue committed
such a sacriledge, abusing the Sacramentes
with such vntrueths. For we are assured by
their notice, who were more internal & cō-
uersant with them both, than the authors
of this confession euer coulde be, that they
are sufficiently enformed of the estates of
Catholikes, the one by experience, the o-
ther by continuall reports of those that goe
ouer. And therefore neither in pollicy, in
which they are noe punies, nor honesty on
which their creeit doth lye, would they deliuer such follies into Princes eares, which
all protestantes hearing by so many attur-
neies, (as all protestants doe) were able to
disproue them of falsehood, for neither are
the restraints, and number of Catholikes so
secret, nor the course to suppresse them so
vnknown, but euery Prince seeth it an impossibility for them to doe any thing, being
as before is shewed, so naked and needy, &
                                    euery

euery way fo vnprouided. Neither woulde
they in difcreation, (if they were as they
are not) the motioners of the Kings comming, feede them with a vaine hope of thē,
whom they at leaft knewe to be a kinde of
broken reeds, fith the more helpe he expe-
cteth,, the leffe he would bring, & happilie
builde a maimed plotte vppon a falfe
fuppofall , to his fecond ouerthrowe : and
if this preparation be greater than euer, why
fhuld he thē truft to our leffe ability, & the
Laws daily weakening our ftrength, & time
hourely encreafeth his more than he did at
the firft affault, whē not any Prieft nor Catholike in *Englande*, was acquainted with his
cōming, nor fure of his intent, til the cōmon
voice bruted it , & our prouifions afcertai-
ned his purpofes, & vnleffe they were our
enimies they would not in cōmon wifdome
fhewe fcrolles of our names, or promife our
afsiftance, fith they knewe not howe ready
our aduerfaries at home would be vpō leffe
matters to feeke our fubuerfion, yea though
they fhuld as we are fure they wil not (paffe
fo fond promifes) yet could not Catholikes
but hazarde all their eftates in their vncer-
tainecies of forraine war, feeing fpecially his
laft ouerthrow, & knowing the enterprife to

E 4   be

be such, that eyther the King must stand
vpon the strength of his owne force, or the
sorrie addition of theyr impotent succour,
which can neuer inable him to contriue his
endeuours. Finally, both *Cardinal Allen*, and
Father *Parsons*, are knowne generally to be
men of excellent gifts, and no such nouices
in the knowledge of Princes intelligencers,
as in the weighty pointes of alteration of
States, & inuasion of Kingdomes, to presume to delude them with impudent asser-
tions, knowen to themselues to be false, as
the informer acknowledgeth this to bee.
And if effects, the most infallible testimonies of intentions, may beare the deserued
credit against naked & vnprouided words
of this partiall Inditor, Father *Parsons* hath
by euident demonstrations of a loyal mind,
sufficiently cleared himselfe from such vn-
due suspitions: for hauing by his wisedome
& rare parts, purchased more then ordinary credit with the King of Spaine. All that
haue bin eye witnesses of his proceedinges,
can auouch, that he hath vsed the kings fauour euery way to the benefit, but no vvay
to the preiudice of your Maiesties subiects.
The souldiers that in your seruice lost their
liberties, and expected no other entertain-
me nt,

ment, but the cuſtomarie pay of profeſſed
hoſtility, was by his meanes an interceſsi-
on, not only pardoned their liues, but with
new apparrell & monie in theyr purſes, en-
franchiſed to their full liberties, eyther to
ſtay in the Countrie, if they ſo fancied, or to
returne to their owne, if they were ſo better
pleaſed; yea whereas by long continued
breaches, betweene Spaine and England,
the name of an Engliſh-man was in moſt
parts of thoſe kingdomes, farre leſſe loued
then knowne: he hath vſed ſuch meanes for
the mittigation of theyr enmity towardes
vs, that now wee are no leſſe welcome a-
mongſt them, and more charitably vſed,
then in moſt other Nations : whereof not
only the quiet of Marchaunts, the admit-
tance of our Studentes, euen in the hart of
our Realme, (both things vnuſual in ſo iea-
lous and ſuſpitious times) but the ſinguler
curteſie towards theyr profeſſed & known
enymies, who are actually taken in a violent enterpriſe againſt them, gaue proofe to
your Maieſtie, witneſſing how much Father *Parſons* hath quallified the diſlikes, that
wars bringeth forth: for euen the *Athalan-*
tado or cheefe Gouernour of the Galleyes
of ſpaine, to make manifeſt that neither the
king,

king, nor his Nobles had in the heate of
their Martiall broyles, loſt the feeling of
theyr auncient League with our Countrie,
ſent into the Gallies of our Engliſh Cap-
taines, the plate and meate from their owne
table, that the world by theſe friendlineſſe
know, how much better they can vſe theyr
enimies, then ſome of your Maieſties vn-
worthy Maieſtrates, your naturall ſubiects,
and loyall friendes. And though it reſt not
in a priuate mans power, to ſtay the endeuours of ſo mightie a Prince, in ſo generall,
and important an enterpriſe, as is war with
England. Yet this vvithout preſumption
may be truely ſaid, that if euer hee ſhould
preuaile in that deſignement, (as the caſu-
alties of warre are moſt vncertaine, and only ouer ruled by God) Father PARSON's
aſsiſted vvith Cardinall ALLENS authoritie, hath done that in our Countries behalfe, for which his moſt bitter enimies, &
generally all your Maieſties Subiects, ſhall
haue cauſe to thanke him for his ſeruicea-
ble endeuours; ſo farre hath hee inclined
furie to clemeneie, and rage to compaſsion.
The conſicent therfore that gaue out theſe
confeſsions, did it but to ſooth vp ſuch credulous auditors as they knewe verie apt to
enter-

entertaine any rumors againſt the credit of
Catholiks, hoping of likelihood to ſell them
theſe fables for ſome benefice of more im-
portance.

No no moſt GRATIOVS Soueraigne,
it is not the authoritie of two priuate men,
that can carrie away Princes, ſo readie to
imploy the manie forces, if they haue not
motiues of greater conſequence: and who-
ſoeuer conſidereth our ſurpriſing of the
Kinges Townes in Flaunders, or inuading
his Countries in Spaine, and Portingale,
our aſsiſting his enimies againſt his daugh-
ters right in Brittaine, our continnall inter-
cepting his treaſure, warring with his fleets,
and annoying his Indies: ſhall finde other
cauſes of his comming, euen ſince his laſt
repulſe, then the ſlender hope of a fewe
beggerlie Catholickes, or the fainte per-
ſwation of two baniſhed men. It is alſo no
ſmall iniurie that is offered to your Highneſſe, in making your SACRED hand,
guided by ſuch thoughts as ſcorne to haue
vntruthes the patrone of your actions,
to ſeeme the Authour of this Sentence:
That manye men of wealth profeſsing in
your realme a contrary religiō, are knowne
not to be empeached for the ſame, either in
their

their liues, landes, goods, or liberties, but only by paying a pecuniary fumme, as a penalty for the time, that ther refufe to come to Churches. If this be as truely, as confidentlye fpoken, why were the venerable Prelates, and other Prieftes, and Gentlemen depriued of their Liuings, and pyned in *Wisbiche*: why are all the principall Catholikes committed to *Elye*, knowne to the minifters, then to *Banbury*, afterwardes to their owne houfes with a fhort compaffe about them, beeing nowe only let loofe to verifie a part of this proclamation, and to be eaflyer enfnared in the perills thereof, to which euery child may fee, they are more fubiecte at home, than they woulde be in prifon, and if they chance not to be fo wary not to be entrapped, effectes will foone proue, (if your Maiefties fauor preuent not the intention of others, that this libertie was) for a purpofe, iuft at the comming forth of the proclamation graunted, fith order will foone be taken, that they fhall not furfet of being fo long free, and if this faying be true, that none are troubled for religiō, what keepeth at this houre at London, Yorke, and other places, great numbers of manie poore Catholikes in prifon,

                                                  fome

some of them languishing a-way with the
commodities of their inclosure, haue by a
patient death obtained the best liberty, o-
thers yet after many yeeres indurance, for
no other cause but for Religion, beeing offered liberty if they would goe to Church.
Pining still in painefull restraint, witnesseth
to the worlde, with their lingring miseries,
the manifest falsenes of this assertion. Was
it not punishment for Religion, when a cō-
panie of Honorable & Worshipful Ladies
and Gentlewomen were most vnciuilly led
through Cheapside, with their Priests before them, only for hearing M A S S E, and
that before Priesthood was enacted to be
Treason. Is not that very statute a most
heauy oppression, now when the most of
these Queene M A R I E S Fathers that are
left, are become so oulde and impotent,
that they can not possibly supply Catholiks speciall necessities, to make it by Law
fellony to receiue young Priests. Are not
Catholiks shortned by this means frō such
helps to which their conscience and Religion bindeth them, a torment to vertuous
minds, more afflictiue than any outward
punishment? Are they not by this tied to
this wounding and bitter choise, either to
liue

liue like Heathens vvithout the Rites of
Chriſtian and neceſſarie S A C R A M E N T S,
for theyr ſoules health, or to purchaſe them
at the rigorous price of hazarding theyr
Liberties, Liues, Landes, and Poſterities,
as in caſe of fellonie. In points alſo of our
credit, hovv deepely vvee are incurred in
reſpecte of our Religion, hovv many ex-
periences make it moſt manifeſt? Wee are
made the common Theame of euery ray-
ling declaymer, abuſed vvithout meanes
or hope of remedie, by euerie wretch with
moſt infamous names: no tongue ſo forſworne, but it is of credit againſt vs: none
ſo true, but it is thought falſe in our defence; our ſlaunders are common workes
for idle preſſes, and our credits are daylie ſould at the Stationers ſtaules, euerie
Libeller repayring his vvantes, vvith im-
payring our honours, being ſure that vvhen
all other matters faile, any Pamphlets a-
gainſt vs ſhall euer be vvelcomed, vvith
ſeene, as allowed. If vvee keepe Hoſpi-
talitie vvee are cenſured to be too popular:
if vvee forbeare, vvee hoarde vppe monie
for ſecret purpoſes: if vvee be merrie, vve
are fedde vvith forraine hopes: if ſad, vvee
are male-content vvith the ſtate at home:

If

If vvee subscribe to Articles, it must be
called Hipocrisie : if vve refuse disloyaltie,
in some wee are measured by the eyes and
tongues, of such vvhome wee can no vvaie
please, but by being miserable : yea, the
verie name of a Catholike, as they in theyr
new Testament terme it a Papiste, is so
knowne a vantage for euerie one, that either oweth them monie, or offereth them
iniurie, that they can neyther claime their
right, nor right theyr vvronges : but their
aduersaries straight leauing the maine-
pointe, pleadeth against them for theyr
Recusancie. And thus trauersing theyr
suites, often causeth theyr persons to be
committed to prison. If any displeasing accident fall out, whereof the authors are eyther vnknowne or ashamed, Catholikes are
made common Fathers to such infamous
Orphanes, as though none vvere so fit slu-
ces as they, to let out of euerie mans sinke,
these vnsauorie reproches: not so much but
the casuall fires that sometimes happen in
London, the late vprores betweene Gen-
tlemē & aprentises, were laid to our charge,
thogh the occasioners of both were known
so wel that the report against vs, could not
but issue from an vndeserued malice: yea
Hacket a

a man fo far from our Faith, as Infidelitie it
felfe, and a little before fo notorious a Pu-
ritane, that he was of cheefe reckoning a-
mong them;when hys blafphemies grew fo
great, hys articles fo impious, that they
made Chriftians eares to glow, and his ad-
herents to blufh: then was hee pofted ouer
to vs for a Papift, and fo named to vulgar
fort; fo common a practife it is to beftowe
vpon vs, the infamies of all offenders. I o-
mitte the vniformed fhame and contempt,
that the very lawes lay vpon vs, condemning the chiefe function of our Religion,
partly for treafonable, partly for punifha-
ble faultes: And pretending an auncient
faith honoured in all former ages, to be fo
deteftable a thing, that it fhould by a folemne Statute be thought neceffarie to
make it treafon,to perfwade any vnto it. I
leaue the flaunders forged againft Priefts,
after theyr Executions, purpofely referued
till the parties were paft anfwering, & then
deuulged to make them hatefull. It vvere
infinite to lay before your Maiefties eyes,
all the croffes that in this world wee beare:
which to men, whom eyther gentry or nobility maketh tender ouer theyr honours,
cannot be but moft bitter corrifiues: for
they

neither dare reuenge their own quarrels for
fear of double offence to god & your highnesse,nor hope to haue redresse in ordinary
course,so far hath disfauor excluded them,
from all needfull remedies : yet must your
Maiesty be informed, (so vncharitable are
our enimies) that we suffer nothing for Religion, whom onely in respecte of Religion
these neglected miseries haue made most
contemptible euery one doing vs wrong,to
please our superiours,whom they see care-
lesse in yeelding vs any right. Nowe howe
vndutifull an impeachment it was to the
credit of your Maiesties words & writings,
to publish vnder your Soueraigne title,that
Catholikes for Religion are not impeached
in their goods or lands, I leaue to effects to
proue. And what is our recusancie, or re-
fusall,to be present at their protestants seruice, but a meere matter of conscience, for
as there is none so knowne, or vsuall a way
to distinguishe any religion from other, as
the externall rites and Sacraments peculiar
to euery one, so can none more effectually
denie his owne than by making open confession of a contrary speech by his assistance
& present at the solemnities & seruice proper to it. For not onely he that denieth

F Christ

Chrift in his heart, but he alſo that denieth
or is aſhamed of him, ſhall in the latter day
be denied of him before his Angells. And
ſeeing men iudge beſt of our minds, by our
actions, we cannot poſsibly giue any greater profe vnto them, that we are no Catholikes, than if we ioine with Proteſtantes, in
their Churches & ſeruice, by which, as then
moſt certaine and ſpeciall markes, they thē
ſelues are knowne to be of that opiniō. We
therfore, not gaineſaid by *Caluin, Melancthō,*
or any other learned Proteſtant, in this e-
ſteeme of voluntary preſents, of any in or at
the ſeruice of a contrary ſect, a denial of his
faith before men which being by Chriſt ex-
preſſely prohibited cannot but be iudged a
meere matter of conſcience, & religion, &
as ſuch a one as is by vs refuſed, ſith neither pleaſure nor pollicie could otherwaies
witholde vs, our refuſall redounding to our
ſo great trouble and diſaduantage, for firſt
ther are twenty pounds by the moneth exacted of ſuch as are to pay it after thirteene
moneths by the yere, an account vnuſuall
in all other cauſes, as the lawes commonlye
read Printed and practiſed witneſſeth, and
multitudes of the vnabler ſort of catholikes
daily feele, that al their goods, & third part
of their lands are ceaſed on, for their Recu-

fancie that cannot yeerly pay thirteenscore
pounds for the same. And this is so perscri-
bed,& performed with such rigor, that it is
in the leases of Protestants hands by a spe-
cial prouiso, ordained that recusants shou'd
not be so much as tenantes to their owne
landes, so seuerely is their religion punished
in that behalfe: yea & this lawe hath bin so
seuerely executed, that whereas poore far-
mers and husbandmen, had but one Cowe
for themselues,& many children to liue vpon it, that for their Recusancie hath bin taken from them, & wher both kine & cattle
were wanting, they haue taken their couer-
lets sheets,& blankets frō their bedds, their
victualls & pore prouision frō their houses,
not sparing so much as the very glasse from
their windowes, when they founde nothing
else to serue their turnes withal, which most
pittiful abuses pore souls both in the North
& other countries, haue bin continually cū-
bred, no cōplaints taking place, where these
outrages were, rather commēded for good
seruices, than rebuked for misdemeanours.
So irreuocably are we condemned to a ser-
uile bondage And if your Maiesty did but
knowe what other extreame penury & de-
solation, they ordinarily feel, your merciful
heart

hart, neuer hardned to fee lamētable fpoiles
would rather haue the lawes repealed, than
the execution fo intollerable. It is not pof-
fible to exprefle in words the continual hel
we fuffer by the merciles fearching & ftor-
ming of purfeuants & fuch needy officers,
that care not by whofe fall they rife, not hauing any deferts or other degrees, to clime
to the hight of their ambition, but by the
punifhment & paines of poore Catholikes.
They water their foūtains with the fhowres
of our tenderest vaines, & builde their houfes with the ruines of ours, tempering the
morter of their foundations, with our innocent blod: our liuings are but fnares for the
owners liues, commonly made the fee of e-
ry mercenary mouth, that can by founding
our difgraces into credulous eares, procure
themfelues warrants to feaze vpon our fubftance. They make our willes before we be
ficke, bequeathing to their owne vfes, what
fhare they like, & by difplāting our ofspring
adopt thēfelues to be heirs of our lands, beg-
ing & broking for thē, as if we were either
condēned for fooles, or in perpetuall mino-
rity, & not contented with our wealth, they
perfecute our liues, neuer thinking their
poffeffio fure, til the affurance be feafoned
with

with our death. So easie it is for our enimies
to quench their angry thirste in our blood:
yea we are made so common forage for all
hungry cattell, that euen the theeues with
scutchins & counterfait warrants, haue vnder the pretence of purseuants spoiled vs in
our houses, hauing the officers to assiste thē
in their robberies, so ready they are at euery ones call, to practise their autority to our
vexation, and so well knowne it is to euery
waybeater howe openly Catholikes lye to
the pray. And though some very fewe finde
more fauor being able to follow it with golden petitions, yet al the rest, whose meaner
estates cānot reach the charge of such costly friends, are made common blottes, open
to euery chance of the dice, to giue entry to
their aduersaries, by their displeasing their
owne seruantes & tennantes crowing ouer
them, and vaunting that euerie pawne may
giue their mate to their highest fortune: for
be he neuer so base that play eth with them,
with the least aduantage, he is sure that many will backe him in it, and haue the tricke
with a sure help, thogh it be the son that taketh against his father, or any faulty drudge
that for feare of correction accuseth his master. It were infinite to set downe the labo-
rinth

rinth of our afflictions, in which, what way
soeuer we go, it is but a loosing of our selues
& a vvinding of vs further into an endles
course of calamities. Let this suffice, that
now so heauie is the hand of our superiours
against vs, that we generally are accounted
men, who it is a credit to pursue, a disgrace
to protect, a commodity to spoile, againe to
torture, & a glory to kill. We presume that
your Maiesty seldome or neuer heareth the
truth of our persecutions, your lenitie and
tendernes being knowne to be so professed
an enimy to these cruelties, that you would
neuer permit their countenance, if they
were but expressed to your highnes as they
are practised vpon vs: yet sith we can bring
the ruine of our houses, the consumption of
our goods, the pouerty of our estates, & the
weeping eyes of our desolate families, for
palpable witnesses of the truth of these co-
plaints. Let vs not be so farre exiled out of
the limets of all compassions, as besides all
other euils to haue it confirmed with your
Maiesties hand, that wee suffer no punishment for religion, suffering in proofe all punishments, for nothing els: we haue beene
long enough cut from all comforts, & stin-
ted by an endlesse taske of sorrowes grow-
ing

ing in griefes, as we grow in yeares, one mi-
fery oretaketh another, as thogh euery one
were but in earneft of a harder paiment; we
haue fome fmall hope that our continued
patience, and quiet effufion of our bloodat
your Maiefties feete, would haue kindled
fome fparke of remorfe towards vs: but ftill
we fee that wee are not yet at the depth of
our misfortunes, we muft yet tread the reftles maze of new agreeuance, fith wee per-
ceaue by this Proclamation, that our caufe
is too farre for being pittied, that it is not fo
much as knowne, where it can only be re-
dreffed : yet fith help neuer commeth too
late, to fo helples creatures, who dayly are
drawen neerely to the brinke of a generall
diftruction, vvhich fome that giue ayme to
your Maiefty, feeme willing that you fhuld
difcharge vpõ vs: we are forced to deuulge
our petitions by many mouthes to opē vnto your Highnes our humble fuits: for neither our felues to prefent thē in perfon (being terrified by the prefident of imprifon-
ment, that laft attempted it) nor hauing the
fauour of any fuch patron, as would be willing to make himfelfe our mediator to your
Maieftie: we are forced to commit it to the
multitude, hoping that amõg fo many, that

fhall

shall peruse this short & true relation of our troubles, GOD will touch some mercifull hart, to let your highnes vnderstand the extremitie of the, which if we were once sure to haue beene effectually performed, wee might either set vp our rest, in an vnflexable sentence of misery, which we hope shall neuer proceed from so easie and gratious a Iudge, as your sacred selfe, or either expect some lenity to allay the anger of our smart, a thing more incident vnto the milde temper of so excellent a minde. In the meane season, we humbly craue pardō of this forced defence, & necessary supplicatiō, which was extorted from vs by open & vnsupportable vntruthes, no lesse needfull for your maiesty to know, thē for vs to disproue; imploying the vndeserued touch of your Maiesties word, & playning the direct path, to our intended subuersion; Accept it therefore (most mercifull Princesse) and all our humble duties & faithes with it, which with most loyall thoughts, & seruiceable resolutions, are vnfainedlie betrothed to your Maiesties defence. God of his infinite goodnes prosper and preserue you to his glorie, your subiects comfort, and your own, both temporall and eternall happinesse. *December* 14. *Anno.* 1595. FINIS.